# A GUIDE TO GARDEN DESIGN

# A GUIDE TO GARDEN DESIGN

Eric Vidal

The Book Guild Ltd
Sussex, England

First published in Great Britain in 2002 by
The Book Guild Ltd
25 High Street,
Lewes, East Sussex
BN7 2LU

Typesetting in Times by
Keyboard Services, Luton, Bedfordshire

Printed in Great Britain by
Bookcraft (Bath) Ltd, Avon

A catalogue record for this book is available from
The British Library

ISBN 1 85776 626 1

*This book is dedicated to my wife, Mary,*
*for her considerable help in its production*

# CONTENTS

A Testimonial ix

Introduction xi

1 Preliminary Area Investigations and Assessments 1

2 Detailed Site Investigations and Assessments 3

3 Garden Design Considerations Including Initial Ground Survey 7

4 Detailed Designs and Key to Symbols 27

5 Designing and Constructing a New Garden 188

as from
G.L.C.
Director for Recreation
and the Arts.
County Hall SE1.

24·iii·86

To whom it May Concern

This is to pay tribute
to the work of Eric Vidal for
this Department. He has served
the G.L.C. for over sixteen years.
In my own experience over the
last six he has achieved an
astonishing amount for the
landscape of London. I know
of no-one with a more passionate
concern for the trees of London,
and especially of its Green Belt.
He has, single-handed, done more
for the trees he understands and
loves so well than many whole

groups of conservationists. His
concern has been made the
more acute by the long-standing
neglect of the treescape of
outer London. His own surveys
have done much to alert
conservationists to the dangers
of failing to replace trees as
they grow aged and infirm
I emphasise his role as an
arboriculturalist but Mr Vidal's
interests and skills are wider
than that. His vision of good
husbandry and land management
has been an asset to the
Greater London Council and a
boon to London in its widest
sense.

Birkett

# INTRODUCTION

After more than fifty years of being involved in many aspects of horticulture, I felt the experience gained would be of help and guidance to those who appreciate the value of their gardens to their quality of life, i.e. relaxation, enjoyment, and the feeling of creativeness. A garden is a living extension of a house.

Going right back to my boyhood, when I was at school, I was asked to organise the school vegetable garden as the output of vegetables helped so much in those days of wartime rationing. Just before joining the Royal Navy in 1943, I spent some time at the East Malling Research Station, near Maidstone, where I learnt much about fruit and hop growing, and this gave me a determination to make horticulture my lifetime's work, all being well, when the war ended.

Upon demobilisation in 1946 I went to Wye College in Kent and, after three years, gained my degree, Bsc Hort.London. I shall always be indebted to those who taught me what I learned there. It is an excellent place of horticultural education. Between terms of instruction I went to many different parts of the country to get first-hand working experience of vegetable, flower, and glasshouse growing. This was followed by my managing different horticultural holdings and enterprises. I mention this because, with the practical knowledge gained and experience of the wider aspects of horticulture such as landscape design, contractual and construction work, site management, arboricultural techniques, etc., I built up steadily an increasing range of knowledge.

Halfway through my working life I changed from the private to the public sector and joined the Greater London Council. I was engaged in the landscape designing of areas of public open spaces and large housing developments such as the Queensmere Road project in Wimbledon, together with extensive building developments such as that on the old Kidbrooke airfield. Frequently the considerable practical knowledge I had obtained in my earlier life influenced the designs of soft and hard landscapes.

Within a couple of years I was appointed Conservation Officer for the huge Thamesmead development down river from Woolwich, which was formerly the Woolwich Arsenal. This was a very interesting job, lasting ten years, as I was to play a very active part in researching the history of the site, the detailed planning of the five lakes and interconnecting canals and their soft edge treatment, including the planting of marginal aquatic plants, the integration of school and housing projects, open spaces, the river wall, road network, and locations of the statutory services, pathways and cycle tracks, all of which could have their location and design influenced by the existing topography and ecology, especially the retention, whenever possible, of the existing trees. All these factors influenced the design of the areas to be landscaped.

For the last five years of my employment, I looked after the environmental concerns of the Green Belt land owned by the Greater London Council. For example, it included land adjacent to the M25, north of London from Denham in the west to Brentwood in the east, and I worked in an advisory capacity with several London boroughs in matters of conservation techniques including extensive tree planting and arboreal husbandry.

Before and after retirement I designed and constructed myself the gardens of our four successive homes, one small terraced house in the London suburbs, a thatched cottage in the countryside, a new bungalow and, finally, because age takes its toll, a small garden for a house in an estate to cater for partial disablement. I have included many photographs of these varied gardens.

So far this introduction resembles a potted autobiography. It is, however, intended to demonstrate how all experience within one's chosen career can be used to help others by passing on as much practical knowledge as possible.

Individual chapters deal with the following:

1. Preliminary Area Assessments and Investigations
2. Detailed Site Investigations and Assessments
3. Garden design considerations including initial ground surveys
4. Eighty dyeline designs at 1:20, 1:50, 1:100 and 1:200 scales with accompanying descriptions and alphabetical key
5. Design, construction and planting of the garden of the house in which I now live.

Photographs of different gardens with which I have been involved are also included.

I have intentionally excluded details of actual constructional activities as these are amply described in DIY and other publications. Apart from mentioning a few trees, shrubs and plants where appropriate I have not included comprehensive planting schemes or specifications as these, too, are well described in various books, magazines and associated articles.

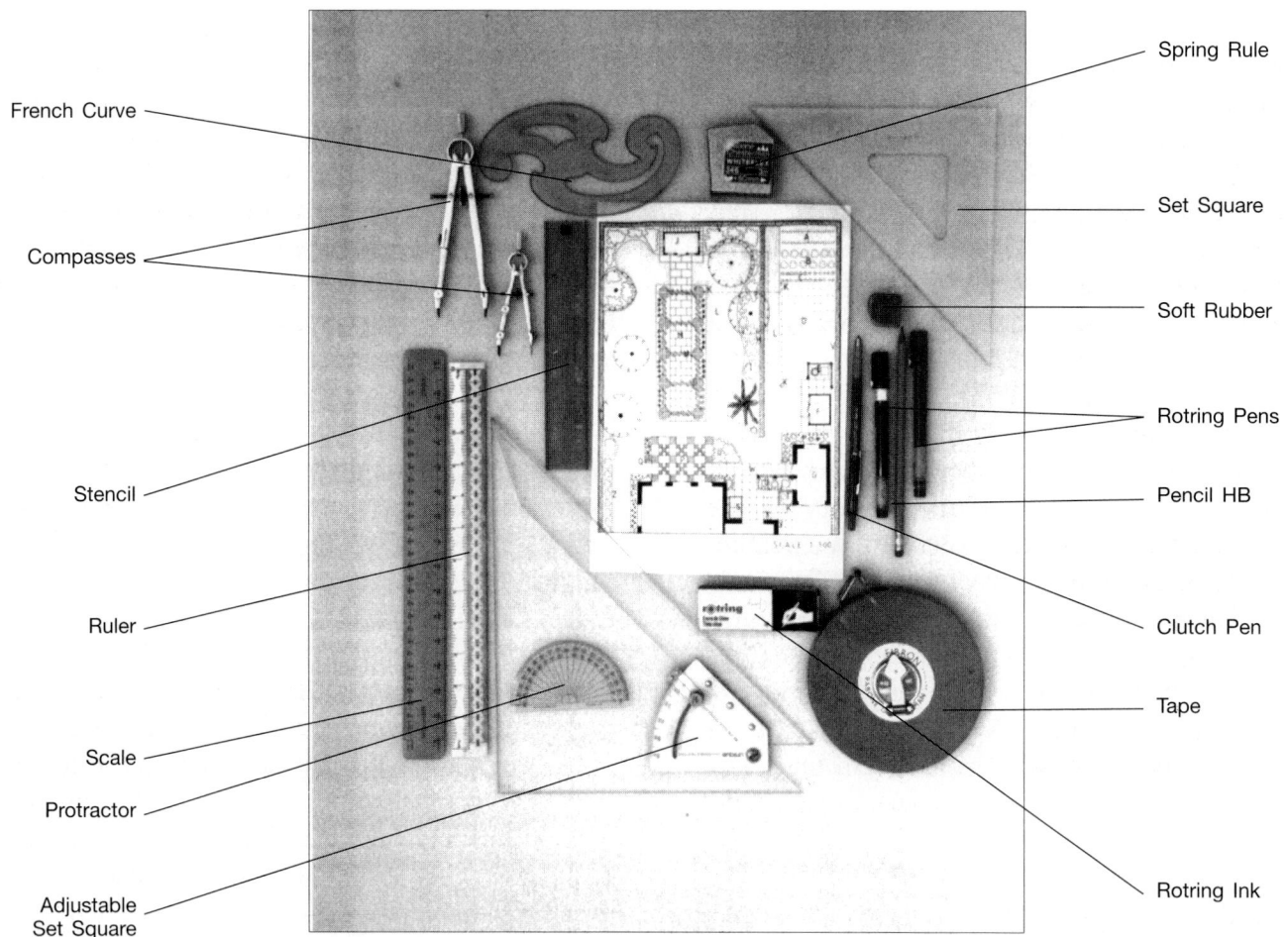

Various drawing instruments

# 1

## *Preliminary Area Investigations and Assessments*

Few people have the good fortune to be able to choose where they live, except perhaps in retirement, and most of us have to locate ourselves near to our work, with the added considerations of availability of children's education, health and mobility, etc.

In addition to all that is the overwhelming necessity to live within our earning capacity, whether in or out of employment. It is with this in mind that there must be a differentiation between homes which are leasehold, freehold or tenanted, because this has a very big influence on the size and type of garden attainable.

It is also necessary to distinguish between the potentials within the occupation of a flat with small garden, a building conversion, detached or semi-detached, period, old or modern, any of which could be in an urban or rural location. Is it a historic building in a conservation zone and listed Grade I or II? Having said this, the following must be addressed:

(a) What is the history of the area, i.e., industrial, rural, archaeological? The local authority may be able to advise. In addition, investigation of church records, museum artefacts, old land surveys, and local maps could be useful, as well as the local knowledge of residents who have lived in the neighbourhood for most of their lives.

(b) It is vital to consult the local authority for all possible information on local development plans, road widening schemes, improvement of statutory service installations, and whether there are bridleways, and permissive or definitive footpaths in the vicinity. Try to arrange a meeting with the Duty Planning Officer. If there is the slightest rumour of contamination such as an old factory, gasworks, garage, or other industrial complex, further enquiries should be made without delay.

(c) An appraisal of the topography and ecology of the area would be advantageous together with a study of soil types. The Geology Survey Museum at South Kensington, London SW7 2DE, produces soil and drift maps of the geology of most areas and these will provide much useful data – chalk, sand, clay, loam, rock, alluvial, peat, etc. For example, in quite a short distance in the Dorking/Reigate area of Surrey, when going from north to south, chalk downland changes to Upper and Lower Greensand, Greensand (including Hastings and Bargate sands), Atherfield clay, and then on to Weald clay.

(d) An examination of the appropriate ordnance survey at 1:50000 scale followed by a more detailed look at the 1:25000 survey would help to show the altitudes and contours of the land, its gradient, water courses, and likely flood plains, the proximity to pylons, roads, railways and canals.

(e) There are many large-scale housing developments of mixed density, and it is important to determine whether the design of the buildings is repetitive or a good mixture of styles and elevations. If most are the same, the character of garden design and landscaping could be more complicated. Far better is a garden designed to blend with the location and type of dwelling especially if there is an open planning factor.

If it is in a low density development how many of the existing trees have been safely retained? Has there been a change of levels, undercutting of the root systems, or bark and branch damage? The use of existing trees gives an immediate landscaping effect.

(f) Try to arrange a meeting with the Duty Officer of the local Environment Agency to get as acquainted with the area as possible.

I cannot stress too greatly the initiative that should be taken by the prospective purchaser in pursuing the overall investigations in whatever directions are required. Hasty purchasing without delving deeply into all these matters could prove disastrous.

Once the prospective purchaser is satisfied with these preliminary area investigations and assessments, it is appropriate to move on to the detailed site investigation and assessment.

# 2

## *Detailed Site Investigations and Assessments*

This next stage covers a wide range of points, on the assumption that a particular property, which is available, is of serious interest and merits greater investigations and appraisal.

The subject matter is so diverse and quite considerable that a form of check list is perhaps the best way forward on first viewing. Most of the points mentioned can have an influence on the treatment of your garden layout.

### Check List

What kind of property is it and how has it been constructed? If possible, try to get the builder's layout plans at 1:500 and 1:100 scales, including elevations and floor plans.

What materials have been used in its construction? These could well influence the character and blending of the garden features to the appearance of the dwelling, e.g., natural or pre-cast stone blocks, brick, knapped flint, pebble-dash, rendered and coloured concrete blocks, half-tiled, as in Sussex, painted weatherboard as in Kent, a pargeted finish as found in East Anglia, cedar shingles as in a timber building, cob and thatch such as is found in the West Country. What kind of roof is there (old or new), thatch, slate or flat (felted)?

What are the neighbouring properties like? Do they overlook, hence the need for screening with trees? Possible noise factor night visits might be required to check. Problem of barking dogs? Proximity of other dwellings – will they inhibit peace and quiet and the desire for seclusion? The experts on problems of acoustics and noise reduction are Cambridge Architectural Research Limited, The Eden Centre, 47 City Road, Cambridge CB1 1DP (01223 460 475).

Information should be obtained from the local council about local bye-laws. Ask them for the booklet on planning produced by the DEFRA without charge. It is absolutely essential to seek planning guidance at the earliest stage.

Check the terrain of the property, e.g., is it on a hill, a flood plain, in a valley or on a plateau?

What is the housing density and does it reduce the individuality of the property?

Determine the ownership of the boundaries. Are there any 'T' marks shown? If so, if the 'T' is marked within 'your' property then the boundary is in 'your' ownership. It could be joint ownership and there could be conflict on matters of access, maintenance and repair. Boundary ownership can cause more problems between neighbours than most other. It is vital to get this established as it can be a great influence on the design and embellishment of 'your' garden. Sometimes deeds or land registration documents show only a red/pink felt pen line to delineate the boundaries and this could be inadequate and unsafe. Information may also be found in title deeds.

Are there any covenants or conditions which apply to the property? Your solicitor should advise about this when they are carrying out local searches – Form CON9 (2000). Are there any trees in the garden or in the gardens of your neighbours which are subject to a Tree Preservation Order? In addition to this what is the age and condition of existing trees? Are they *Cupressocyparis leylandii*? Is there any disturbance to existing hard surfaces from root growth? Is there overhang from neighbouring trees? Do any neighbours' trees prevent adequate sunshine from reaching your garden and are any in possible danger of being uprooted or subject to limb fracture? What condition, pathologically, are these trees in? What is their estimated lifespan before reaching their climacteric? Is there any evidence of honey fungus from rotten tree tissue or tree stumps? If surgery is at any time required, how can it be carried out? It is strongly recommended that these matters should be resolved before new landscape construction and new planting begins.

Is the garden in a frost pocket? What is the altitude? On a hill the temperature on a winter morning could be very different from that in a low-lying area. Consider the wind chill factor and the effect on foliage and blossom. From which direction is the prevailing wind likely to be, and what will be its effect? Is the property near the sea and what will be the effect of salt on plants, e.g., Euonymus and Tamarisk are fairly tolerant.

The growth of lichen on stone and branches would indicate clean air. Have a look at a local churchyard for these indicators.

What is the average rainfall, e.g., the east has far less rain than the west.

Lack of rain in drought conditions, with the likelihood of hosepipe/irrigation bans could perhaps be disastrous to some plants in certain soils.

What do the annual tables show for the average amount of sunshine/rainfall?

Is there a problem of smoke from nearby properties or smell from factories?

How much intrusion is there from traffic noise?

### Statutory services

*Electricity*: How is this supplied – overhead or underground? If the latter, how? Sheathed, armoured, piped in conduit, earthing? Where is the meter – inside or outside the dwelling? If the garden is going to be adjusted to new levels, will the cables be nearer to the new surface or exposed, with resultant danger?

*Water*: Where is the supply? Is it in galvanised pipes, alkathene or similar? Where is the stopcock? If necessary, can the supply be drained out and by what method? Is it supplied from a well?

*Gas*: Where is the supply and at what depth? Again, where is the meter, inside or outside? In emergency where can the supply be cut off and how easy is it to get to the equipment, i.e., extensive shrubberies making access difficult and time-consuming.

*Telephone*: Is the line below ground? If so where, and at what depth, and how protected? If above ground, are the wires likely to be put in jeopardy by tree growth?

*Television cables*: The above observations apply.

In the case of electricity and telephone, are there poles situated in the garden? How is maintenance access achieved? Are there any wayleaves in force?

*Drainage*: What is the disposal of foul drainage? Where are the locations of pipes, inspection chambers and rodding eyes? Again, all these factors can influence the design of the garden in many ways.

If there is a septic tank or cesspool, where is it, in what form is it constructed, and how is access obtained for routine work? Where is the overflow likely to be? If in a large grassy area there is often a vigorous growth of nettles, as evidence of outfall. These are a wildlife resource and a food plant for the caterpillars of the peacock and other butterflies. If the outfall is into a pond, albeit some distance away, then the high nitrogen content could be reduced by the massed planting of great reedmace, rushes and phragmytes.

What installations are there for the disposal of rain-water? Where are the soakaways, for this water must not go into the foul drainage pipework? Where is the location of the soil pipes? How would they be affected by changes of soil levels? Are the soakaways properly constructed and covered? If not, earth will soon get in and make them defective with the result that there will be seepage into areas where it is unwanted. Of course, there is a big problem if the subsoil is impermeable clay.

Are S or P gullies or bottle gullies in place at the bottom of roof rain-water downpipes to remove sediment? Is there a grid or grating on top to stop leaves getting in? Is there a brick or stone surround to the gully to prevent adjacent soil getting in? Downpipe gutters should be fitted at the top with wire balloons to stop leaves and twigs from blocking them up. Is there any land drainage in existence, e.g., to accommodate 'run-off' from a neighbour's garden at a higher level?

What information can be obtained about the water table if on low ground, and if there is a problem, what are the implications?

*Other factors*

If modification or alterations are likely to be required to the dwelling, what is the work sequence in relation to garden and construction activities? What is the likely disturbance?

Is there street lighting and does it affect the property in any way? Is its efficiency masked by tall trees when in full leaf?

Are there any eyesores near the property, e.g., rusting barns, factory chimneys, pylons, telephone or telegraph poles? Can they be screened by suitable tree planting? For example, poles could be partly screened by the fastigiate cherry *Prunus amanogawa* or hornbeam *Carpinus pyramidalis*.

What is the aspect? Has the pole star been located on a starlit night and recorded on plan to confirm the north point?

What are the long-distance views? Mountains, hillocks, lakes, rocky outcrops, open fields, estate land with specimen trees? How could the sight of these be incorporated into a garden design?

Is it possible to measure the limits of sun shade and shadow at different times of the year? What are the changes of level within the property curtilage?

Try to get an assessment of the problem of perennial intrusive weeds such as oxalis, couch, twitch, convolvulus (bindweed), ground elder, Japanese knotweed, marestail, creeping thistle. How can it be dealt with? Some may well be invisible during winter dormancy.

What is the likelihood of vandalism? Do hedges on the roadside require prevention of trespass by planting with *Berberis gagnepainii* or similar?

What is the condition of boundaries – stone, brick or timber? What might be involved if work is required upon them?

Are there symptoms of plant nutrient deficiency such as chlorosis in Pieris or magnesium as in Skimmia. These can be remedied by the application of iron chelate (sequestrene) or magnesium sulphate (Epsom salts).

It is helpful to see what assets there are that can be utilised in situ or, in the case of smaller specimens of hedging, trees and shrubs, transplanted to a more favourable location, for example: hedging, trees, shrubs, stone outcrops, stream, ponds, adjacent copses or woodlands – the possibility of wildlife.

How adequate is the vehicular and pedestrian access to the property? Are there good sight lines? Are there any legal considerations in relation to the property? Is there joint ownership of the access – maintenance, obstruction, landscape treatment of verges, space for vehicles manoeuvring, the problem of wash-down facilities?

What local planning restrictions are in force, e.g., regarding the construction of a conservatory? What is the proximity of adjacent buildings and how can that issue have an influence on the garden design, outbuildings, planting, etc?

Do you have a copy of local building regulations? If not, it is wise to ask for one from your local authority as it provides information on planning aspects including properties within a conservation zone relative to the restraints that there may be in a garden and, hence, its design.

Another factor to consider in certain circumstances is whether one must conform to a communal planting scheme, regulations or covenant, i.e., a single tree (what species?), and whether a boundary hedge in the front is permitted. If so, what species and height specifications? When does such a restriction or covenant cease, allowing you to plant up later?

If the property you have in mind is terraced, how easy will it be to get supplies into the back garden? This could mean everything being carried through the front door and living quarters. Will it be possible to offload supplies in bulk if there is no pavement? How can it be dealt with? Consider the problems, cost and permissions required when hiring a skip to remove unwanted materials such as subsoil and sundry rubbish.

## The soil

It is desirable to ascertain the pH of the soil, i.e., acid or alkaline status. The optimum is about 6.5. A soil testing kit can easily be purchased and soil samples should be taken some 200mm down, since the topsoil status could well be altered by application of lime or peat. A lot of moss and buttercups could indicate cold damp soil in winter with a high clay faction. Scarlet pimpernel in summer could point to an impoverished soil. A profile of the soil should be taken using either a soil auger or by digging a wider trench up to a metre with a spade. This will reveal the podsol showing the strata of topsoil to subsoil and below, and indications of poor drainage.

*Types of soil*: hold the sample near to the ear to listen to the sound when rubbing it between your finger and thumb.

- Sand: Gritty, cannot be formed into a ball. Does not take a polish when rubbed between forefinger and thumb.
- Sandy loam: Gritty, can be rolled into a ball but not a cylinder, does not take a polish.
- Silty loam: Smooth, silky, does take a slight polish.
- Sandy clay loam: Gritty and sticky, does take a polish.
- Clay loam: Sticky, does take a polish.
- Clay: Sticky, easily moulded.

Assess the specific heat of the topsoil. Sandy soils will warm up more quickly with resultant improved root growth and seed germination. The colloidal or humus content of the soil is very important in that it retains chemicals such as artificial fertilisers in the soil. Sandy soils are easily subject to leaching.

Soil texture is equally important, i.e., an adequate content of grit assists drainage structure and improves the aerobic capability. Soil bacteria such as nitrobacter and nitrosomanus will thrive better in a good soil texture.

## Diseases

Inspect any existing fruit trees and bushes for disease. Retention or removal could influence the ultimate design. For example, canker in apples, silverleaf in plums, bacterial stem canker in cherries, leaf curl in peaches and nectarines, big bud in blackcurrants, mildew in gooseberries, red core disease in strawberries, leaf virus in raspberries.

Inspect ornamental trees for disease such as Dutch elm or Wanstead disease in sycamores.

Soil Auger and Spade

6

# 3

## *Garden Design Considerations Including Initial Ground Survey*

Having carried out the activities and searches mentioned earlier to your satisfaction, and purchased the property, now is the appropriate time to carry out an accurate and measured survey of your garden and, in the following pages, I have tried to demonstrate the simple method of doing this, including triangulation and offset measurement. It is preferable to have two people doing this, plus some bamboo canes for use as sight lines and stations. It is really applied geometry.

I have shown, using different scales, typically shaped houses and garages located in various plot shapes. Existing features, such as large trees, should also be picked up, plus manholes, inspection covers, rodding eyes, and any other permanent fixtures. Boundaries and gates should be recorded. It is beneficial to have available a clipboard for recording measurements, which should be obtained by using a long tape, preferably 30m long, and several bamboo canes about 1m long, together with a carpenter's square, easily constructed, measurements in the proportions of 5 hypotenuse, of 4 base line, of 3 vertical (in Imperial measurements – 5 ft hypotenuse, 4 ft base line, 3 ft by vertical line). This is useful when obtaining offset measurements.

Using a suitable scale, a pair of compasses, a ruler, French curves, a set square, and HB or 2B pencils, draw out the plan, possibly on squared paper, A4 or A3 size, which can be photocopied, to the scale selected according to the size of the plot. When the provisional plan is checked for its accuracy the details can be inked in, followed by another tracing showing only the outlines of the plot and house without the stations or numerical data.

## Site Triangulation Survey (A) 1:00 scale:
## A Hypothetical Example

*Method and procedure*

1. Plot the outline of the dwelling, first locating the corners and, by offsets, the position of doors and windows, proceeding in a clockwise direction if you are right-handed, holding the metric tape in the left hand or, conversely, in an anti-clockwise direction if you are left-handed holding the metric tape in the right hand.

It is helpful to have an assistant to hold the end of the tape as you proceed and insert bamboo canes as required, for example:

At D record doorway and window and corner C of building
At C record two windows and corner B
At B record one window and corner A
At A record doorway and corner H
At H record window and corner G
At G record one doorway and one window and corner F
At F record one garage entrance and window and corner E
At E record one window and corner D

If you have a builder's floor plan this could be useful.

An example of metric tape readings along FE 0.7, 2.8 (garage) 4.2, 5.9 (window), 6.6 corner E (metres).

2. Having plotted the outline, the next stage is to survey with your assistant the corner of the plot and boundaries, e.g., Measure the radial distances:

FO and EO
EL and CL
BI and AI
AR and GR

and then plot them using a pair of compasses, adjusted to 1:100 scale.

3. To ensure the boundaries are straight, monitor check your measurements in (2), measure CK, BJ, BT, AS, GQ, FP, FN, EM. Note the use of bamboo canes (line EM) to obtain accuracy of sighting the building wall face.

If all your calculations and recordings are drawn correctly then you have the finished survey. Note: if you wish to use larger size paper then use 1:50 scale.

4. Survey/plot any existing pathways, gates, hard-standing and driveways, e.g., FV, EV, & EU, FU, and UV (driveway gates) plus inspection covers and rodding eyes.

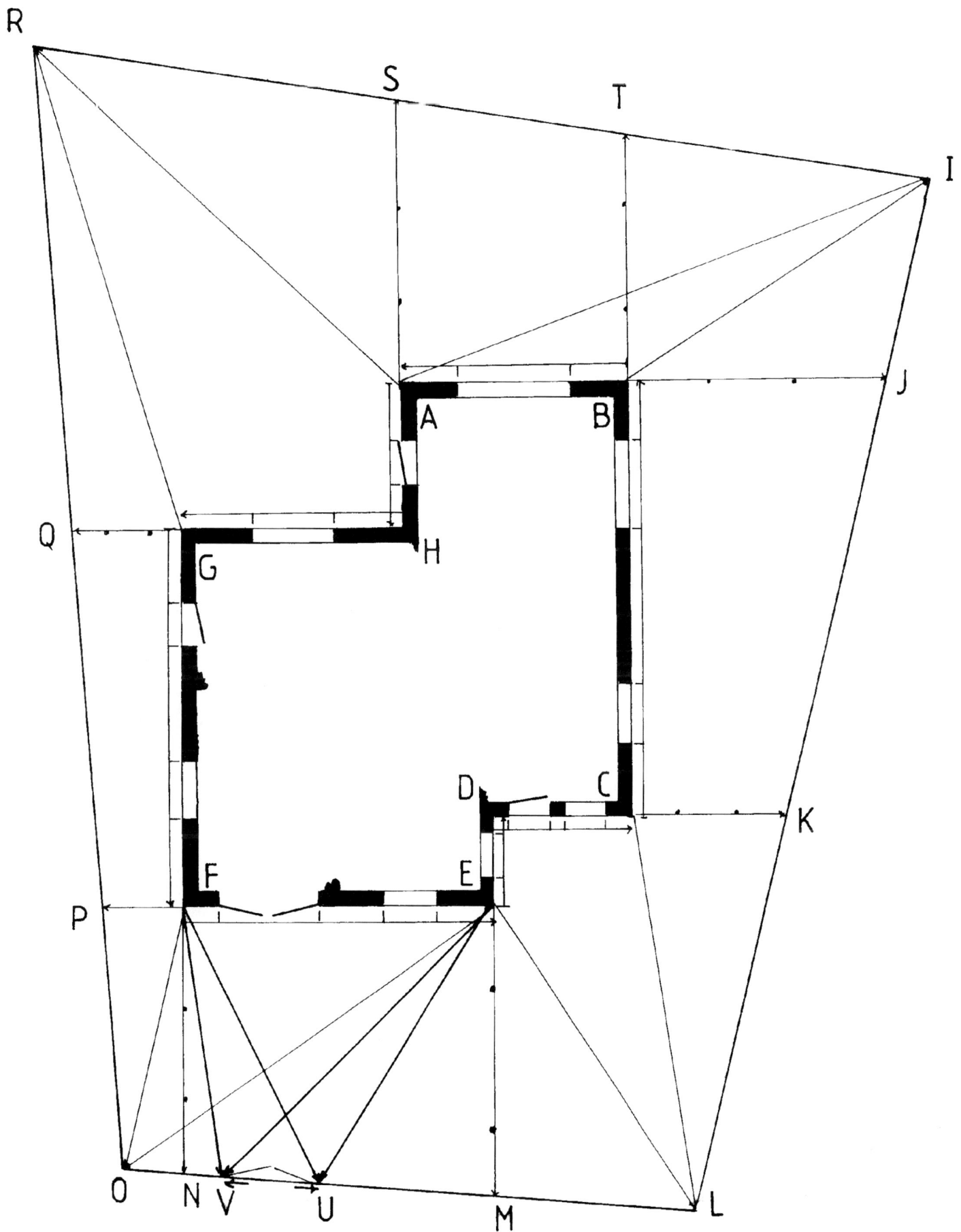

SITE TRIANGULATION SURVEY 1:100 SCALE

9

## Site Triangulation Survey (B) 1:200 scale: A Hypothetical Example

*Method and procedure*

1. Plot the outline of the dwelling, first locating the corners and, by offsets, the position of doors and windows, proceeding in a clockwise direction if you are right-handed, holding the metric tape in the left hand, or, conversely, in an anti-clockwise direction if you are left-handed, holding the metric tape in the right hand.

It is helpful to have an assistant to hold the end of the tape as you proceed and to insert bamboo canes as required, for example:

At A record one window and corner P
At P record one window and corner O
At O record three windows, one door and corner N
At N record one window and corner M
At M record one window and corner L
At L record three windows, one door, and corner K
At K record corner J
At J record one window and corner I
At I record five windows, two bay window corners, and corner D
At H record one window and corner G
At F record one window and corner E
At D record one window, one french window and corner C
At C record corner B
At B record two windows and corner A
At O record distance to Q
At U record distance to R
At R record one window, two doors, and corner Q

At Q record two windows and corner K
At K record one window and corner S
At S record two garage doors and corner S

If you have a builder's floor plan at the same scale this could be useful.

An example of metric tape recording using DC 0.5, 2.7 window, 3.4, 4.9 French window, and 5.6 corner C (metres). Then hammer in the two stations, n and o, at convenient locations.

2. Having plotted the outline using 1:200 scale, the next stage is to survey, with your assistant, the plot boundaries and the two existing trees using stations, n and o, e.g., measure the radial distance Do, Oo, On and Dn.

After fixing these then measure and plot Jf, If, Dc, oc, na, Qa, Ri, Mi, plus Ao, Bc, nc, ao, Tn.

The location of the trees is then measured and plotted mn, mo, nl, lo, ml, with a pair of compasses or boom compass.

3. To ensure the boundaries are straight, check your measurements in (2) measure Jg, Ie, Dd, Ab, Ok, Uj, Mh.

Note the use of bamboo canes (line Jg) to obtain accuracy of sighting the building wall face.

If all your calculations and recordings are drawn correctly then you have a finished survey.

4. Survey/plot any existing pathways, hardstanding and driveways.

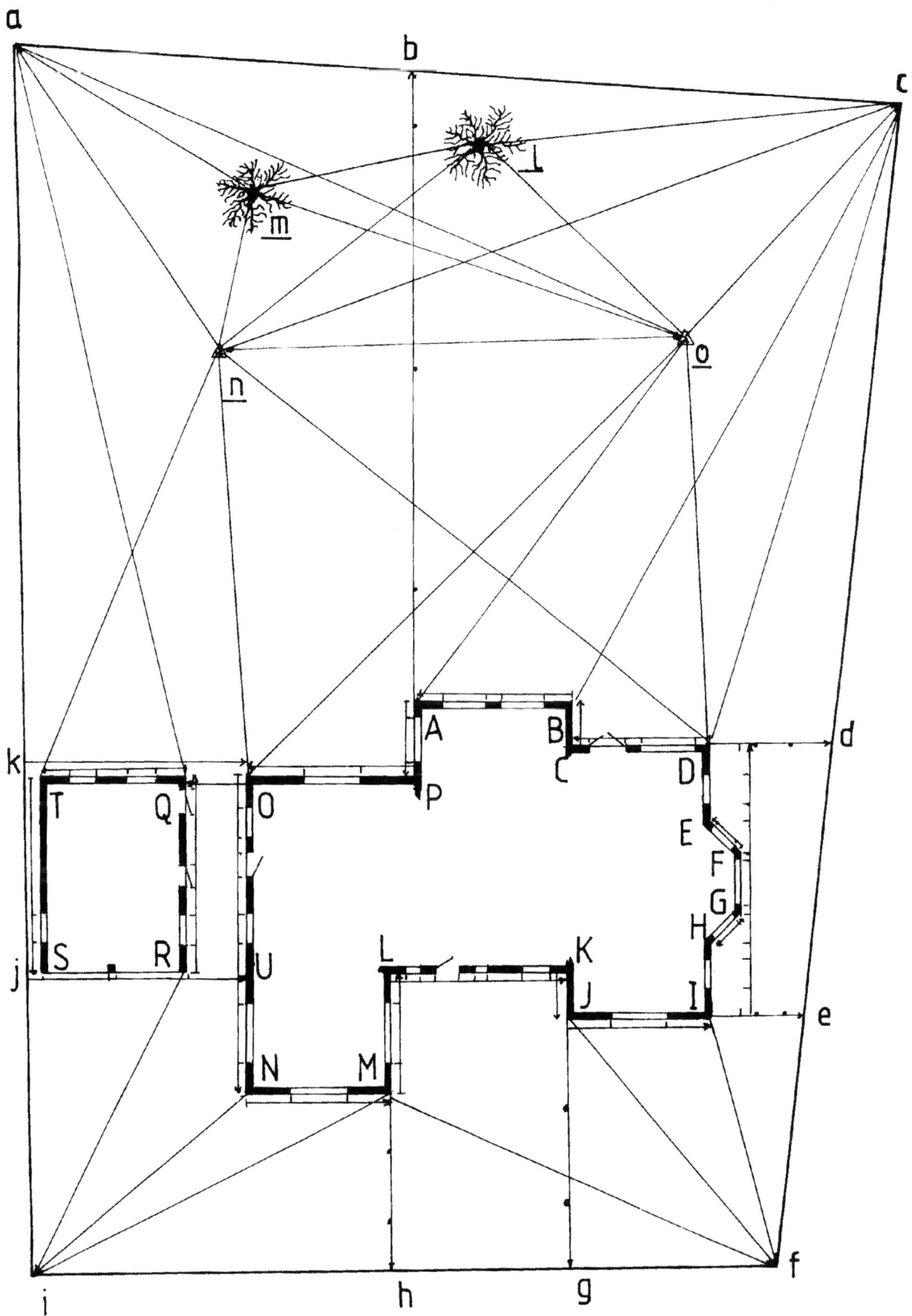

SITE TRIANGULATION SURVEY 1:200 SCALE

**Site Triangulation Survey (C) 1:200 scale:
A Hypothetical Example**

*Method and procedure*

1. Plot the outline of the dwelling as described in the previous examples A and B, paragraph 1.

If you have a builder's floor plan at the same scale, this could be useful.

2. Having plotted the outline using 1:200 scale the next stage is to survey with your assistant the plot, boundaries and two stations, j and k, especially required since part of the garden, b,c,d,e, cannot be adequately seen from the dwelling. Measure the radial distance Aa, Aj, Ak, Bk, Ah, Eh, Fg, Bg, plus, in line with the house walls, Ai, El, Bf and ek and kj which are intentionally in a straight line, then jc, kc, jd and kd, and ultimately bj at right angles to the boundary, ac. This activity will ensure that the boundaries are straight.

3. An additional check is to measure the boundaries after the initial plotting, i.e., ab, bc, cd, de, ef, fg, gl, lh, hi, and ia.

Note the use of bamboo canes to obtain accuracy of the sighting of the building wall face.

If all your calculations and recordings are drawn correctly then you have a finished survey.

4. Survey/plot any existing pathways, hardstanding and driveways.

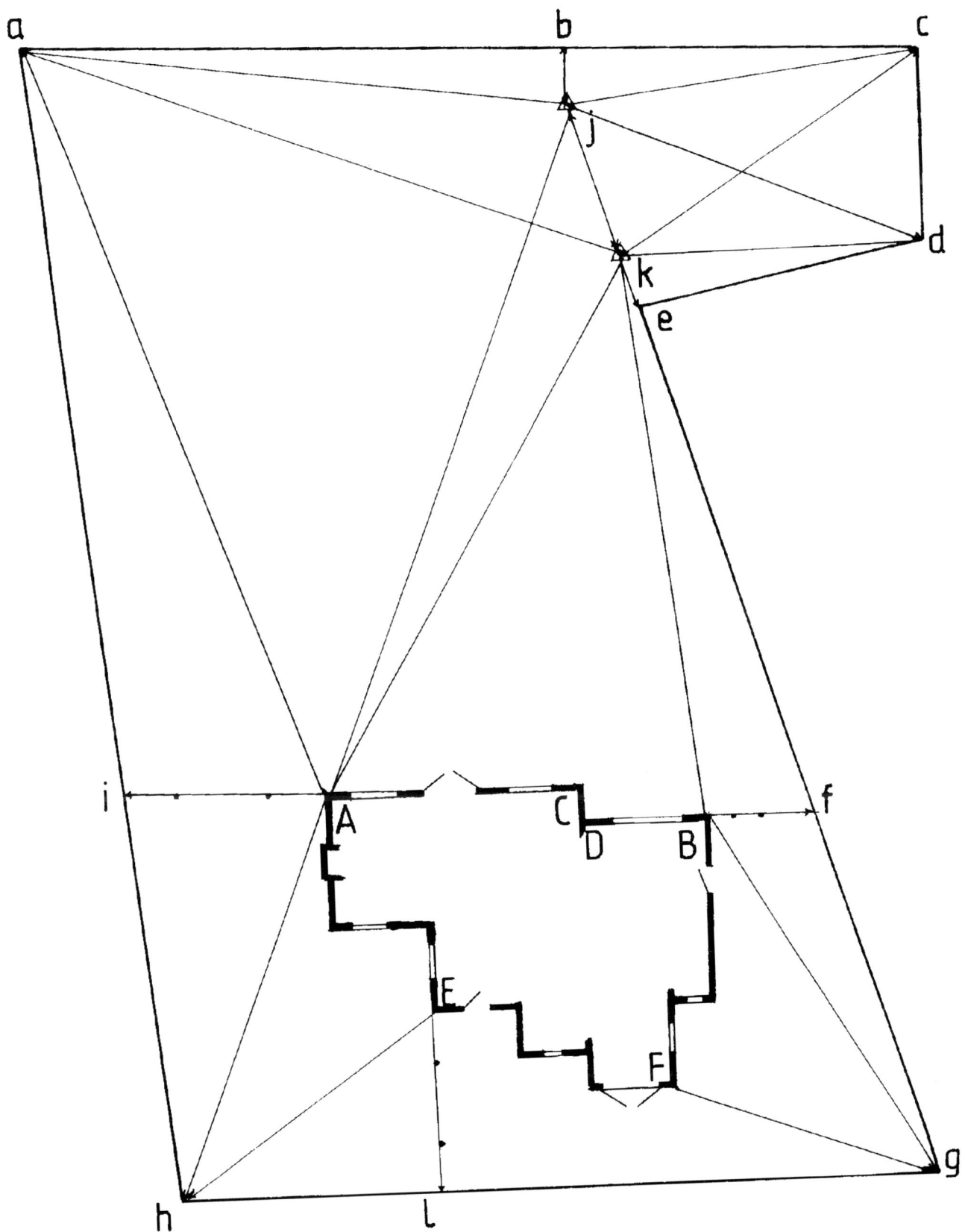

SITE TRIANGULATION   SURVEY 1:200 SCALE

13

## Design Considerations

Having completed the basic survey and for the purpose of this study in 1:100 and 1:200 scales (A4 size), it is desirable to make several photocopies for conceptual sketches, completing them preferably coloured in crayon.

There must be sympathy between the design and the characteristics of the house. This is an opportunity to use your creative flair and potential. All parts of these design components should be in proportion to the dwelling and especially with any colour schemes. It is important to have a list of any restraints which could influence the design in any way. Garden design uses many skills and these include a working knowledge of stone, wood, metal, building materials, zoology, botany, chemistry, geometry, engineering, artistry, plant growth and form, soil science and horticulture.

At some stage in the production of conceptual designs, the use of thick coloured paper (say light green for grass, dark green for planting areas, brown for base earth, yellow for paths, grey for terraces, blue for water spaces, black or purple for different kinds of buildings, pink for garages and drives) will be advantageous, cut and shaped carefully to scale as basic components to form templates which can be arranged and rearranged to suit. They can be temporarily stuck down with Blu-Tack or double-sided tape. When one of the conceptual drawings is short-listed, it is often a good idea to make a three-dimensional scale model of the base plan (coloured) and buildings to height and size. This can be done by using balsa wood as in aeroplane modelling. It cuts easily with a razor blade and pieces can be glued together. Trees can be constructed out of matchsticks or similar, with tufts of green foam glued to the top. By doing this it will be possible to view the model from several different angles.

It is desirable to make a list of likes and dislikes and what you want that could be incorporated in the design. Existing features within the plot such as large trees must be shown. Using another sheet of A3 paper, superimpose your A4 conceptual design in the middle of the A3 paper, and this will permit you to sketch in features which are outside the perimeter of your plot. They can only be approximate and notional, for obvious reasons, but it will assist the production of an overall plan, i.e., other existing trees, dwellings, greenhouses, sheds, etc., in neighbouring gardens. Plot also the prevailing wind direction, having recorded the north point on a starlit night. Simple contouring of a sloped site may also be possible. Points of access should be emphasised, i.e., gates, rear entrance, and restraints such as the proximity of problem structures and eyesores.

It might even be possible to plot land drain networks if these are known. I have experienced the discovery of these on different sites in very dry conditions since there is a discoloration of the grass. In some cases, where there have been years of settlement, distinct, longitudinal depressions can be observed. All these factors and others could be within the scope of site intelligence. Areas of grass growing over old foundations or broken up concrete would also show up in drought conditions. An example of this phenomenon is where an existing path constructed in gravel has been soiled over and turfed.

It is extremely important to have a knowledge of plant form, habit, growth factors and characteristics because, while the garden design to all intents is stable, all plant growth will change over the years, i.e., a shrub border will become overgrown, a hedge will encroach on a pathway, trees become too big, and rob the ground below of nutrition.

Before listing many items of interest which could be considered in the preparation of garden design, I would suggest that you consult the local planning authority with your final conceptual plan to ensure that there is nothing which might contravene planning or building controls. In certain cases, it may be desirable to request a written confirmation of provisional agreement and initialling of plans before any contract is made with a landscape contractor or work started by you, the purchaser.

This is particularly important in the case of fencing, walls and gates, or where there are open plan conditions or restrictions which it may be possible to have relaxed or removed. Sometimes even hard-standing for parking a commercial vehicle or for storing goods in connection with a business may require planning permission. If you are in a listed building or in a conservation zone, National Park, or Area of Outstanding Natural Beauty, there are even more stringent controls over many items, and consultation with the local authority planning department is even more important. It can be a criminal offence to carry out work which requires listed building consent without obtaining it beforehand.

Designing a garden where it is only necessary to decide on limited activity, like paths and planting, is relatively simple, but when it involves structures such as sheds, greenhouses, conservatories, outbuildings, kennels, etc., to be incorporated into a design, then I cannot stress too much the need to get professional advice and approval first. It may be necessary to prepare an outline application. Observations may be required to be made by your neighbours in case they wish to raise objections or, conversely, express their support for your proposals. Many trees are covered by Tree Protection Orders. Ask the council for a copy of the Department's free leaflet *Protected Trees – A Guide to Tree Preservation Procedures*, and the Planning Department's free booklet, *Outdoor Advertisements and Signs*, such as 'Beware of the Dog'. Also ask for a copy of the schedule if you have a tree upon which there is a TPO. Dead, dying or dangerous trees within TPOs can be removed without permission and a replacement tree planted. It could be a 'grey' area, so be prudent and consult the local authority first.

*Wildlife*: Some properties may hold roosts of bats or other protected species, either in the dwelling itself or in old hollow trees, old walls and structures. Other species which must be conserved are badgers and their setts, newts, and, in the plant world, orchids, etc. It is strongly recommended that, in such areas, reference is made to the Countryside and Wildlife Act.

*Boundaries and access*: If changes to these are required it is paramount to consult the local authority Highways Department. Owners of adjacent properties may be under no obligation to repair fencing unless this is covered by relevant documents. They could, however, be liable for damage arising from the collapse of fencing and walls. Restrictive covenants should also

be examined. Materials and light factors may be subject to restraint within a garden in some cases.

An owner has no right of way across a neighbour's land without his or her permission, even to repair his own walls. Sometimes the point is mentioned in property deeds. If the neighbour refuses access, it may be necessary to apply for an order gaining entry under the Access to Neighbouring Land Act 1992. Damage to your neighbour's property has to be made good. It is believed that some insurance companies do now offer boundary fence damage cover.

The problem of the condition of a neighbouring garden, i.e., neglected or overgrown, is difficult and there is little or nothing that can be done unless it poses a nuisance or health hazard, e.g., rats. In certain cases local councils have powers under the Town & Country Planning Acts to order such a garden to be cleaned up.

The Weeds Act 1959 lists certain weeds, e.g., spear thistle, broad-leaved dock, and ragwort, that have to be controlled. The seed heads (clocks) of dandelion and willow herbs are a big problem and any other plants that have wind dispersal for their seeds. One can only hope that neighbours who have these in their gardens will recognise their responsibilities.

I realise that I have dwelt at some length on various legal aspects but I cannot emphasise too strongly that it is of paramount importance to carry out full researches before conceptual designing.

**Conceptual Design Drawings**

We now move to the stage of producing conceptual design drawings. There are many points to mention. To try to place them in any order or bracket them in any particular subject is almost impossible because of the likely overlap. I have therefore decided to list them as they come to mind.

Garden design, in all its facets, can be compared to interior decoration and the placing of furniture. It is essential to design the infrastructure first, namely, path and terrace network, and coupled with the requirements of structures, i.e., sheds, greenhouses, cold frames, outbuildings, fuel bunkers, oil tanks, fruit cages, etc., and the provision of water and electricity supplies.

Whenever possible there should be a sense of discovery in the various locations within the ornamental garden.

All the time, when designing, it is beneficial to keep in mind the saleability of the property and its garden, besides merely making it satisfactorily for oneself. Choosing the composition of the ornamental garden, colour schemes and planting plans can be likened to making the selection of carpets, curtains, and furnishings within the property.

Even at this stage one should have thought of final embellishments such as lighting (tree branch tracery and emphasis of colour), garden furniture, containers like tubs, troughs, window-boxes, flower pouches, hanging baskets, mangers, barrels with plant-holes, and large ornamental pots. Old agricultural implements, cart wheels, wooden wheelbarrows, cast iron urns, cross-cut saws, feeding and drinking troughs, hay racks, staddle stones, scuttles and sink gardens, can also play a part in the design.

Examine the effect of light and shade on the garden and the glowing beauty of a sunrise and sunset on structures and plants, as well as the bark of trees and shrubs, e.g., snake bark acer, *Prunus serula*, *Betula jaquemontii*, and different varieties of dogwood, *Cornus alba*. There must be a feeling of intimacy within the ornamental part of the garden that reflects, as far as is possible, the character and aspiration of the occupier.

Consider the impact of the front garden on passers-by, arousing their admiration and even, perhaps, mild envy of how beautiful your creation has become and how much pleasure it gives to others. I would mention here the magnificence of the floral decorations in Brittany and other parts of France and the Black Forest in Germany, and, in contrast, the different and rather austere compositions found in parts of Holland. Think how often we are drawn to a pub or restaurant by the attractiveness of its exterior floral decorations.

Your garden should be one of which, given the resources, you can be justly proud.

In certain situations the designs should be specifically conceived for deaf, blind and disabled people as well as for children and animals. Check that the pathways are wide enough for two people to walk alongside each other, that there is wheelchair access and gates which are wide enough and which will swing back adequately. Remember too the danger of low branches of trees. Following on from this, bring into mind the importance of scent (rosemary, lavender, etc.), and feel and touch, the fragrance of Philadelphus (mock orange) and Syringa (lilac) in the summer, together with Nicotiana and honeysuckle in the evening.

If you are an apiarist get the best possible information on plant choice from the Director of the International Bee Research Station. Similarly, the RSPB will advise on the best plants for attracting birds into your garden.

Consider the benefit to plants generally if members of the leguminosae are included for their part in the action of bacteria rhizobium, such as *Cytissus battandieri* and *Genista hispanica*. Don't forget that the seeds of Laburnum are very poisonous.

If you are a lover of butterflies short-list Buddleias, Syringas, and Lavandula, and for moths various honeysuckles.

The choice of plant material can substantially influence the final design and should be given very careful research when preparing planting plans.

Have a thought for the conversion, in later years, of a feature such as a sandpit into another, like a paddling pool, without a radical redesign being necessary with the consequent upheaval and constructional costs.

In the matter of your health and physical condition now and in future, give thought to the ability to bend, climb steps, or dig. The ageing factor should be taken into account in certain cases when designing.

If any of the existing trees are covered in ivy do not try to pull it off when it is alive because the stems will break into little pieces. Much better to sever the network at ground level, allow it to die and dry out (say 3 or 4 months) when the adventitious roots will wither, and whole long pieces can be easily removed without leaving many small pieces.

When considering tree planting, position bamboo canes approximately 2.25m long to indicate temporarily the optimum location, not only for yourself but for the impact on your neighbour's possible loss of views. In some cases, however, evergreen trees might hide eyesores for all concerned.

If, after the construction of walling, it is desired to speed the weathering effect by algae or moss, then repeated watering-can applications, using a rose, of liquid farm manure, will rapidly assist the process.

If security is a serious problem, gravel pathways around the house are good acoustic alarms.

While inspecting trees assess the location of the drip-line, i.e., the tips of the branches. This indicates not only the extent of partial shade but the likely zones of the feeding roots. Trees are very important as besides giving shade, they filter dust, help to baffle noise, and assist in screening unwanted features. They can also provide autumn colour and bark splendour, and assist in the process of photosynthesis. Adversely, however, their soil water transpiration rate is considerable, especially in the large-leaved species. Worse still is their root penetration of drain runs, especially so in the case of willow.

If the branches of a neighbour's tree overhang your property you are legally entitled to reduce them to the vertical line of the boundary, but you are bound to offer them to your neighbour first, as the pieces are his property. Surgery like this may imbalance and disfigure the tree. Mutual consultation first is preferable, if possible. If there is disagreement as has happened in many cases of *Cupressus leylandii*, you may require the advice of a solicitor. For a copy of *The Right Hedge for You*, write to DTLR, PO Box 236, Wetherby LS23 7NB.

Don't forget to think about the ease of access for the postman, paper-boy, and milkman. If papers are left on the doorstep they risk getting wet or blown about. In the case of milk, the bottles or containers should be placed in the shade. Give thought to even these minor requirements within the smaller intricacies of the design.

It is wise to assess the ability to maintain a property, i.e., ladder and step placement for action on windows, boarding or roofwork, likewise wall decoration and window-cleaning, so plan the location of your wall and bushy shrub planting to cater for this, together with hard surfaces to support a ladder.

When planting trees money can be saved by using salvaged vehicle seat belts, cut to size, as tree ties.

In order to provide pockets for draping alpines on new walls of brick or stone, place used toilet roll or kitchen towel inner tubes in with the cement work; make sure the hidden end connects with the back-filled soil. After a couple of days they can be removed by unwinding and it will now be possible to insert a plug of soil round the plant root, place it in the hole, and carefully firm in. It is a cheap but very effective method instead of trying to drill out holes later.

If tree stumps are a problem, review the access for a mechanised stump chopper to be used. If access is impossible then providing it is safe to use an alternative method, make large diameter holes with a brace and bit as deep as possible and fill with chili saltpetre, i.e. sodium nitrate. This substance is deliquescent, i.e., it will soon dissolve and be absorbed slowly by the root timber. Topping up of the holes should be done frequently. Then, in the hoped-for dryness of the summer, light a small fire and the wood will gradually smoulder away. It is wise to have a bucket of water nearby in case it is required. Removal by mattock, saw and bill-hook is a very laborious business. Consider the possibility of honey fungus occurring later in the fragments of root still left in the ground.

When planting trees it is prudent to position tree guards around the main trunk to guard against damage by rabbits and, more important, claw tearing by cats. The latter can easily damage tree tissue and this could be expensive. Provide scratching posts instead.

Also, when planting trees, insert the tree stake first in the planting hole, then offer the tree on the leeward side to the prevailing wind (usually a south-westerly). Align the tree branching to the post and reduce the height of the post if required to eliminate bark grazing. Use a block to distance the tree from the post. If the tree is large, then two posts with a cross-bar add greater strength. This method might also be preferable if the tree is multi-branched instead of a single trunk, such as a feathered birch or larch, chosen for naturalising.

When designing, try to avoid the possibility of short cuts when moving between two points as there is a risk of wearing the grass or trampling down the soil.

Corners of buildings should always be softened from the severity of line by appropriate planting of wall shrubs, especially those species which are not too prolific in growth. It is prudent to affix trellis or straining wire secured by vine screw eyes to the wall surfaces before offering plant tissue to be tied in. Future pruning is made simpler by it being possible to tie in new growth immediately. I have frequently observed cases where wisteria, loosely secured to a wall, has come away in a storm, and the branches are too rigid to re-train. Years of flowering growth would then be lost.

If a pond is to be incorporated into the design, and if it is at all possible, slope the sides, for this will assist ice to move upwards when expanding. Another useful tip at that time of year is to throw in some large old rubber balls or rotten logs which will absorb the expansion factor of the ice. Never break the ice if there are fish in the pond; it can be harmful to them.

When constructing an archway or pergola it is strongly recommended that tanalised timber be used. Larch may look more rustic but soon disintegrates with rot. Silver birch, which I have seen used, rots even quicker. It is wise to locate the upright posts far enough apart to allow for the growth of roses, etc., otherwise clothes could be damaged when passing through an archway.

When installing a large wooden water butt or one made in plastic, fit a tap for watering but place the butt on concrete blocks some 300mm off the ground to enable watering cans to be placed under the tap and filled easily. Also, fit an internal pipe to act as an overflow. It is preferable to locate the butt over a drain gully with a cover to stop leaves and twigs falling in. Don't forget to drain the butt if hard frosts are forecast. In addition, place another cover over the top of the butt, making sure it is cut out for a downpipe to go through it.

Similarly, if the garden is designed with standpipes, plumb in a method of draining the whole system when it is cut off from the main supply in the late autumn by a submerged stopcock some 500mm below ground. Don't forget to open all standpipe taps at the same time in the process to safeguard them. The system, if laid without a constant fall, may require more than one draining plug.

If there is only a tap on the side of the house, turn off the stopcock valve inside the house near the rising main and open up the outside tap completely to dry out. To make doubly safe wrap all taps with dry sacking, covering that with good polythene to prevent the sacking getting wet, and bind with synthetic string.

It is also important to consider electrical supplies, lighting and power, to sheds, greenhouses (bench soil heating, tubular heating and lighting), fountains and water pumps, lighting brackets or columns near steps, etc., and waterproof power points for electric appliances, courtyard lighting and swimming pools, tennis court illuminations, etc. Plot exactly to scale where these locations are. Supplies should be safely installed before any other construction takes place.

If your garden contains a septic tank or cesspool it can often be disguised by an arched canopy made of strong galvanised cattle wire secured into the ground, upon which can be grown a suitable climber such as *Clematis Montana*, honeysuckle, or, if not too rampant, Russian creeper, *Polygonum baldschuanicum*, although that plant is better suited to smothering an outhouse. It can be pruned hard. Make sure, however, to retain access to any inspection covers and/or mica breathers.

Honeysuckle shoots twist round the wire, likewise Clematis leaf stalks.

In connection with mulching there are mixed opinions as to whether black sheets of polythene should be used. They can soon look unsightly and, if not properly anchored, are susceptible to dislodgement by strong winds. Torn areas could become a haven for snails and slugs. Bark chippings are occasionally used and while they do the job reasonably well, they can look untidy, and there is always the risk of infected wood tissue, such as honey fungus, not being eliminated by sterilisation.

Manure and compost which has not been heated properly could well contain a high percentage of weed seed, but that risk should be balanced against the nutritional benefits. The best manure for most purposes is well rotted horse manure if it is obtainable. Small stone chippings to form a kind of scree is another method to consider in the case of alpines, quite apart from the advantage of a drier, more aerated medium in which to grow them.

Sphagnum and sedge peats are excellent but nowadays there is a strong tendency not to use this valuable natural resource, supplies of which are finite.

Referring to slugs again, weathered boiler ash can be used around but not on top of delphinium plants for a partial mulch, but of greater importance is the abrasiveness of the ash particles, inhibiting snail and slug movement during the dormant months.

If a pond is envisaged, make sure there are small areas on the sloped sides which are level, upon which can be placed perforated plant baskets for marginal aquatics. If there are going to be fish, arrange for a large hide on the bottom using one or two very large paving slabs placed on small brick piers to provide shade and, more importantly, a refuge against attack by herons. On the bottom of the pond there can be further planting of oxygenating plants plus waterliles if there is enough water depth (choose the variety carefully, consulting a specialist firm's catalogue). The slabs, if just below the water surface, give opportunities for birds to drink and preen, while any surface mud offers swallows and martins a resource for nest-building.

Very occasionally a property is purchased which has a long frontage. Although planning permission for a new building plot may not be granted immediately, even under the classification of in-filling, permission might be obtained in later years which may well prove a financial benefit. It is therefore wise to consider a new imaginary boundary fence being created to hive off the plot, i.e., a line of pegs hammered in just above the grass levels. With that in mind, perhaps grass down most of it and plant new trees in locations which are unlikely to be disturbed during any future building work, e.g., away from sight lines, drain runs, access, building line, etc., and the establishment of a new hedge. Then your own garden can be designed in a more detailed and permanent way, always allowing for contingencies. The fact that the secondary plot has the elements of a new garden gives it greater selling value.

There is a tendency for higher density building developments to have smaller gardens. There may not be clauses, in the overall planning permission, for small open spaces within the general layout, for trees to be planted for passive recreation. If this is so, it increases the importance of planting suitable trees and shrubs in your own garden. Hence the influence on your conceptual design.

When designing and incorporating rock, do try to set your rocks in a way that is natural, i.e., as in outcrops. A rockery where the stones have been dropped down in place at all sorts of angles, like almonds on a cake, looks awful.

When choosing slabs try to select non-slip products or riven or exposed aggregate. Smooth surface types, although cheaper, can bring about serious injury in wet weather, due to their sliminess, and the perimeters may be bevelled which can allow the cement pointing to come out in icy weather, or in wet/dry conditions. This is particularly so if the slabs have not been spot-bedded down on a good hardcore base, preferably with a concrete finish, i.e., to reduce the likelihood of movement because of inadequate site preparation. It is very easy to trip over a badly laid paving slab.

The use of pea-grade beach shingle is sometimes an unwise decision for, if next to a grassy area, some of it may be inadvertently kicked up and this puts in jeopardy the blades of a cylinder mower. Beach shingle will also adhere to muddy footwear and can be transferred to undesirable locations.

When planting a hedge next to a field where there is farm stock, consider a mixture of beech and thorn. Never use laurel or yew which are poisonous to animals. Thorn on the field side will act as a deterrent to cattle and beech on the inside will provide a screen and windbreak. If the hedge is trimmed in late July or early August the beech leaves will stay on, due to the non-formation of the abscission layer in the leaf stalk, and the hedge will turn beautifully brown in the autumn. The thorn and beech will grow into each other to give a good effect. If horses are in the field they will soon damage gorse by eating it.

In parts of East Anglia and France, for example, old brick walls are to be found which have a wavy pattern, known as crinkle-crankle, which were used for growing peaches and nectarines, and to shelter other sensitive plants. The thick brickwork retained the day temperature and inhibited the risk of frost at blossom time, and also assisted in the ripening process. Even nowadays in large new gardens this method of growing is used, the wall often being capped by suitable ridge tiles to deflect the rain.

In many coastal districts hazel wattle is often used to diffuse the fierce winds. Hurdles dipped in creosote first will last a lot longer. If willow hurdles are used it is possible that they might take root.

In more recent times plastic netting of different mesh sizes is used, although it can look unsightly.

When considering the planting of climbers, it is often possible to mix the species to advantage, for example, *Wisteria sinensis* (grafted, not a hybrid seedling) and Laburnum (both leguminosae family) which will flower at the same time, also Clematis, e.g., *jackmanii* and 'Ernest Markham' (in this case to achieve a longer period of flowering).

It is wise to visit plant nurseries and garden centres frequently during the growing season to record flowering times, blossom characteristics, berry and fruit formation, and leaf colour, in order to make lists for planting in due course. Much disappointment from choosing wrongly, due to impulse buying, can thus be avoided.

Sometimes, to make an area seem more natural, i.e., when it is desired to plant a mixture of ferns, logs can be used which have a diameter of some 250mm and a length of 1500mm. They will be heavy and difficult to handle, but are necessary to hold back and retain the earth behind them. Try to use oak as it will last much longer. It is interesting to note that in the Fens and other peat bog zones, old oak trees have retained their original state, even after thousands of years, when erosion has revealed them. Birch is one of the worst timbers which will rot down very quickly. In Glasgow there is a municipal park in which there are fossilised tree stumps and roots on display under large glasshouses.

Railway sleepers have a prolonged lifespan as they have been impregnated with preservative after being cut to length. Old ones can form a useful edging material in some cases.

When designing your garden, give a great deal of thought to the precision installation of water to required standpipe locations and also the method of installing trickle irrigation systems especially for greenhouse growing. This activity should occur before any other construction work.

When choosing young trees try to obtain feathered maidens as they will provide much better plant material to train and provide bud selection. When dormancy breaks, young buds which point in a direction that is not required or are too close to each other can be rubbed out at this very early stage in their development.

Likewise, when choosing half-standard or standard trees try to obtain delayed open centre trees and not open centre ones as the branch structure will be so much stronger. I have seen many large open centre fruit trees, i.e., all branches coming from one location, split in half when in full fruit or in very stormy weather. It is far better to choose and label these personally at a tree nursery during the growing season. Getting the right tree in its infancy is extremely important. Badly shaped ones are very likely to grow into an unsatisfactory branch network.

Soil fertility must be considered. It is absolutely essential over a period of time to build up the humus content or colloidal status. This medium materially affects the retention of nutrients. It is a complete waste of money to add inorganic chemicals to an impoverished soil because they will soon get washed out into the ground water by leaching. In association with this, a heavy soil such as clay, should be opened up with coarse horticultural grit or similar.

Applications on top of winter-dug soil can be of great benefit since frosts followed by rain will erode the surface soil particles and assist naturally in their mixing. This forms what is known as the crumb structure. It provides a far better growing medium for root growth and assists rapid drainage after flash floods or down-pours. Bonfire ash, if handled as soon as it is dry, is partly suitable for soil structuring. Any potash (potassium carbonate) will be rapidly leached out in rain and therefore, as a fertiliser, is more or less useless. Organic fertilisers such as bonemeal and hoof and horn, although expensive, are much better and give slow release of nutrients by the action of bacteria.

If earth has to be backfilled during construction it is advisable to add layers of compost or humus in strata as there are bound to be air pockets and young roots will soon dry out and perish.

In addition, in cases of, say, a metre deep of fill, even with periodic foot-treading while building up the levels, it could take a year or more to finally settle. To use any heavier equipment to press it down is not advisable and will be counterproductive as it will cause panning, possible waterlogging, and unsatisfactory root development.

Another factor of importance is the worm population and that is why well rotted farm manure is so beneficial. It provides a good colloidal state, a reserve of organic nutrients, and the worm runs help drainage, quite apart from the digestive activities of the worm's alimentary canal or intestine.

A further matter to be stressed is that subsoil should be graded to have a good crossfall to drains or weepholes before the addition of topsoil, otherwise good drainage will be impeded. This is especially important when preparing a site for grassing down when it is largely clay. By careful grading and gentle consolidation by foot-treading, not with a heavy roller, the likelihood of small areas ponding is reduced. A layer of some 50mm thick of raked horticultural grit will take up the minor depressions in the final levelling before turf laying and the rooting of new turf will be speeded up.

For shrub and some herbaceous plants some 500mm of topsoil is required, if possible, while tree pits will need much more for real benefit. A word of warning, however – don't dig tree pits in clay as in winter they will fill up with water (clay is, for the most part, impermeable) and the tree is likely to die in due course.

When constructing a cold frame or shelter,

consider the use of polycarbonate sheets which are sold in standard sizes. Being almost unbreakable, this material may be more appropriate when there are young children and large animals moving about.

Having discovered any inspection covers or rodding eyes during the survey of the garden it is important to try and grease the rims, screws or bolts against rusting.

When taking into account all airbricks, etc., around the property, make sure that soil cannot come nearer to the damp proof course than 150mm, assuming that there is one. Some very old properties do not have them and therefore it is prudent to incorporate in the design a low brick wall at soil level with about 100mm gap between that and the house wall, to make it possible to use a handbrush to remove leaves and similar.

When carrying out hard landscape construction note the following:
The differential between invert levels should be at least 1:50.
The differential between drainage channels should be at least 1:250.
The differential between longitudinal paths should be at least 1:250.
The differential between crossfalls of rough surfaces such as in situ concrete should be at least 1:30.
The differential between crossfalls of rough surfaces should be at least 1:40.
Other useful data: to convert metres to Imperial feet multiply by 3.2810. To convert yards to metres, multiply by 0.9144.

Before final designing, the selection of materials could depend on the availability of acquiring old materials, say from demolition sites or the modernising of old buildings, for example, handmade paving bricks, rope-twist edging tiles, tiles for tessellated paths, stable and panel pavers. These old materials are likely to have a well weathered appearance and are preferential for blending into old or brick constructions. Occasionally one can find firms that specialise in stocking and selling such items.

Visits to local branches of builders' merchants are advisable to see what kind of materials are stocked such as paving slabs, bricks, stone and aggregates.

When organising your composting arrangements a slatted wooden container is desirable for aeration. It is also beneficial to place some land drains, if available, or perforated plastic pipe at the bottom because they speed up the drainage of excess water and, again, assist aeration. To reduce the likelihood of the top layers drying out and to assist the rotting, a piece of thick carpet cut exactly to size does a good job when placed on top. When starting a new bay try to incorporate a bucket of old compost because that will have a nucleus of earthworms and other invertebrates and bacteria, essential for the decomposition process.

When designing, give thought to the possibility of putting up different types of nest-boxes and bat boxes, sited as far away as possible from prowling cats and rodents. Pre-cast concrete swallow nests could be fitted if there is adequate space under the roof eaves.

By placing feeding trays in strategic locations there is immense enjoyment to be had from watching different bird species and, in any case, it is sound conservation policy. Another benefit is that birds feed off insects, aphids, wireworm, leather-jackets and cutworms. The downside is that some species eat worms.

If you have a special wish to plant certain species, spend a little time observing neighbouring gardens to see what is best suited, i.e., sandy, acid soil, plant rhododendrons, azaleas and heathers and, if dry, roses, etc.

If, in your garden, there is any existing overgrown laurel, thorn, privet, or *Lonicera nitida* hedging that could be utilised if drastically reduced, then cut it hard back to about 300mm off ground level during the winter dormancy period when the plant's nitrogen is in the root system. In the spring the meristematic tissue will soon burst into new growth. A heavy application in the spring of dried blood, an organic fertiliser, around the feeding root areas will speed up the process considerably. This is when the sap rises. When the new growth has reached the desired height, remove the growing tips to stimulate branching and thus hedge thickening.

Either during or after a final design it is wise to consider what the next step is, i.e., employ a contractor to carry out all the work? There are benefits to this but there are also drawbacks. The owner may have little control over work sequence, delivery and timing of materials and, perhaps more important, it may be costly to have a change of mind. The second choice is to find a person who will carry out part or all of the work. In this case the owner will have a greater input into what is to be done and when. Variations can be made if that person is working on an hourly rate/materials supplied basis with weekly progress payments. The person who does the work can place the orders for materials or the owner, in consultation with this person, will order and book delivery of the material, sometimes in reverse order as they are required, and the owner will be responsible for paying the supplier.

The third choice is to do the work yourself. The snags here are that if the owner is in full-time employment, finding the opportunity to do the work, the problem of bad weather causing delay, and being in attendance for delivery of materials and to ensure that they are placed where required, make for some difficulty. If you are retired, there are advantages, providing you are strong enough and have the skills and a good working knowledge of construction. Then you are in full control over whatever needs to be done.

There is then the business of making sure the builders' merchants will deliver as requested and can deliver easily, i.e., tip or side offload, whether temporary red and white bollards are needed, and whether the public road or pathway is strong enough to take a large truck with a full load. Who would be liable if there is damage to the road surface? Incidentally, you should check what kind of inspection cover you have in the drive; if it is cast iron it could easily break, and therefore you will require a strengthened sheet metal galvanised type to withstand wheel and axle weight. To prevent spoiling the surface of a public road, have ready heavy-duty polythene sheeting. Old hessian sacks will keep the frost out of bricks, sand, etc., if the work is being carried out during the winter months.

Whatever method is finally chosen, I cannot stress too strongly that the constructional work should be done properly so that it will last for a long time. An example of this is slabs laid on sand on a weak base. In no time they will lip and become unstable. Likewise, using too weak a cement mix only stores up problems for later. Foundations of walls must be of adequate depth, width and material proportions in the concrete. It is often wise to incorporate lengths of reinforcing rods especially on corners. For wall strength don't try to get by with single brickwork with occasional buttresses. If appropriate use bricks or stone to face the walling and cheaper concrete blocks to back it. But this will only be possible in most cases if the wall is an earth-retaining one.

Build in the necessary safeguards against the action of root growth and land settlement, especially if, during the construction of the property, there has been disturbance to the original site. It is frequently possible to see walls built by a contractor which lean over because of the lateral force of the earth behind them, or which have split because of large tree roots nearby that, over the years, have expanded in girth. Sometimes walls are built of inferior quality bricks which disintegrate in time from frosting and weather. If drains are laid near trees, bed them down and haunch them in concrete to prevent root penetration and ultimate clogging. These defects represent a waste of money and more money will have to be found to put right what should have been done in the first place. Another example is that of tall interwoven wood panel fencing, which has a high factor of wind resistance, being blown aside, just because preserved posts of inadequate cross-section have been used and not secured by concrete dollies. This also applies to concrete posts if they have merely been placed in a hole and backfilled with rammed hardcore and earth.

Frequently, fencing components, sheds, etc., are offered for sale where ordinary wire nails instead of galvanised ones have been used, or a heavy duty staple gun has been used for instant effect. Similarly, panel components that have been sprayed with preservative after assembly instead of properly immersing them in a preservative, like creosote, in a suitable trough first, are likely to deteriorate rapidly. Check them by easing the panels apart to look for colour difference. Use galvanised gate furniture instead of painted metal which will not pass the test of time, and galvanised screws, nails and bolts.

When stapling wire into wooden posts don't drive the staples in completely as they are easier to remove and less likely to pinch and sever the wire.

Another factor which must not be forgotten is the use and ultimate disposal of top and subsoil. There are bound to be pieces of brick, stone or paving which have another use, i.e. hardcore. Therefore the storage of this kind of material during construction must be thought out well in advance. Work sequence and planning is vital.

Lastly, but of the greatest importance, is the question of finance. Whichever design is decided upon, how is it to be paid for? Can the work be staggered? Consider what items are the most important. For example, in pricing up bills of quantities for a greenhouse or shed, should the base be constructed first and then a year or so later the product itself purchased? Early research into the cost of greenhouses and other buildings is imperative to build up a picture of likely expenditure.

How wise it is, if required, to lay in water and electricity to pre-planned locations rather than to discover that they are needed later, requiring much disturbance and unwanted additional costs. Work out your itemised costings.

Instead of large-scale tree and shrub planting, perhaps make do with bedding plants and packets of seeds in the first year or two. Take the long-term view. Remember that seeing a new garden evolve with progressional photographs is deeply satisfying. But in the case of older people, time is of the essence and it may not be appropriate to buy young plants which may take a while to mature and to be in their glory.

Each project should be considered on its merits and there are so many alternatives to weigh up. But, on the other hand, beware of the instant garden where a contractor has perhaps rotavated an area containing couch, bindweed, and the like, to give an immediate effect and many troubles are stored up for later. There is an old adage which is sometimes wise

– make haste slowly, and discover during the year what is in the ground. This is especially so in the case of bulbs or dormant roots of intrusive perennial weeds.

At this point I imagine the reader might be saying – what a lot there is to think about! Part of the purpose of this book is to alert those wishing to design and make a garden to some of the essential components and problems that might arise along the way.

Once the survey is completed the next stage is to consider the scale in which you wish to plot items and start designing. I would strongly suggest that you use squared graph paper which will help you in many ways, whether you decide to work at 1:20, 1:50, or 1:100 scale. The larger the drawing the better but, of course, after A3 size, photocopying in its entirety is impossible unless you are producing a dyeline negative which can then be printed professionally. It all depends on the amount of precision detail you desire.

For those who want a greater degree of precision in setting out a design in situ, the next stage would be to draw a metric grid on a copy of your scaled design so that it is possible to create a 'mock-up' within your garden. Place bamboo canes at every metre point on the perimeter and then join up as indicated with strong string. Sand can then be dribbled to define construction zones and an assessment made to see if what you have designed is compatible with locations and your wishes.

Sometimes white or silver paint spray can be used to advantage in forming design lines on the soil.

It is wise to obtain several copies of your final design for use on site or for note-taking, or even to hand to the person who is doing the construction work.

Before planning to start work by whatever method, it is essential to prepare an approximate bill of quantities as far as it can be judged, and cost it up, i.e., $x$ paving slabs @ ..., $y$ bricks @ ..., $z$ stone for walling, rockery, water and electricity installations, plus individual items such as shed, greenhouses, etc.

See if it can all be budgeted for immediately or in staggered expenditure. If it is the latter then decisions have to be made, i.e., what to proceed with and what may be deferred. In any case, it is recommended that 10% of the estimated costs are set aside for any unexpected outlay.

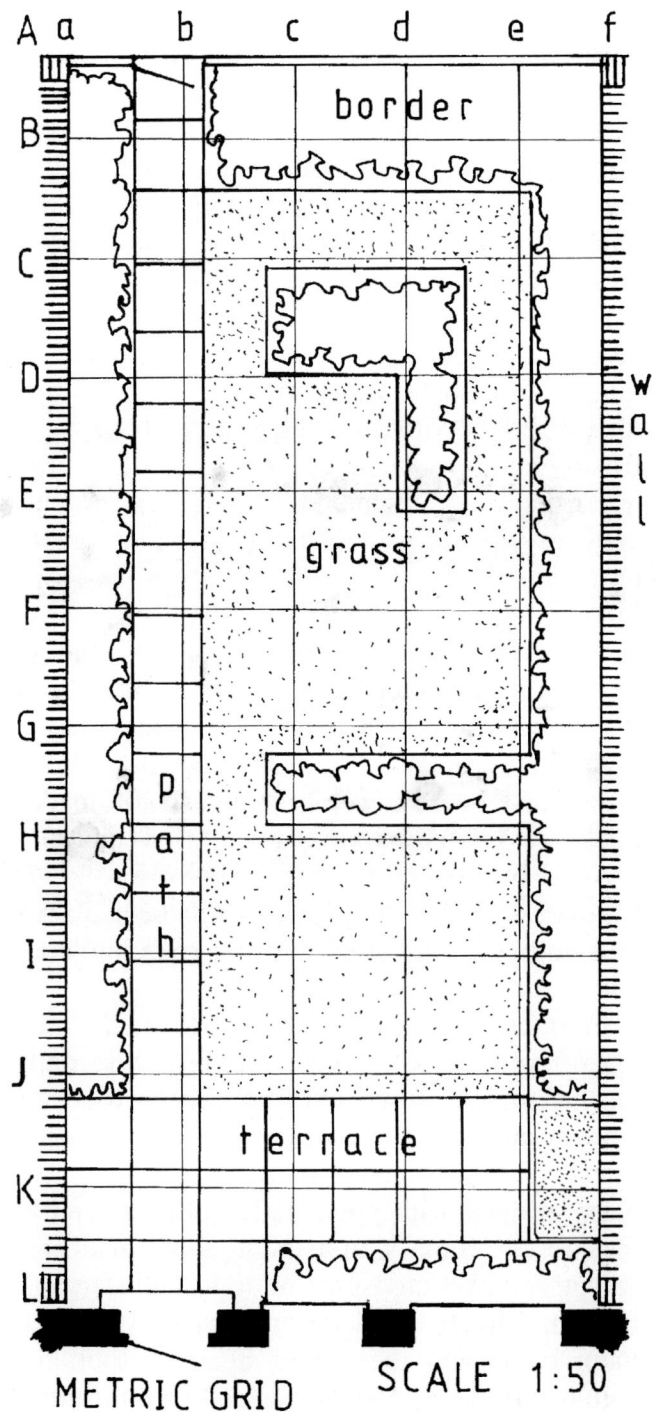

METRIC GRID          SCALE 1:50

# The small terraced house in the London suburbs

Front of house before improvements

Front of house after improvements. Georgian type portico fencing and boundary trellis

Front of house paved area, brick wall, raised beds of flowers

Front of house showing window boxes and climbing rose

Rear of house, small pond next to paved area and surrounding flower beds

Rear of house, raised flower beds with seat

# The thatched cottage in the countryside

Construction of largest pond in concrete with lip stone and surrounding beds

Main pond with plant pots and crazy paving surround

The two smaller ponds with crazy paving surround and associated pathways

View of pond complex

View of pond complex in full flower

View of smaller ponds with seat in background surrounded by flowering shrubs

# The thatched cottage in the countryside

Kitchen garden-construction of service path leading to garden shed and installation of irrigation network

View of extensive fruit cage, frames for Dutch lights and screening pergola with archway

Front garden showing principal flower borders and crazy paving edging to lawn

Pathway adjacent to cottage with low retaining wall planted with mixed alpines

Front entrance with gate and fence leading to pergola system

The front pergola resplendent with Wisteria and Laburnum in full flower

# The new bungalow

The rear garden, just grass and boundary fence

The rear garden after landscaping and erection of wall trellis

The rear garden in its pre-landscaped state

The rear garden showing the newly constructed base with low walling for the lean-to conservatory

The construction of a service path to divide the flower and shrub border from the small vegetable garden. Note the two strong washing line poles.

The lean-to conservatory with adjacent trellis and flower borders

# The rear garden of the small house in a modern estate - sequence of work

Rear garden upon occupation.
View from point U showing part of
fence A C

Rear garden construction of raised
borders H I Z. Note mowing strip
along H I and drain surround at J.
Terrace G H Z used as a temporary
stock-piling area

Rear garden view along path T U from
U showing paving and raised flower
beds X. Note weep hole

# The rear garden of the small house in a modern estate - sequence of work

Stone block surround to seating area G with brick on edge finish adjacent to paved terrace

Crinkle-crankle type curved raised bed Y for shrubs and tree planting with wide curved steps to higher lawn area R P W O. Note pockets for alpines in curved wall

View of curved border Y prior to turfing lower lawn G N I H. Note weepholes and double staking for trees

# The rear garden of the small house in a modern estate - sequence of work

Rear garden facing house showing borders H I Z and part of X, window box at J, rotary washing line at M

Rear garden view of French window L with adjacent Clematis secured to plastic covered wire between vine-screw eyes

Rear garden view of border X in full flower and part of path T U

# The rear garden of the small house in a modern estate - sequence of work

Rear garden view from first floor showing raised flower bed Y, W and part of X, steps N O and part of lower lawn N I H G. Note turf trimmed to mowing strip

Rear garden view from point V showing part of raised flower bed X towards upper lawn and surrounding beds W showing extensive tree planting of silver birch with twin post tree staking

Rear garden view from lower lawn G H I N towards point A, shows seat R, border Y, steps N O, border W and boundary fence A C

# 4

## *Detailed Designs*

In this section of the book I have prepared 80 different conceptual scaled designs at 1:20, 1:50, 1:100 and 1:200 scale. As far as is possible I have shown most components to scale, i.e., paving, walls, etc., so that the reader can benefit from it by using a scale. This method can then be used in preparation of your design, with the plot having been dimensioned using a survey by triangulation as previously described. The designs vary from town houses, basements, old farmyards, open plan and individual house developments, courtyards, open

countryside, even to a garden with a model railway, a caravan site, and a waterside property.

I suggest you examine each design and hopefully get inspiration from some of them. Indeed, there may be just one feature in a particular design which merits, with others, inclusion in your own conceptual design. If it stimulates you to put pen to paper, apart from the hard physical work that follows, you should obtain considerable satisfaction from creating just the garden you want.

## Contents for this chapter

| | |
|---|---|
| A small basement front garden | 28 |
| A garden on two levels | 30 |
| Terraced town house garden | 32 |
| Labour-saving cottage garden | 34 |
| A spider's web design | 36 |
| A small urban garden overhung by a tree | 38 |
| A shady town garden with a tree seat | 40 |
| End of terrace mews garden | 42 |
| Georgian house on a corner plot | 44 |
| A long narrow front garden | 46 |
| Courtyard garden | 48 |
| A town house forecourt | 50 |
| A practical caravan park garden | 52 |
| Screening for traffic noise in an urban kitchen garden | 54 |
| A levelled platform on a sloping site | 56 |
| Two lawns on a slope | 58 |
| Paving and steps | 60 |
| A secluded terrace | 62 |
| Formal rose garden on clay soil | 64 |
| A loggia and barbecue | 66 |
| Two plots in one | 68 |
| Dealing with a long driveway | 70 |
| Garden near a railway embankment | 72 |

| | |
|---|---|
| Vegetables and flowering trees | 74 |
| Large kitchen garden and fruit cage | 76 |
| Sloping site with 'cut-and-fill' | 78 |
| An asymmetrical shape | 80 |
| Gardening on two levels | 82 |
| A central vista | 84 |
| A circular lawn bordered by steps | 86 |
| Perimeter problems: a shared drive | 88 |
| Paved areas and a beech hedge | 90 |
| A corner plot | 92 |
| Curved borders – infill site | 94 |
| A feature pond | 96 |
| Mounded island bed | 98 |
| House set back in its garden | 100 |
| A wide plot | 102 |
| Play area with mixed planting | 104 |
| Open plan garden | 106 |
| Low-maintenance garden | 108 |
| Tricky levels | 110 |
| Difficult surface water drainage | 112 |
| A hammerhead driveway | 114 |
| Three interlinked ponds | 116 |
| Urban walled garden | 118 |
| Plot for a partially disabled gardener | 120 |

| | | | | |
|---|---|---|---|---|
| Large front garden | 122 | | Yew hedges and a swimming pool | 156 |
| Terrace with alpines | 124 | | A peaceful orchard | 158 |
| A front door at the back! | 126 | | A design incorporating large existing trees | 160 |
| Walkway and feature pool | 128 | | A modern country house garden | 162 |
| A modern house with a small garden | 130 | | An irregular-shaped plot with a long drive | 164 |
| A family garden | 132 | | A sunken garden | 166 |
| Urban garden with screening | 134 | | Triangular site | 168 |
| One-third functional, two-thirds ornamental | 136 | | Formal garden with pond and beech hedges | 170 |
| Patterns of paving on a large terrace | 138 | | A ranch-style chalet on clay soil | 172 |
| Crazy paving terrace | 140 | | A former farmyard redesigned | 174 |
| Garden for a partially sighted person | 142 | | Large-scale formal garden | 176 |
| A feeling of seclusion | 144 | | Low-maintenance gardening on a large | |
| A woodland garden for a mobile home | 146 | | scale | 178 |
| Mews house with a roof garden | 148 | | Creating a large natural pond | 180 |
| Riverside garden with slipway | 150 | | Large lawns and a panoramic view | 182 |
| Lakeside garden with terrace | 152 | | Heathland planting | 184 |
| Garden for a model railway enthusiast | 154 | | Two semis sharing a communal garden | 186 |

# Key to symbols

| Symbol | Description | Symbol | Description |
|---|---|---|---|
| — · · — | Electricity | — · · — | Contours |
| — · — | Water | ⊕ | Incinerator |
| ◦ · ◦ · | Oil | ⊓ | Compost bay |
| + + + | Gas | ⁄⁄ | Rockery |
| ⇒ | Drains and direction of fall | ⊛ | New deciduous tree |
| · · · · · · | Chain link fencing | ✳ | Existing deciduous tree |
| OXOXOXO | Post and wire fencing | ✳ | New conifer |
| ━━ | Interwoven wood panel fence | ⚜ | Marginal aquatic |
| ▭—▭—▭ | Post and rail fencing | | Long grass |
| ▄ ▄ ▄ | Palisade fencing | | Waterlily |
| x x x x x | Close-boarded fencing | ◇ | Rotary washing line |
| ◦—◦— | Post and single wire fencing | ⊠ | Lamp post |
| ◦◦◦◦◦◦ | Post and chain fencing | ⊙ | Sundial |
| ⁄⁄⁄⁄⁄⁄⁄ | Ranch type fencing | ⊠ | Bird table |
| ▮···········▮ | Trellis | ◎ | Bird bath |
| ▭ | Wooden steps | ≋ | Hedging |
| | Macadam | v v v v | Vegetable garden |
| | Grass | ++++ | Cane fruit |
| ◉ | Rodding eye | 8⊙◯ | Soft fruit |
| ☖ | Water standpipe | | Plants |
| + + + | Concrete | | Small plants – alpines, etc. |

## A small basement front garden

This design makes the best possible use of the very small basement front garden. Access for constructional work has inevitably had to be through the dwelling or over the wall, using a small crane.

There must be an adequate crossfall to allow for surface water to reach the soakaway at (X) and a suitable pipe under the raised bed (Q) in the corner near the plant tub at (S). There is a concentration of large plant containers of different kinds, all of which must have suitable drainage holes in case of hard frosts.

In order to break up the uniformity of paving levels, a low border with trellis (L) that can be seen through is situated in a strategic location.

Wall shrubs, low-growing shrubs, and draping alpines embellish the other raised angular border. There is an opportunity for flower troughs at (R).

If the garden has a southerly aspect, the temperatures could become quite high and therefore plants which can cope with a hot dry situation should be chosen. If, on the other hand, it faces north, then the plant choice is limited, concentrating perhaps on foliar species, even ferns.

---

**Key**

| | |
|---|---|
| A | Dustbin or other refuse container |
| B | Close-boarded gate to refuse area |
| C | Inspection cover |
| D | Rectangular non-slip paving slabs, different sizes |
| E | Paving bricks, assorted patterns |
| F | Barrel with holes for hanging plants |
| G | Weepholes through low walling for soil drainage |
| H | Shallow brick wall |
| I | Access to dwelling |
| J | Small flower border with wall shrubs attached to wire between vine screw eyes |
| K | Small brick pillar with cap |
| L | Strong trellis |
| M | Bricks on edge |
| N | Assorted large pots and ornamental urns |
| O | Container with side handles |
| P | Raised planting area with stone walling |
| Q | Reconstituted stone walling with coping |
| R | Plant trough |
| S | Plant tubs |
| T | Manger for trailing plants |
| U | Cobble infill |
| V | Brick wall sides to refuse area |
| W | Large plant container on stand |
| X | Drainage grid over soakaway |
| Y | Small pots for specimen miniature plants |
| Z | Perimeter walling |

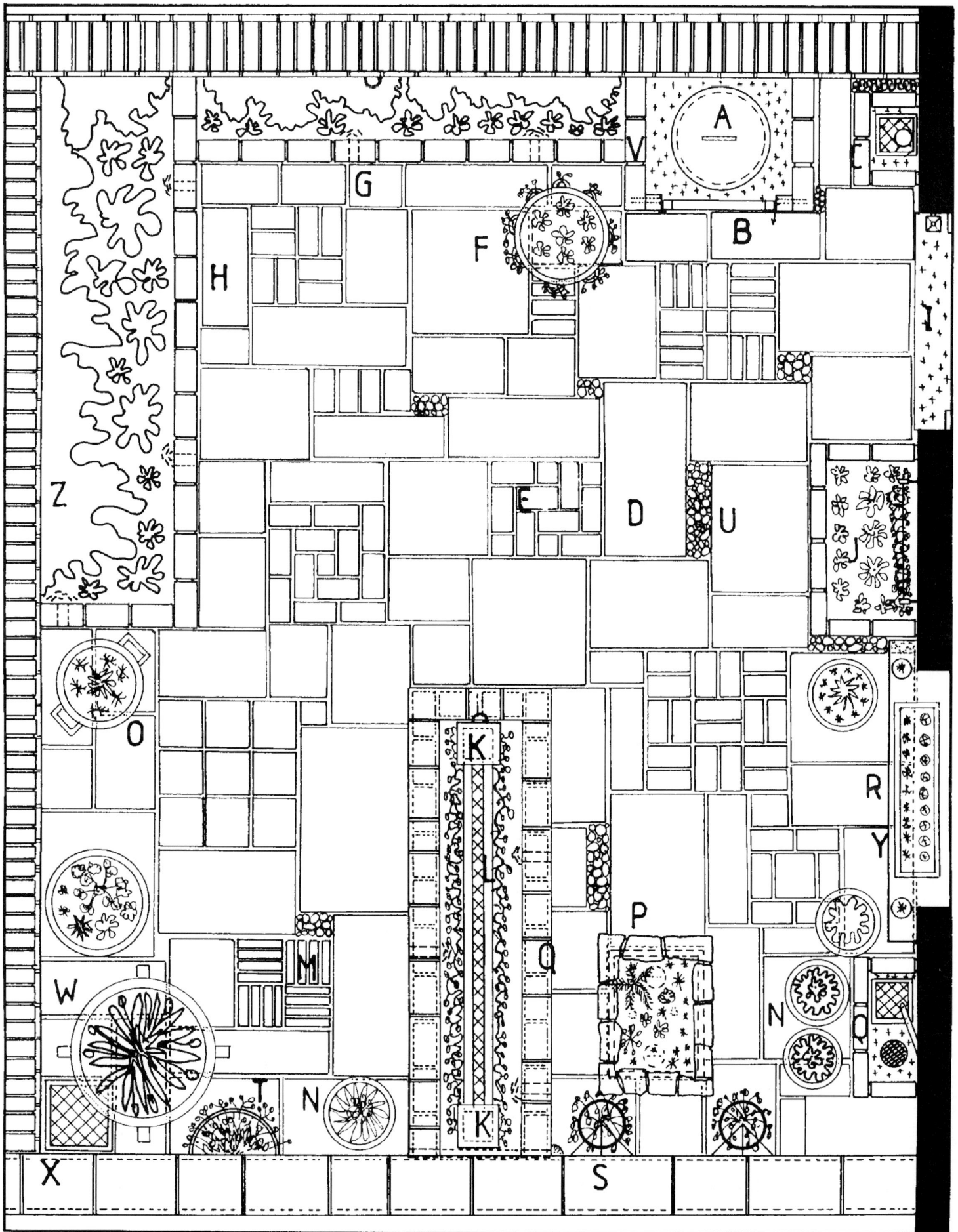

A B C D E F G H I K L M N O P Q R S T U V W X Y Z

SCALE 1: 20

**A garden on two levels**

The garden of this property has given much opportunity for two levels of landscaping, made more interesting by the house being broadside on. Near to the house is a narrow lawn adjacent to a service path on the house side and opposite is a fairly substantial bed containing large rocks, well placed (B). To retain this is a low stone wall (C). If the soil is acid (i.e., low pH) then it can be planted up with heathers, prostrate brooms, and Japanese azaleas, etc. To reach the lower lawn there are some curved steps (O) from the terrace (P) being the principal viewpoint. At one end of the lawn there is a kidney-shaped pond (K) with a surround of crazy paving (M) well secured by cement. However, note that surface water from the terrace (P) is taken by an underground pipe (R) to refill the pond with an overflow (S) to a soakaway (L). To provide a focal point there is a long seat (J) on slabbing which also provides a panoramic view of the rockery and house.

At the other side of the garden there is a sloped non-slip path down to a paved area in which is situated an incinerator, compost bay and water tap (D). Conifers and a tall tree (perhaps birch) screen this area which is located adjacent to a brick retaining wall with weepholes, in addition to the telegraph pole and overhead wires. The ground adjacent to the path (A) is sloped, upon which there is a thick thorn hedge and on the other side a field and roofed animal shelter. This grassy slope gives an opportunity for spring bulbs, primroses, etc.

**Key**

| | | | |
|---|---|---|---|
| A | Sloped path | O | Curved steps |
| B | Rockery | P | Terrace |
| C | Retaining wall | Q | Small bed edged with stone including weepholes |
| D | Tap | | |
| E | Compost bay | R | Underground pipe from terrace to pond |
| F | Incinerator | S | Pond overflow pipe |
| G | Telegraph pole | T | Upper lawn |
| H | Thick hedge | U | Lower lawn |
| I | Conifer screen | V | Cobbles |
| J | Long seat on slabbing | W | Brick retaining wall |
| K | Pond | X | Sloped grass bank |
| L | Soakaway | Y | Gully with dirt trap at lowest point of terrace, i.e., adequate crossfall |
| M | Crazy paving surround | | |
| N | Rockery | Z | Trellis secured to brick retaining wall |

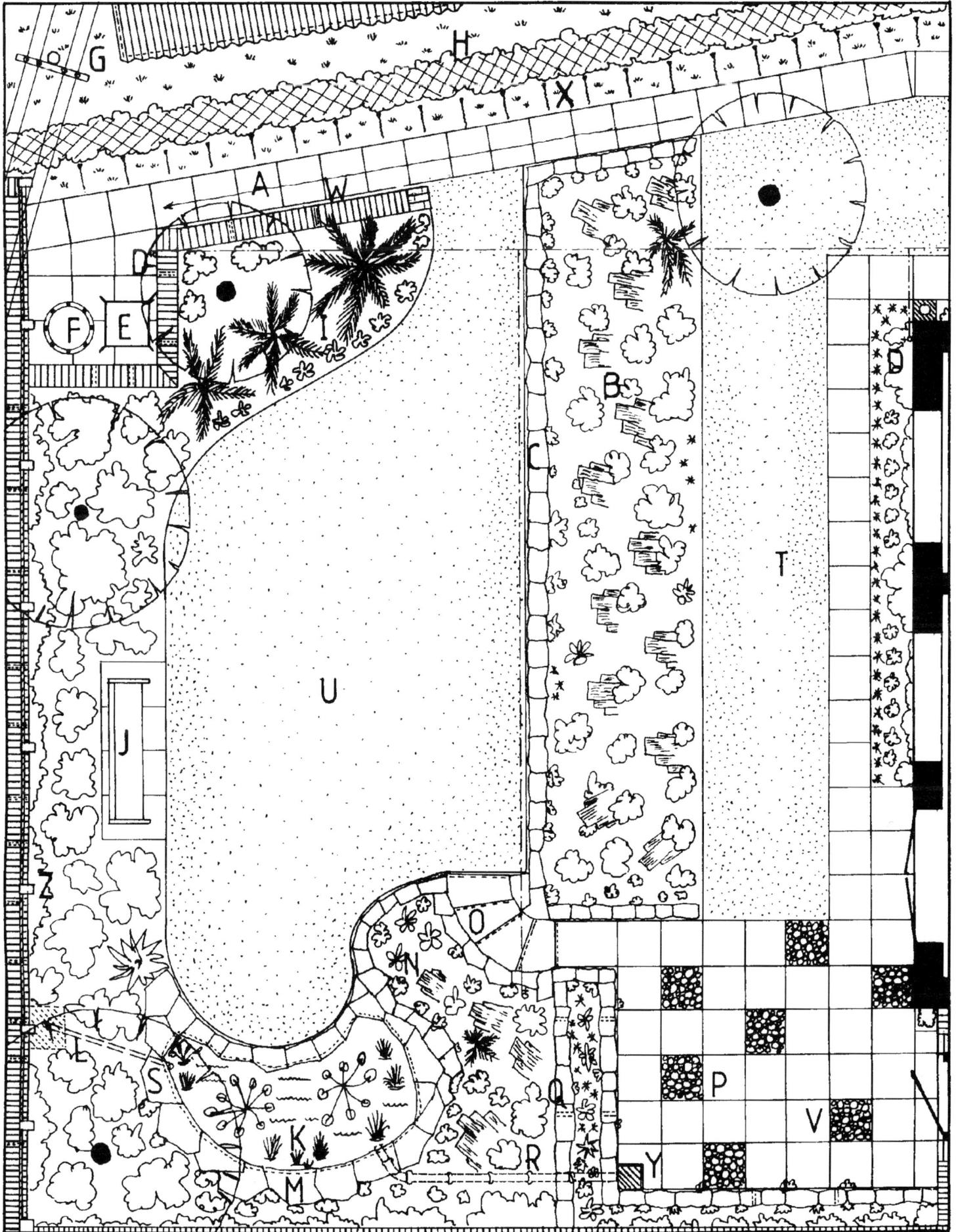

G

H

X

A

W

D

F E

I

B

C

T

D

U

J

Z

O

N

L

S

Q

P

K

V

M

R

Y

SCALE 1:50

## Terraced town house garden

Occasionally in towns and cities terraced houses are to be found with basements. With imagination and flair they can be made very attractive. In this case it is a corner plot. Steps made of in-situ concrete lead down from the pavement, curving at the bottom. On the inside there is a stepped down brick wall upon which, on one section, is a trough with low-growing flowers. The window-sills (A) are embellished with large troughs which, because the windows are of the sash type, enable fairly tall flowers to be used, i.e., the windows cannot swing open and damage the flowers. There are many other troughs and tubs here and there, even an old galvanised bath tub (N).

An old-fashioned lamp and bracket (O) helps to illuminate the back door area leading to the steps. The refuse container (P) is shielded by a low brick wall and gate. Hanging baskets (W) help to dress the walls. Cast iron railings (D) bedded in concrete, faced by a low brick wall, surround the property. The front door is approached by steps (S) at the top of which there are two tubs planted with topiary bushes. The top of the basement steps is fortunately illuminated by the street lamp post (F). Surface water drains off by adequate crossfalls to the rain-water gully and grid (L).

---

**Key**

| | | | |
|---|---|---|---|
| A | Large flower trough on wide window-sill | N | Old galvanised bath |
| B | Flower trough – could contain bamboo-staked annual climbers | O | Lamp on bracket |
| | | P | Refuse container |
| C | Earth-filled brick trough with weepholes | Q | Wide flower trough |
| | | R | Large flower trough |
| D | Cast iron railings | S | Steps to front door |
| E | Pollarded tree, probably sycamore | T | Concrete suitably tamped or stippled to prevent slipping |
| F | Lamp post | | |
| G | Wrought iron gate | U | Drain gully for downpipe with brick surround |
| H | In-situ concreted steps scored to reduce slipping | | |
| I | Wall with bricks on edge, stepped down as required | V | Round flower containers – could be used for culinary herbs |
| J | Narrow flower trough | W | Hanging baskets |
| K | Corner bed in brick | X | Trellis screen of adequate height to give privacy to basement room |
| L | Drain gully with grid | | |
| M | Manhole cover | Y | Corner bed |
| | | Z | Tub |

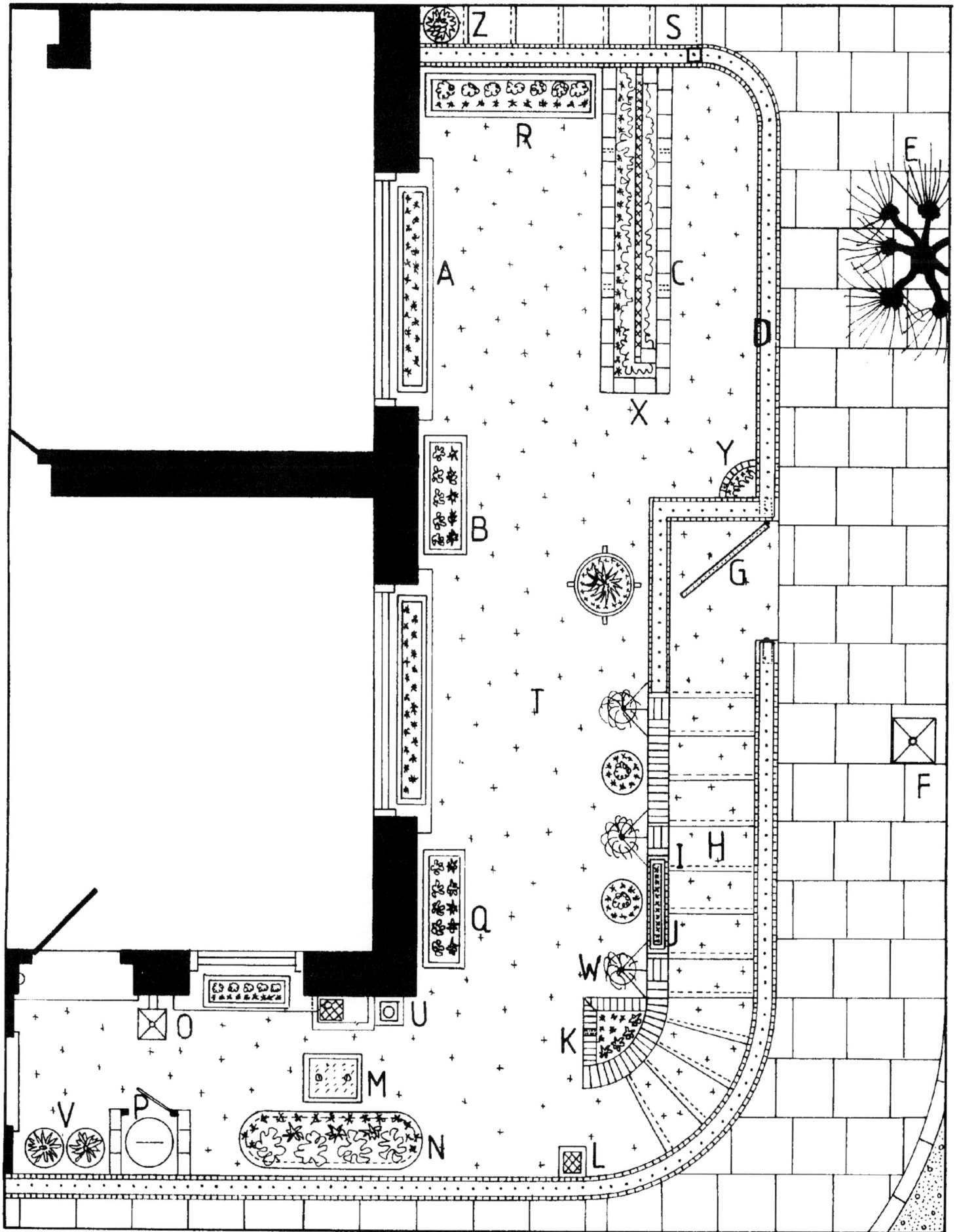

Z    S

R

A    C

X

D

E

B    Y

G

T

I H

F

Q    J

W

O    U    K

M    L

V P    N

SCALE 1:50

## Labour-saving cottage garden

This small garden has had to be designed and constructed simply, with as much labour-saving as possible. The cottage is relatively small and the property is bounded by old stone walls. One boundary wall has had to be buttressed to ensure its stability (Q). In one corner there is an old shed constructed of rough stone which is connected to the house by a path consisting of crazy paving edged with paving bricks leading to an extensive terrace. Several pockets have been left in this terrace for cushioning alpines. There is a small raised bed (note weepholes) as a feature next to the curved seat and adjacent wooden table.

In the corner of the lawn next to the terrace there is a well-shaped ornamental tree to give shade. It must be a non-vigorous species. The small bed adjacent to the terrace window is edged and planted. At the other end of the terrace is a flight of three steps leading to the rear door of the house. There is an opportunity for a sink garden here. From this terrace there is a curved brick path leading to a covered well (O) surrounded by cobbles (W) with the circumference in brick on edge as headers (P).

---

**Key**

| | | | |
|---|---|---|---|
| A | Old stone shed | N | Lawn |
| B | Water butt with tap to take roof water located on bricks for watering-can access | O | Well with roof |
| | | P | Brick on edge surround |
| C | Concrete step | Q | Stone buttress |
| D | Crazy paving edged with brick | R | Fan-shaped fruit trees – plums, pears, etc. |
| E | Small raised planting border with weepholes | | |
| F | Pocket for shade tree | S | Fan-shaped peach or nectarine tree |
| G | Curved seat | T | Small pockets in terrace for alpines |
| H | Wooden garden table | U | Side pathway |
| I | Brick edging to small bed | V | Stone wall |
| J | Flight of steps | W | Cobble |
| K | Entrance to rear of house | X | Wall shrubs against stone wall |
| L | Rectangular area for sink garden surrounded by cobbles | Y | Shallow wall made of large stones to support steps and small terrace |
| M | Curved path of paving bricks | Z | Rain-water downpipe with brick surround |

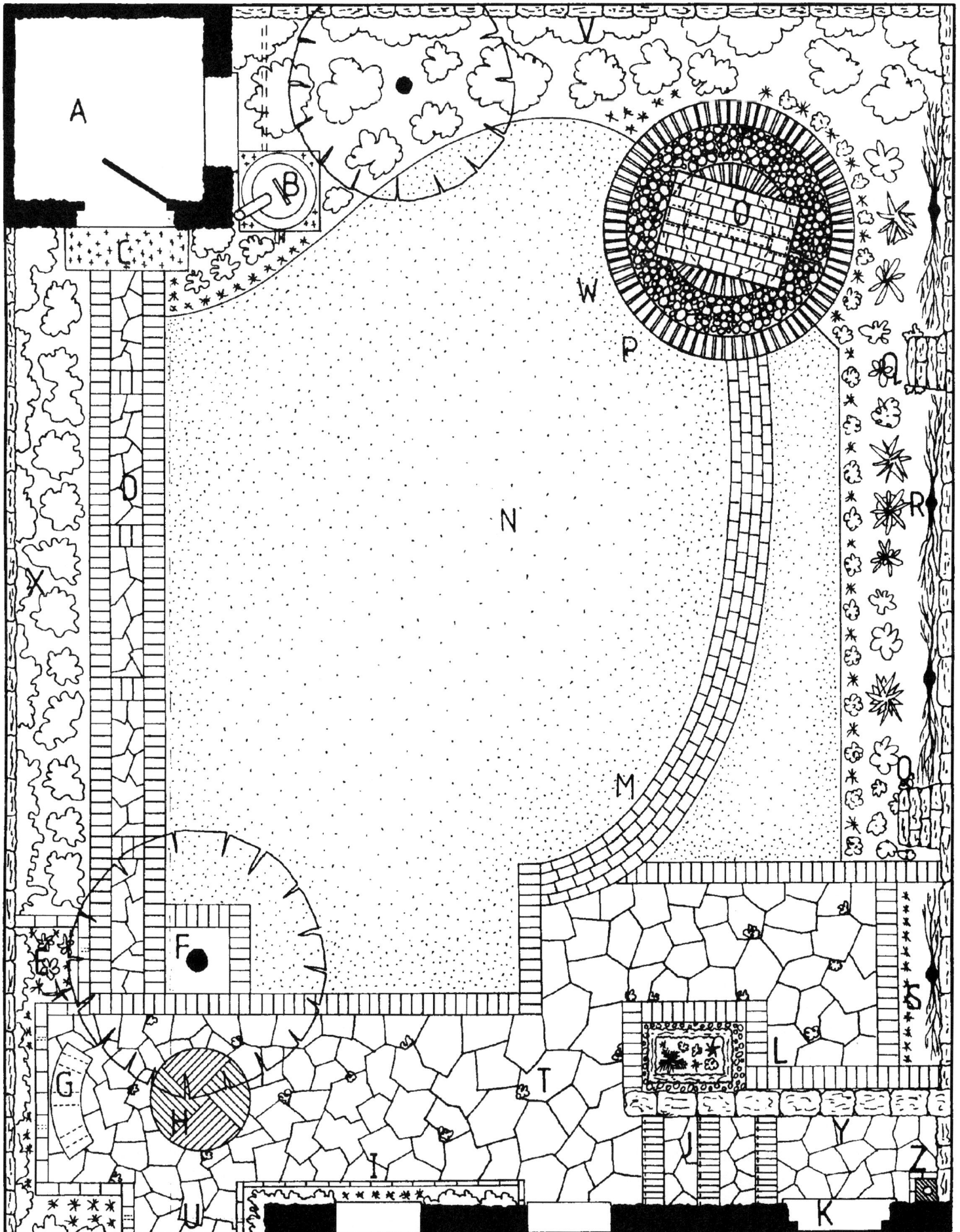

35

SCALE 1:50

## A spider's web design

This urban property has a rear garden of unusual design, i.e., like a spider's web with radial lines of paving from the centre to a broken edge finish, allowing for a diversity of planting. The paving is old York stone (I) with different areas of brick paving (G) and occasional pockets (F) for planting. In the centre is a cobbled area (M) upon which could be set a feature, i.e., an urn, fountain or bird table. Electric cabling in galvanised conduit has been laid before construction of the paving for a connection if required.

The almost rectangular terrace, with small slabs and paving bricks with adequate cross-falls for surface water drainage, is next to the French windows, and has circular steps (D) to lead down to the lower level.

Intentionally this main area has been left more or less bare for the occupier to set out troughs, pots, urns, garden furniture as he/she so desires, and rather like furniture in a large room it can be changed around from time to time.

---

**Key**

A  Wall shrub to soften house corner
B  Brick pillar with capping
C  Earth-filled brick walls
D  Curved steps
E  Alternate brick and tile on edge to form circle
F  Pockets left for alpines and other cushioning plants
G  Brick pavers
H  Coping over wall

I  Electric cable to centre feature installed before construction of paved area
J  Various shrubs – different heights and widths
K  Small non-slip paving slabs
L  Brick pavers laid to specific pattern
M  Cobble centrepiece upon which a small feature could be set, i.e., fountain, bird bath, urn, etc.

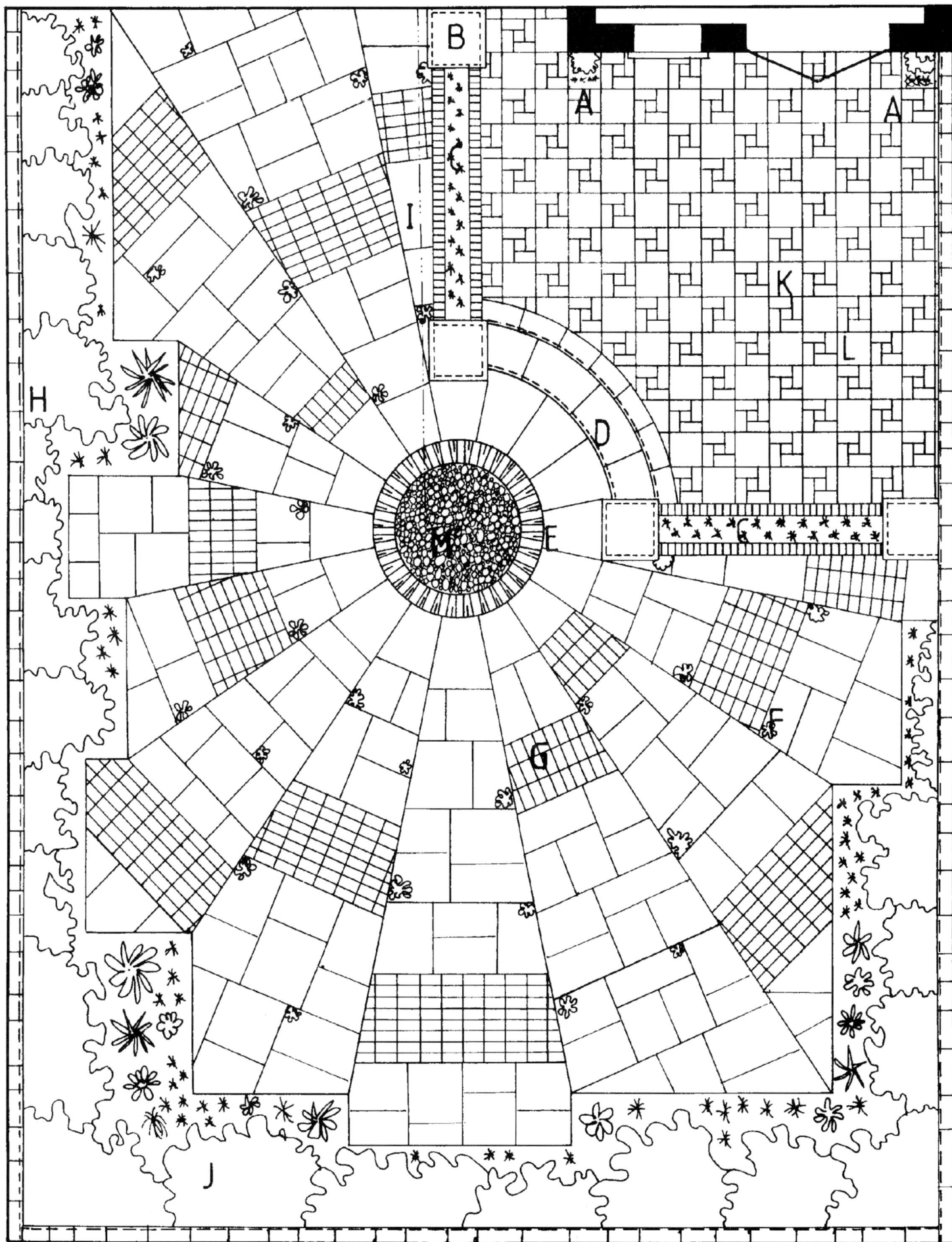

SCALE 1:50

### A small urban garden overhung by a tree

Urban dwellers frequently have to face the problems of a very small garden and, in a few cases, of a large street tree (X) which brings about difficulties of shade and slippery surfaces especially after leaf-fall, together with root growth problems and branch overhang. Limbing, branch balancing, and peripheral pruning may be subject to a Tree Preservation Order imposed by the local authority.

However, the potential of the area can be realised by the inclusion of a wide variety of features both in paving types, structures, and decorative additions such as a formal pond with moving water, sink garden (P) and bird bath (E). Enhancement can be obtained by wall mirrors (M) suitably embellished by wall shrubs, thus providing the impression that the garden in places is larger than it actually is. Especially important is the provision and location of seats (H) + (U) to vary the view of different aspects of the garden.

This garden benefits considerably from three-dimensional planning, i.e., by the judicious use of wall shrubs to adorn the different kinds of walling while occupants enjoy interesting views from the living room and other rear rooms.

---

### Key

| | | | |
|---|---|---|---|
| A | Street lamp post | O | Bird table |
| B | Brick paving, herringbone pattern | P | Stone sink on piers |
| C | Flower tub on stand | Q | Waterlily |
| D | Panel pavers | R | Cascading water feature |
| E | Bird bath | S | Marginal aquatic plants in brick boxes |
| F | Cobbles | T | Coping stone slabs on low wall |
| G | Granite setts | U | Garden seat |
| H | Stone seat on brick pillars | V | Inspection cover |
| I | Broken paving infill | W | Water butt with tap at base of rain-water downpipe |
| J | Paving brick surround | | |
| K | Cushioning alpine plants such as *Campanula carpatica* | X | Street tree – problems of branch overhang and roots |
| L | Non-slip type paving, irregular pattern, different sizes | Y | Small border backed by trellis for wall shrub |
| M | Mirrors secured to walling | Z | Regular pattern of square paving slabs |
| N | Brick paving | | |

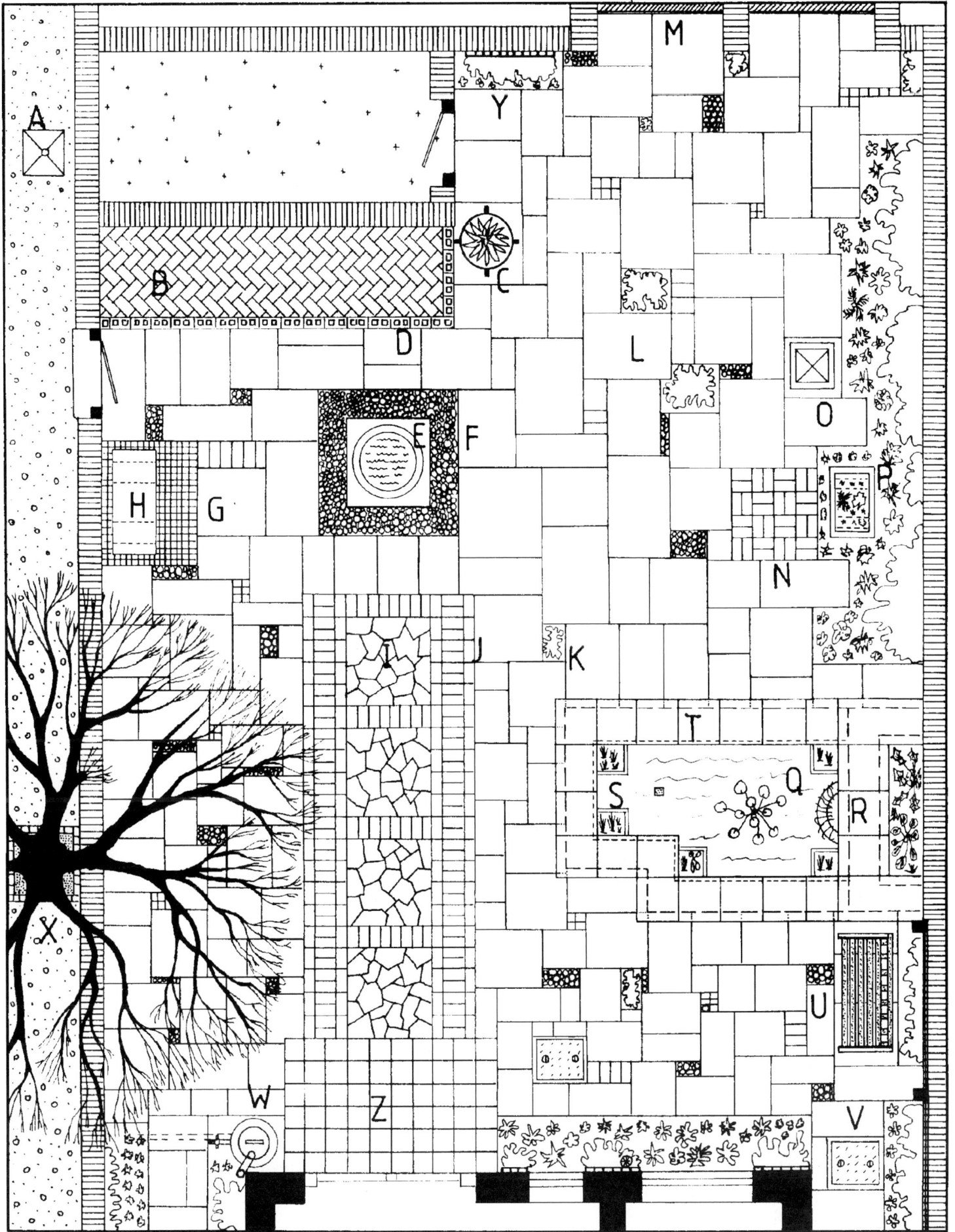

SCALE 1:50

**A shady town garden with a tree seat**

This property is at least 100 years old and has three storeys. It is situated in the residential area of a town. The large tree has a Tree Preservation Order on it. In the pavement outside there are two round drain covers (J), a lamp post (Z), and an old water-filled horse trough (S) as there are old stables nearby. Because of its location greater attention is required to use plants/shrubs which will grow satisfactorily in shady conditions. Grass would be unlikely to grow well here, hence the majority of the garden has been paved. An interesting feature, probably of Victorian origin, is the balcony with appropriate adornments. A little planting is possible but the weight of troughs (D) and pots must be well deployed and limited. The pleached limes (Q) will help to reduce traffic noise and dust from the road.

The paved garden provides opportunities for further plant containers if in optimum locations. The perimeter walls are clad with ivy (self-clinging) and other wall shrubs which will require wiring. There is an opportunity for hanging baskets on the house walls in summer.

**Key**

| | | | |
|---|---|---|---|
| A | Paving, using random rectangular sizes preferably with a non-slip surface, with open joints to assist drainage | N | Trellis approximately 900m high as screen and backing for small formal bed |
| B | Balcony | O | High brick wall, bricks on edge as headers |
| C | Balustrade around balcony | | |
| D | Flower trough with trellis backing | P | Variegated ivies |
| E | Wooden steps from first floor on to balcony with adjacent plant tubs | Q | Pleached lime trees |
| | | R | Curved high brick wall, bricks on edge as headers |
| F | French windows on to garden | | |
| G | Down pipe with wire balloon to prevent leaves blocking it, from balcony guttering | S | Water-filled horse trough |
| | | T | Adjacent house with opaque window |
| | | U | Brick paving |
| H | Concrete hard-standing | V | Strong posts with wires to initially train the pleached limes horizontally |
| I | Entrance gate into garden | | |
| J | Pavement drain hole | W | Fig tree |
| K | Five-sided timber seat around tree | X | Climbing *Hydrangea petiolaris* |
| L | Large tree which has had to be pollarded | Y | Door under balcony |
| M | Bird table | Z | Lamp post |

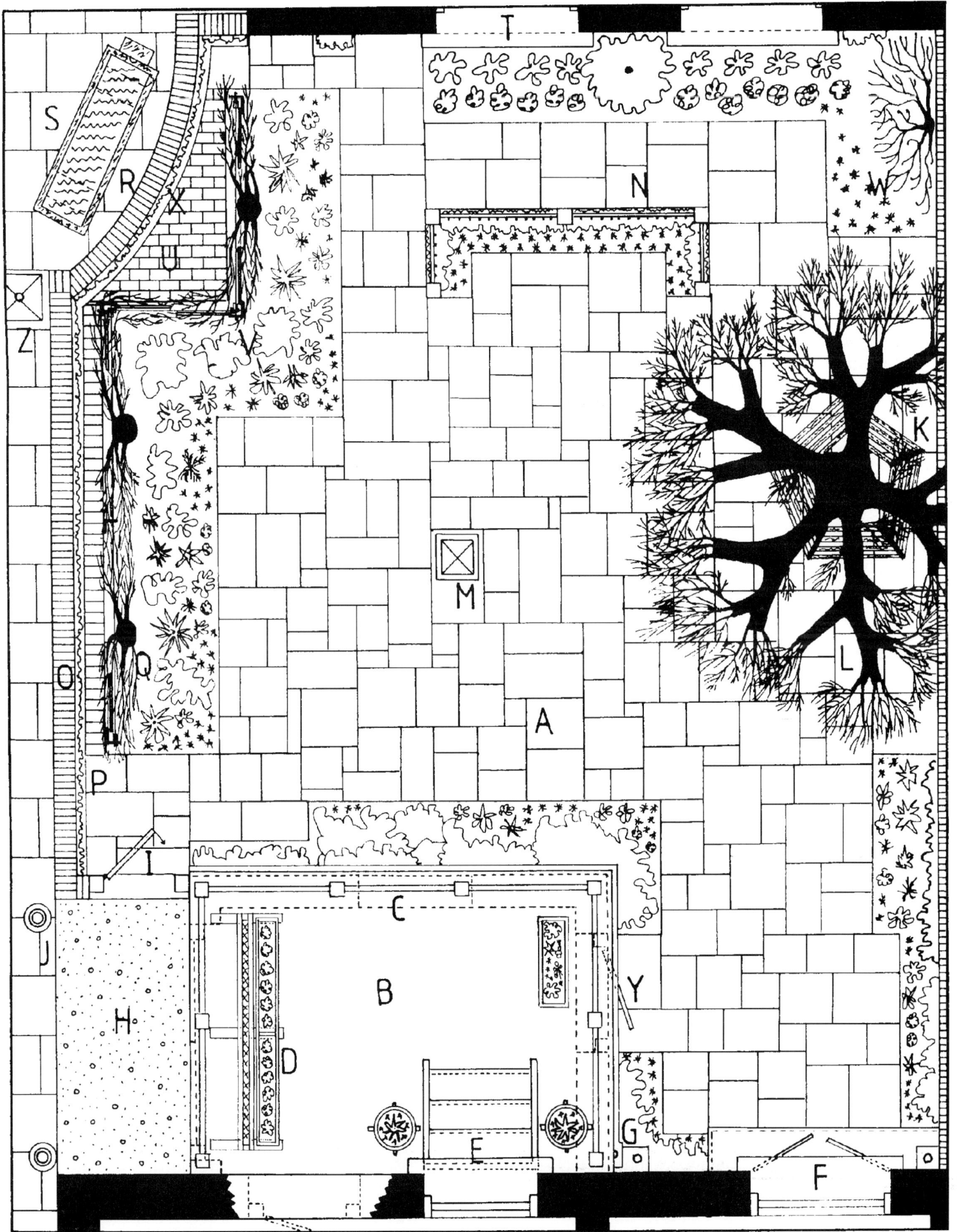

41

SCALE 1:50

## End of terrace mews garden

This small garden is in a mews area and hence the type of garage and approach drive with access pathway through a brick archway to the end of terrace house. The opportunity for a complex layout is small but the curved path with cobble infills breaks up the straight-sided rectangular terrace area. A curved lawn edge adjacent to two shrubs assists this.

The approach path consists of paving bricks as edging within which are slabs laid in an alternate pattern with small cobbles (I), (J). Path (C) is similarly patterned. Steps at (G) plus a small wall at (A) break the monotony of a one-level site. Note that because the house walls are finished in pebble-dash, wall shrubs are not an option and therefore there are no beds by the walls.

Imported plant containers would help to embellish the terrace (F), and to give further interest, the paving has been laid diagonally. Note the concrete posts (R), supporting the close-boarded fence (B). Two well shaped trees are planted as far away from the house as possible to give shade and variation of height supplemented by shrubs. Wall shrubs are secured by wiring to the concrete post structure.

---

**Key**

A    Low wall around raised bed
B    Close-boarded fence secured to concrete posts with gravel boards
C    Paving slab pathway with alternate cobbles
D    Planting area of low-growing shrubs and other plants
E    Entrance to dwelling
F    Patterned diagonal two-colour paving
G    One shallow broad step
H    Square raised border with brick surround and weepholes. Note space between this and house wall to prevent damp
I    Cobble, alternate bonding
J    Rectangular non-slip paving slabs
K    Paving brick edging (to withstand frosts)
L    Lawn
M    Large rectangular paving slabs
N    Door into garage workshop – step down, inward closing
O    Long double garage

P    Brick wall archway and gate
Q    Lower brick wall graded down from archway
R    Concrete posts supporting close-boarded fence
S    Rain-water downpipe to gully with cover against leaves
T    Ornamental tree planted among shrubs
U    Cobble insert between large rectangular paving slabs
V    Workshop end to garage
W    Garage drive with adequate crossfall drainage
X    Small border for flowers or window box
Y    Note – no wall shrubs – impossible because of pebble-dash finish to house walls
Z    Neighbour's rain-water downpipe. The neighbouring house window has opaque glass

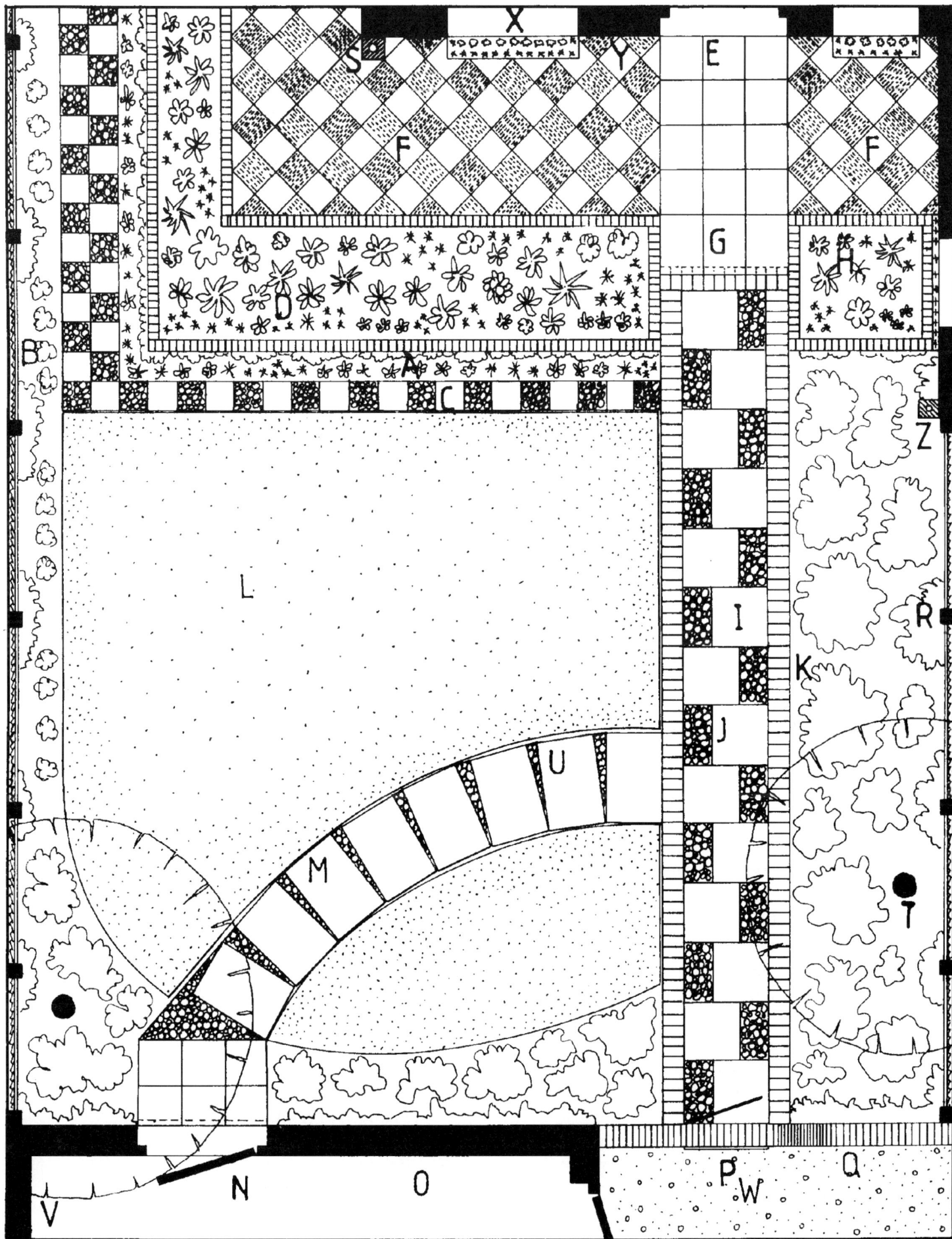

SCALE 1:50

## Georgian house on a corner plot

This beautiful Georgian house is situated on a corner bordered by pavements (C). The entrance, with curved walls (D), has brick pillars with capping and spheres (E and F). There is a very ornate wrought iron gate (S) opening on to a straight formal central path (H) with identical rectangular lawns (T) either side. Nearer the house is a paved stone terrace (Z) upon which are two identical teak containers (L) planted with mophead bay trees. At one end of this terrace there is a teak seat (N) and table (M). At the other end there are triangular steps (Q) leading down to a service area with associated brick walls (X and Y).

Either side of the front door are two antique lanterns. The whole front garden has around it a thick brick wall (G) with coping stones, with massed mixed shrubs (U) between the wall and the lawns.

---

**Key**

| | |
|---|---|
| A | Formal entrance to front garden |
| B | Two large plant containers |
| C | Pavement |
| D | Curved brick walls with shaped coping |
| E | Brick pillars with caps and spheres |
| F | Larger brick pillars with caps and spheres |
| G | Thick brick wall with coping |
| H | Formal central pathway in stone slabs |
| I | Front door lanterns |
| J | Refuse container on lower level |
| K | Door to cellar |
| L | Two teak plant containers planted with mophead bay trees |
| M | Teak table |
| N | L-shaped teak seat |
| O | Low wall shrub such as *Cydonia maulei* |
| P | Flower trough on window-sill |
| Q | Small flight of triangular steps from front terrace to cellar |
| R | Formal curved steps with risers |
| S | Wrought iron entrance gate |
| T | Equal-sized lawns |
| U | Mixed shrubberies |
| V | Standard street-tolerant tree, e.g. *Prunus sargentii* 'Rancho' |
| W | Standard street-tolerant tree |
| X | Brick retaining wall |
| Y | Small brick retaining wall |
| Z | Front terrace |

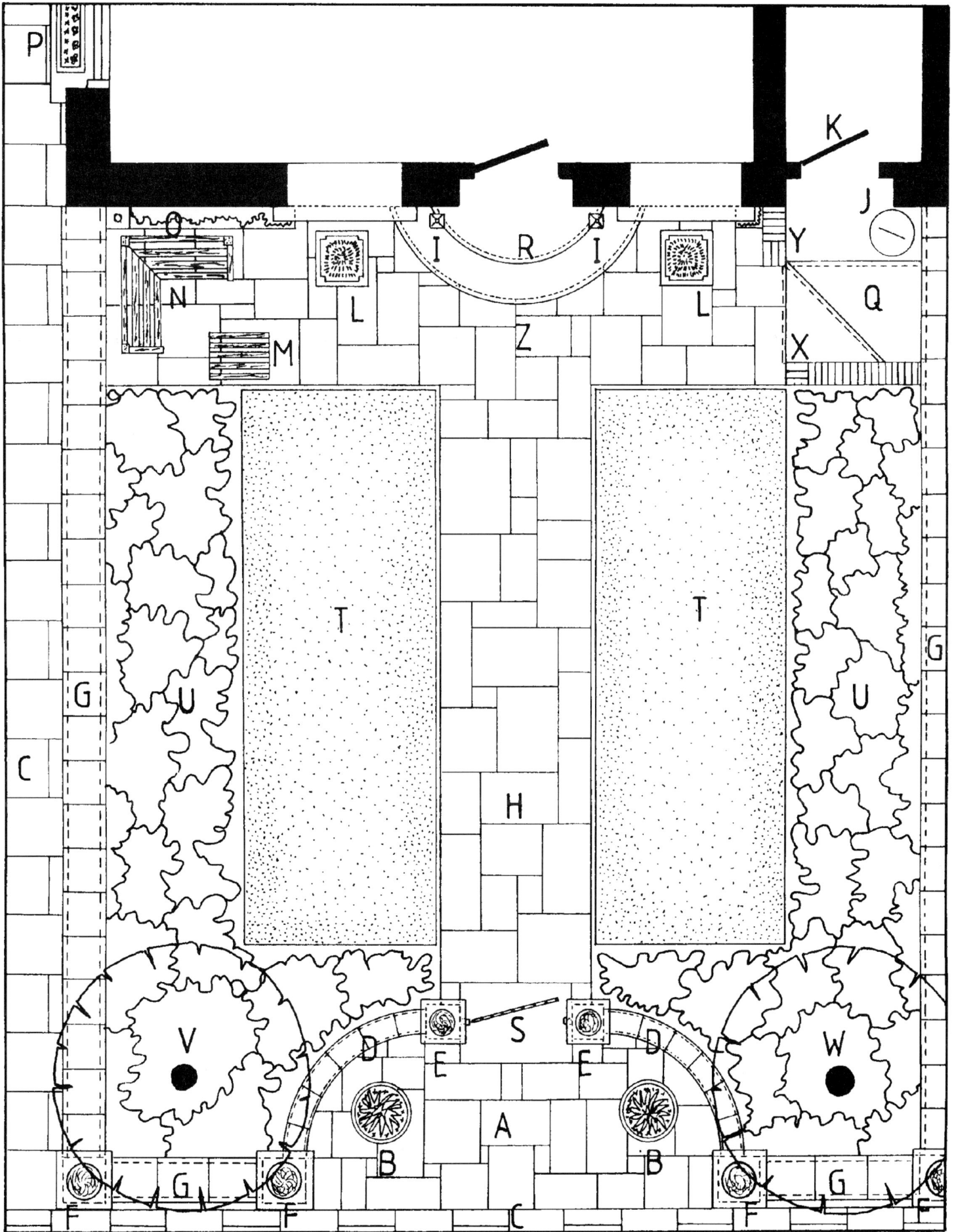

P

K

J

O

I R I

Q

N

L Z L

Y

M

X

G

T

T

G

U

U

C

H

V

D E S E D W

B A B

F G F C F G F

45

SCALE 1:50

## A long narrow front garden

This terraced property has a small rectangular front garden with party brick walls either side. There is no side pathway so that all access to the back garden has to be through the front door. This access must remain clear at all times, which influences floral planting. On the wide window-sills of the sash windows (H) there is an opportunity to place purpose-made wooden troughs constructed of tanalised timber, preferably planed to allow for painting, secured with galvanised screws, with adequate holes in the bottom for drainage.

For approximately one-third of the side walls, wooden trellis (J) some 300mm wide has been secured by brackets upon which to grow suitable climbers to afford better screening to the small terrace. In one corner is a sandpit (I) for children to play in. In the other is a bird table (E). Note: the side walls do not touch the house in order to prevent damp. As it is a very old property there is a possibility of ineffective damp-proofing. In the small bed by the front of the house, vertical slating bedded on to waterproofed cement, may be desirable. Shrubs and climbers are planted either side of the lawn to give colour, berries and foliar interest. A trellis (D) some 1·2m high secured to strong tanalised posts with pillar caps helps to divide the garden and forms a limited screen from passers-by in the street.

A small picket fence backs on to the pavement plus gate to prevent dogs from entering. The L-shaped bed gives an opportunity for formal bedding.

| Key | | | |
|---|---|---|---|
| A | Tallish shrubs preferably evergreen | I | Sandpit |
| B | Bed for formal planting | J | Trellis secured to brick walls |
| C | Paved pathway – non-slip riven surface | K | Low-growing shrubs, mostly |
| D | Trellis between posts | | deciduous |
| E | Bird table | L | Wall shrubs, climbing roses, etc. |
| F | Small trough | M | Pavement |
| G | Small terrace in front of house | N | Lawn |
| H | Sash windows with flower troughs | O | Front door |

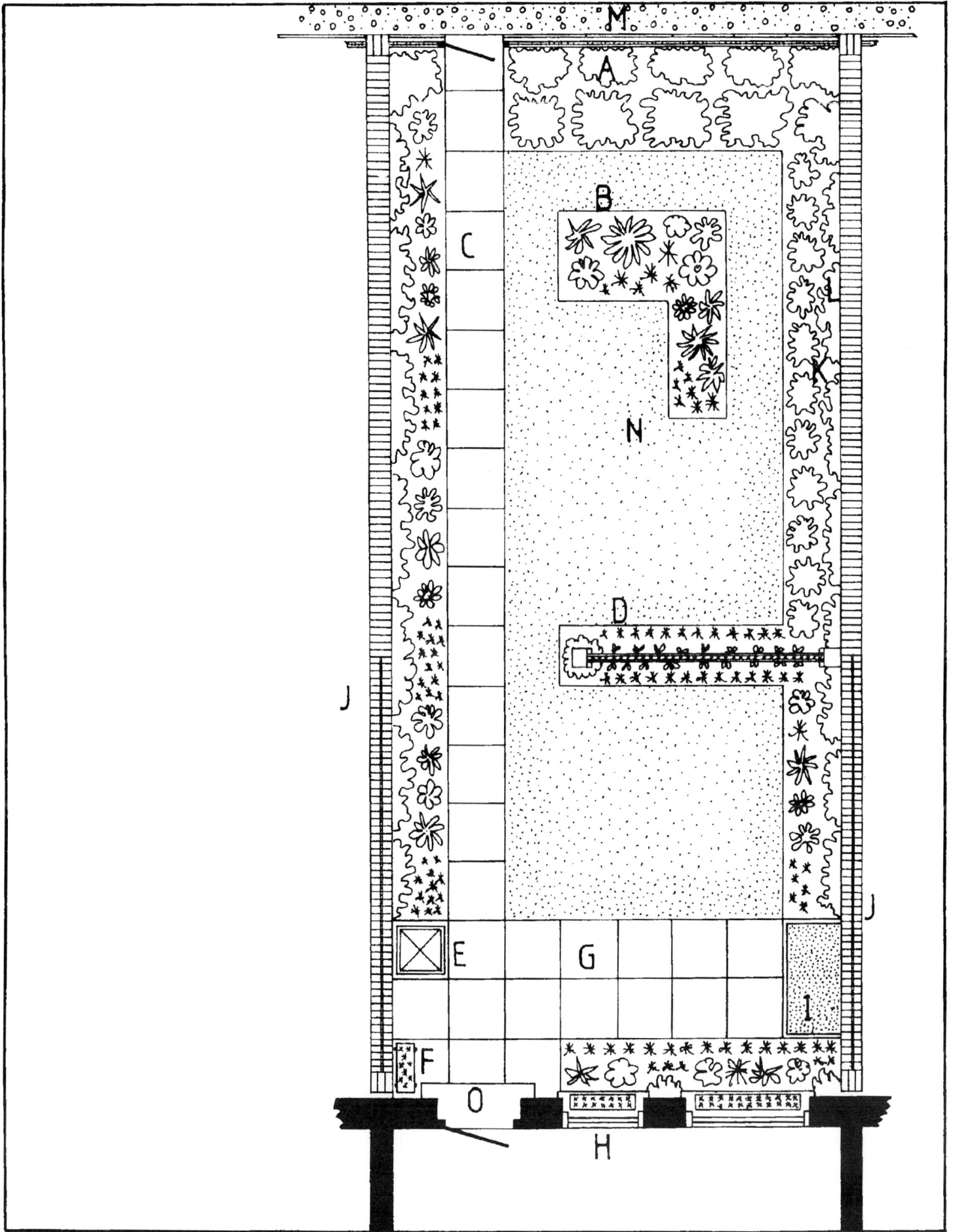

M

A

B

C

L

N

K

D

J

J

E G

I

F

O

H

SCALE 1:50

## Courtyard garden

This older property is situated on the corner of public highways, although one (B) has restricted access because of retractable bollards (A). The courtyard (T) has metal railings (R) on two sides. The courtyard or terrace is completely paved and has steps (J) down to it from a rear door. Adjacent to this is a brick wall (K) upon which hanging baskets (L) and flower tubs (O) help to embellish it.

The roof (X) of the neighbouring property is on one side of the terrace and the rain from it is taken by guttering (G) into a large water butt (F) with tap (Z). Inside this water butt is an overflow pipe which takes excess water via an open gully (V) to an outlet (W). There is a similar open gully (Y) on the opposite side. Both these drain off surface water from the terrace which has been carefully laid to allow adequate crossfalls. Large half-butt barrels with feet are placed around the terrace to give colour and some privacy. In addition there are further flower troughs and tubs next to the house walls together with flower-filled mangers (N) or half-baskets.

---

**Key**

| | | | |
|---|---|---|---|
| A | Retractable square bollards | N | Mangers filled with flowers and moisture-retaining liners |
| B | Macadam pathway | | |
| C | Drain covers | O | Flower tubs |
| D | Raised flower trough on brick pillars | P | Large half barrels, with feet, for flowers, etc. |
| E | Water tap secured to boundary wall | | |
| F | Water butt with protective lid raised on brick to facilitate watering-can access | Q | Flower trough |
| | | R | Railings surround to courtyard |
| G | Guttering on roof of neighbouring building with downpipes into water butt | S | Drain off courtyard to gully |
| | | T | Bonded square paving |
| | | U | Brick boundary wall |
| H | Lantern illuminating courtyard | V | Open gully to receive surface water from paving |
| I | Flower tubs | | |
| J | Steps down on to terrace | W | Outlet to open gully |
| K | Brick wall, approximately 1m high, with bricks on edge on top | X | Roof of neighbouring building |
| | | Y | Open gully to remove surface water from paving |
| L | Hanging baskets | | |
| M | Flower trough | Z | Wooden tap for water from water butt |

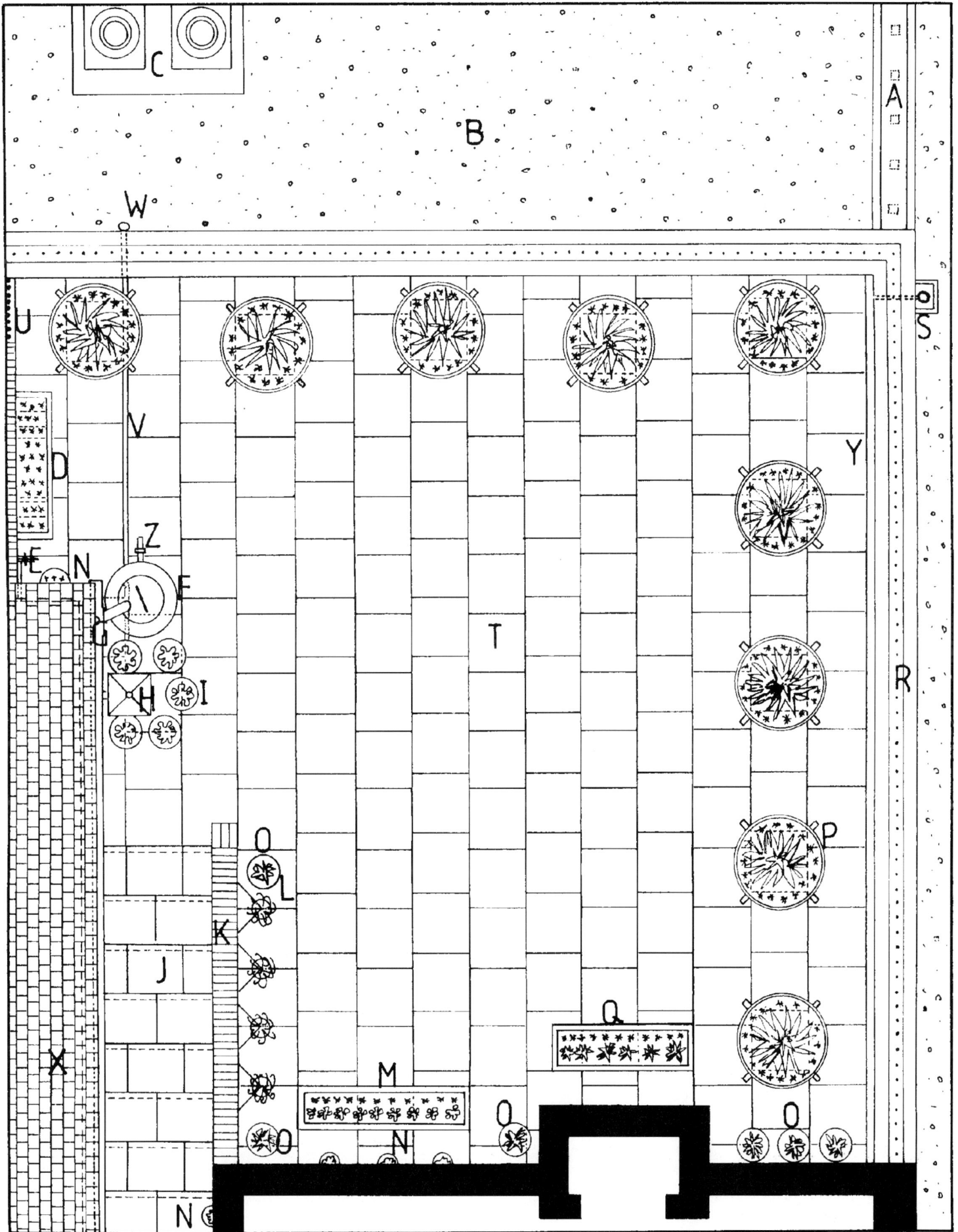

C

A

B

W

U

V

D

Z

*E    N

F

G

H    I

O
L

K

J

X

M

N

O

Q

O

Y

T

R

S

P

O

O

SCALE   1:50

## A town house forecourt

This town house is set back from the pavement (T) and has a forecourt of random rectangular York paving (S) which has been neatly butted up to the straight finish of the pavement. At one end of this pavement there is a large gate (P) leading on to another property which has a young plane tree (L) planted in the lawn (M). There is a brick dividing wall between the two properties. At the side of the house, shown, there is a service area in concrete (J) with refuse container (I) and gate (Z) affixed to timber posts (K) let into the brickwork.

The front door is enhanced by an entrance of quarry tiles (A) either side of which are flower boxes (B). There are other flower boxes (D), troughs (E), flower tubs (H and C) and a seat (G) located in various places on the terrace. The two rain-water downpipes (Y) are partly disguised by planting.

---

**Key**

| | | | |
|---|---|---|---|
| A | Quarry tiled entrance | N | Mowing strip |
| B | Flower troughs | O | Concrete entrance to adjoining property |
| C | Flower tubs with feet | | |
| D | Flower boxes | P | Large gate to adjoining property |
| E | Flower troughs | Q | Brick pillars with capping |
| F | Demarcation line between public pavement and terrace | R | Brick wall with bricks on edge on top |
| | | S | Random reclaimed rectangular paving |
| G | Seat | T | Public pavement |
| H | Flower tubs with feet | U | Kerbstones |
| I | Refuse container | V | Highway |
| J | Concrete service area | W | Drain |
| K | Gate posts | X | Granite setts |
| L | Young plane tree | Y | Rain-water downpipes |
| M | Lawn | Z | Wooden gate |

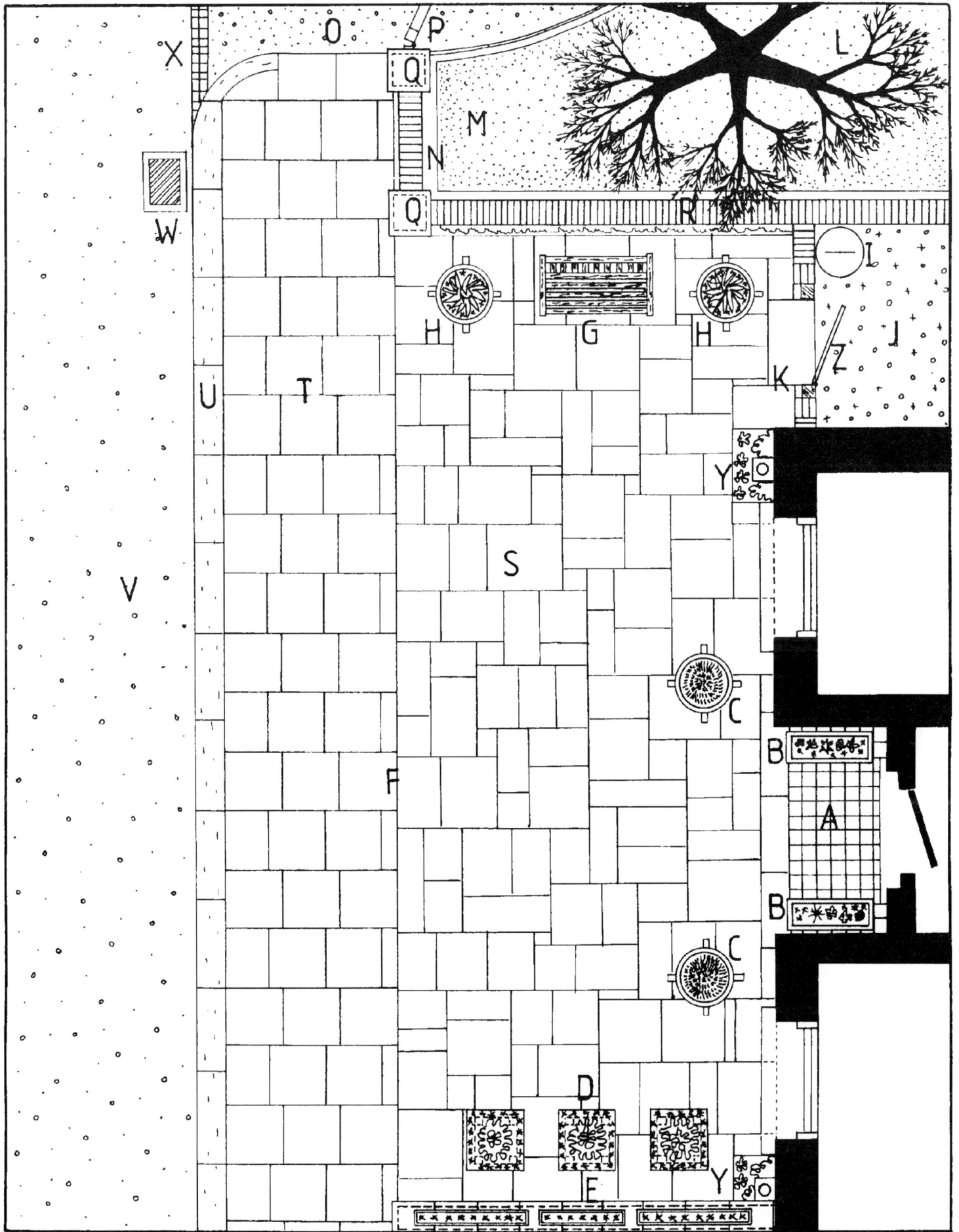

X

O P
Q

L

M

N

Q

R

I

H G H

Z

K

Y O

U T

S

C

V

B

A

F

B

C

D

E Y O

SCALE 1:50

## A practical caravan park garden

This plan shows a caravan parked in a caravan park on a concrete drive (Y) and hard-standing. It is serviced by electricity (X) and water (W) via control lockers (S and R respectively). Flower troughs (H) are set at the four corners to disguise the caravan support legs. The gas cylinder (T) is near the service path which surrounds the caravan. Flower troughs (G) are placed adjacent to the wheels. The caravan door (U) with movable steps, is opposite a small terrace (F) from which a path (E) goes on to a macadamised service path. On that section of the lawn (B) are a table (A) and chairs (V) and paddling pool (C). Adjacent to the table in the corner could be placed a climbing frame. Two flower troughs (J) hide the jockey wheel.

The caravan is screened from the concrete drive by a length of trellis (K) at the end of which is a box (I) on a post for mail, papers, milk, etc. In the corner is a large flower tub (M) screening the walled refuse container area (N) plus a fire bucket (L). In the corner of this lawn (B) is a dog kennel (O), drinking bowl (P) and a strong wire (Q) tethered between two posts upon which to secure a dog's lead.

## Key

| | | | | |
|---|---|---|---|---|
| A | Table | N | Refuse containers |
| B | Lawn | O | Dog kennel |
| C | Paddling pool | P | Drinking bowl |
| D | Hedge, e.g., yellow privet | Q | Wire tether |
| E | Path and gate to service path | R | Service locker for water |
| F | Terrace | S | Service locker for electricity |
| G | Troughs next to wheels | T | Gas cylinder |
| H | Flower tubs | U | Caravan doorstep |
| I | Box for letters, papers, etc. | V | Garden chairs |
| J | Troughs hiding jockey wheel | W | Underground water supply |
| K | Trellis screen | X | Underground electricity supply |
| L | Fire bucket | Y | Concrete drive and hard-standing |
| M | Large flower tub | Z | Macadamised service path |

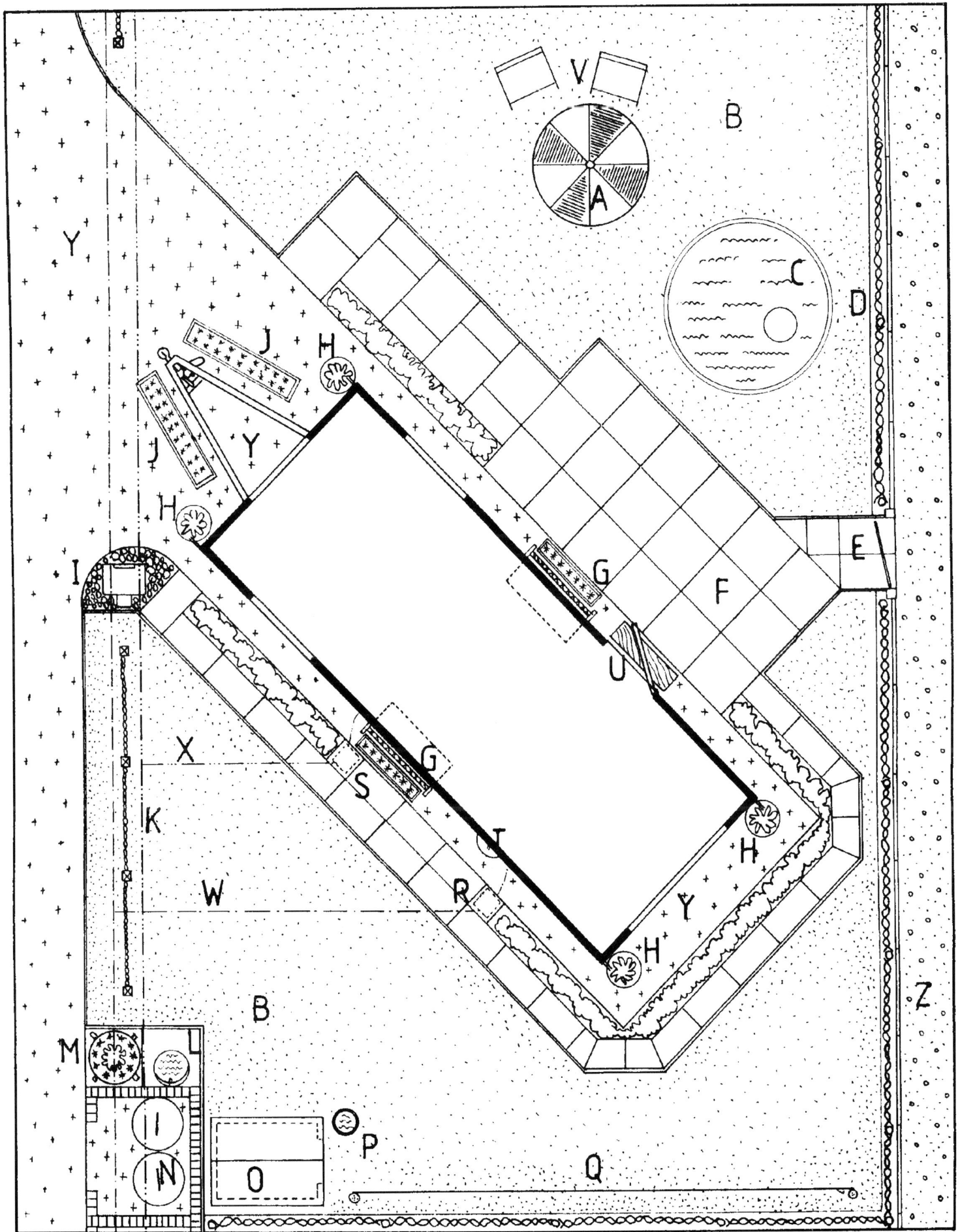

V

B

A

C

D

J

H

Y

J

H

G

F

E

Y

U

I

X

G

K

S

G

H

W

T

R

Y

H

B

H

M

P

Q

Z

N

O

SCALE 1:50

## Screening for traffic noise in an urban kitchen garden

This roadside plot with garage separated from the semi-detached house suitably divides an area which is principally to be used for a kitchen garden, but takes into account French window access to a small formal garden with paving, lawn and narrow borders. The path leading from a roadside entrance to the front door has associated paving intentionally laid in a staggered pattern to give greater interest with small adjacent borders for more formal bedding.

Because it is a corner plot there is a greater need to plant medium-growth trees interspersed with a wide assortment of evergreen shrubs, thus providing a visual and acoustic screen from traffic. Emphasis must be given to adequate fencing (O) along the mutual boundary supported by fairly extensive pergola work.

The kitchen/garage complex requires to be suitably screened by a thick beech hedge or similar, reaching a height of some 0·75m so as not to reduce light to planted areas.

**Key**

| | | | | |
|---|---|---|---|---|
| A | Lawn | | O | Boundary fence, wire, panelling, etc. |
| B | Vegetable garden | | P | Tubs |
| C | Soft fruit garden e.g., currants, gooseberries, raspberries, etc. | | Q | Rose, honeysuckle, etc., pergola as screen or windbreak |
| D | Garage | | R | Lawn |
| E | Workshop | | S | Interwoven wood panelling |
| F | Wall shrubs | | T | Standpipe for water |
| G | Dustbins or wheelie bins | | U | Bottle gully at bottom of rain-water downpipe with brick surround |
| H | Trellis screen | | V | Water inside garage for car washdown |
| I | Low brick boundary wall | | W | Rose border with climbers on pergola to screen buildings |
| J | Propagating cold-frames | | X | Small raised border with stone surround |
| K | Square shrub border with low pergola wall | | Y | Garden shed |
| L | Stone sink | | Z | Low-growing wall shrubs under window-sill |
| M | Bird bath | | | |
| N | Garden seat | | | |

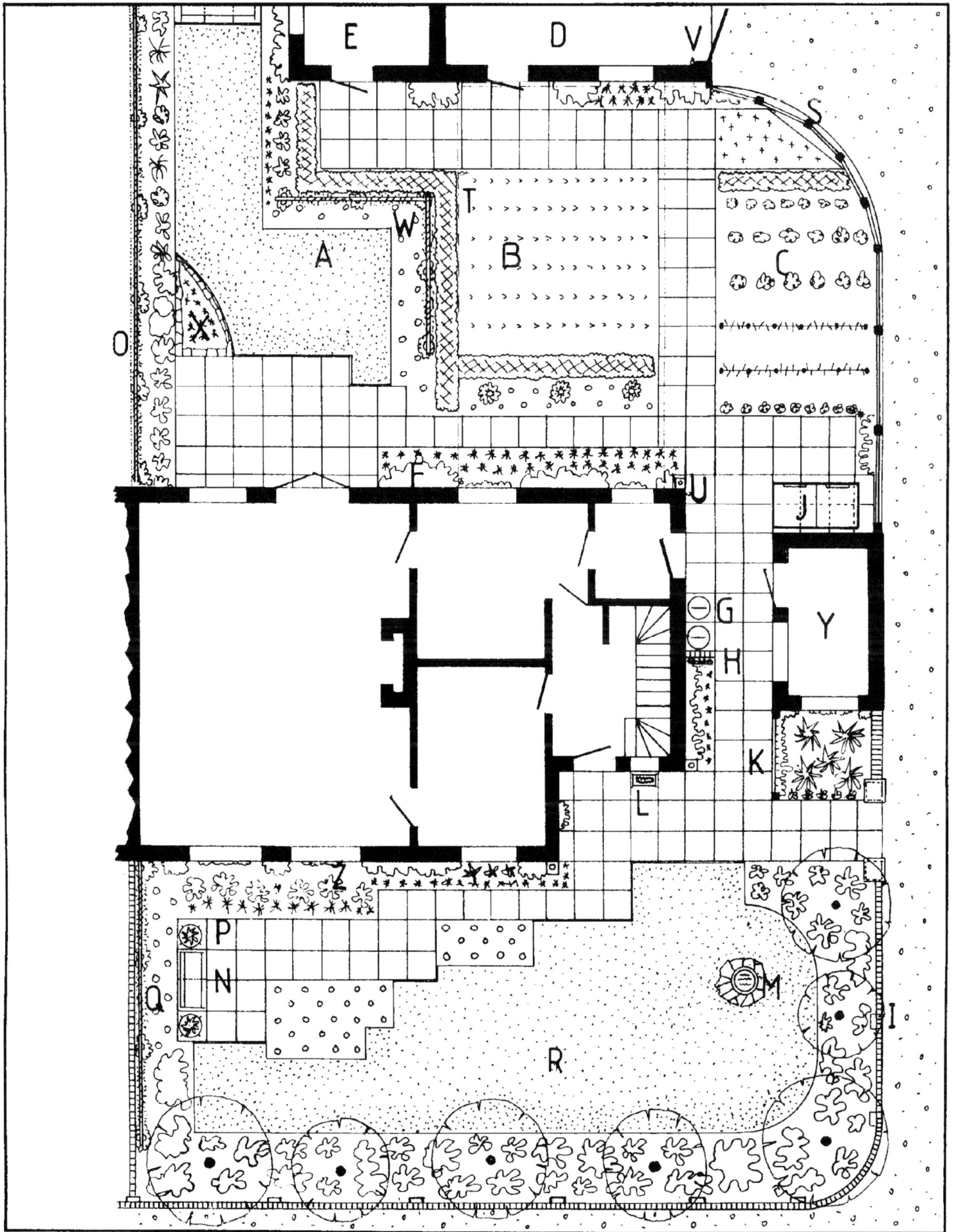

E          D          V

S

T

B          C

W

A

X

O

F          U

J

G          Y

H

K

L

Z

P

N          M          I

Q

R

55          SCALE 1:100

## A levelled platform on a sloping site

This garden highlights the problems of designing and constructing the front garden of a house on a levelled platform on a sloping site. Within the house and surrounding area of paths, excavated material will have been removed off-site, necessitating the re-soiling of borders near the house and associated beds nearby.

A curving path of non-slip paving slabs (I, M, R), with many shallow steps with risers takes up this slope, incorporating a 'pausing' area with seat at (L) and a lantern at (N) for use at night. Note the need to install electricity cable from (N) to house before hard and soft landscaping. Strong retaining walls (concrete foundation and cement bonding with weepholes) with a 15° batter are essential, draped with many different alpines.

Large rockery stones, well keyed into the sloping ground, assist stability and give much character especially if there is bold planting of prostrate and low-growing shrubs supplemented by the occasional flowering tree of low vigour. Additional imported clean topsoil will be a requirement.

The wall (T) requires great strength with a steel-reinforced in-situ concrete backing faced by suitable bricks, not of the cheaper type. There should be plenty of weepholes so that there is the minimum water pressure build-up behind the wall.

---

### Key

| | |
|---|---|
| A | Garden shed |
| B | Oil tank |
| C | Refuse container |
| D | Small rectangular pond with aquatic plants |
| E | Water butt connected to rain-water downpipe |
| F | Tubs |
| G | Raised shrub border with shallow brick wall |
| H | Planted area |
| I | Steps with risers |
| J | Sloped banking with strong brick retaining wall |
| K | Large stones set into sloped land |
| L | Seat in recess – pausing place |
| M | Stone edging to align with curved steps with risers |
| N | Outside lamp with armoured cable to house threaded through galvanised conduit pipe |

| | |
|---|---|
| O | Electricity cable buried under terrace, borders and paving threaded through galvanised conduit pipe |
| P | Seat |
| Q | Thick stone retaining wall with batter laid on concrete foundations and cement jointing, weepholes |
| R | Crazy paving |
| S | Entrance gate between brick pillars with caps |
| T | Thick brick walling with weepholes with brick on edge finish |
| U | Large rockery stones set to levels, well keyed in for bank stability |
| V | Boundary hedge |
| W | Garage |
| X | Macadam pathway surround for maintenance access |
| Y | Bold planting of low-growing shrubs, plants, etc., steep banking consolidated by *Hypericum calycinum* |
| Z | Terrace – mixture of rectangular and triangular pattern |

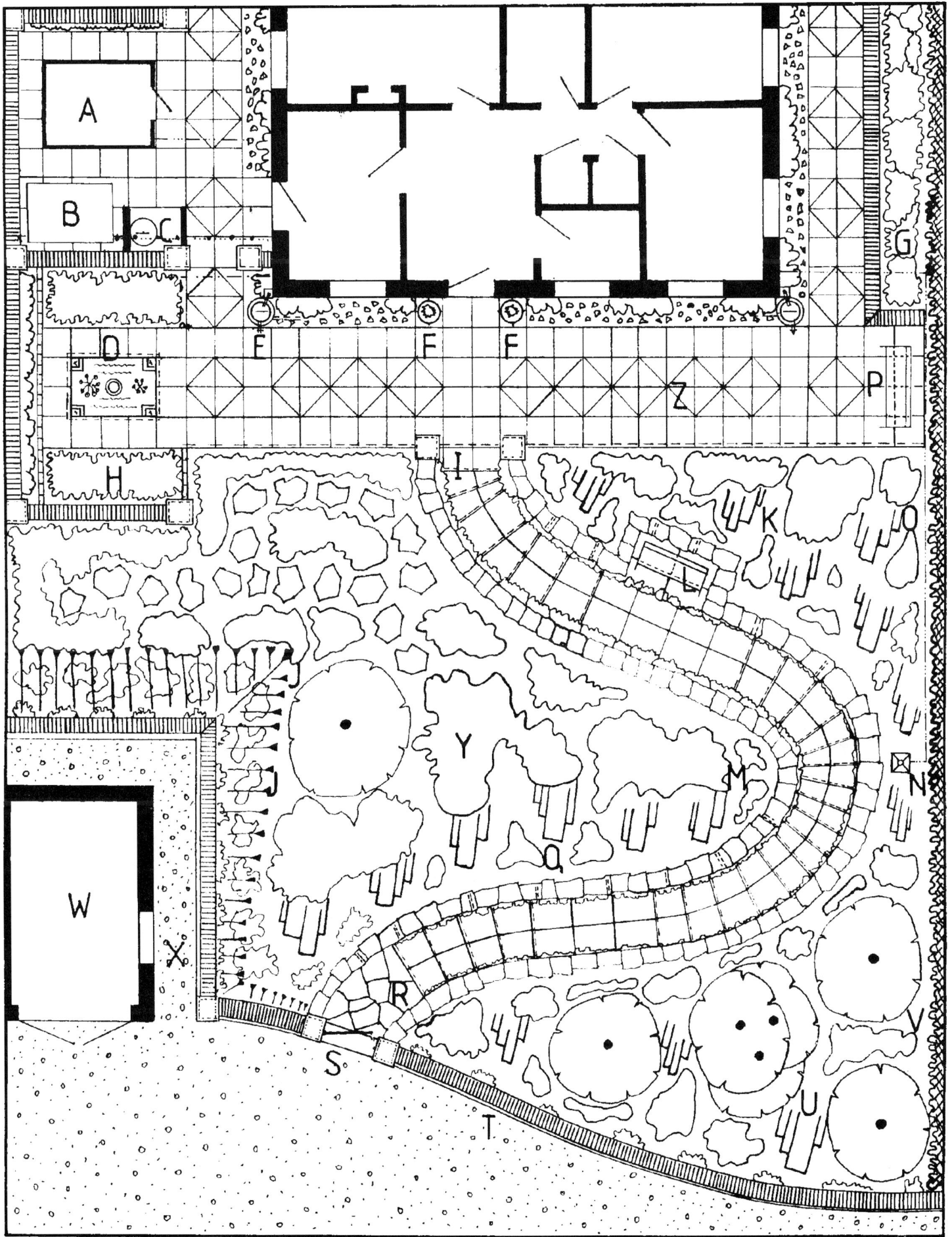

SCALE 1:100

## Two lawns on a slope

This semi-detached property has an awkwardly shaped rear garden with a gentle slope away from the house, see pathway (F). To take up this difference in levels between the two lawns (Y) there is a sloped section (Q) and a low retaining wall with mowing strip (H) encompassing a rockery (T) thickly planted with alpines (I) and a dwarf prostrate conifer (J). In the lawn (Y) nearest the house is a small pond (K) with water plants and crazy paving surround from which an overflow (L) goes towards the rockery into a soakaway. A terrace (N) and long path have been constructed next to the house, at one end of which are fuel bunkers (P) and refuse containers (N).

At the bottom of the garden is a shed (B) with electricity connected, next to the vegetable garden (C). The service path (E) has standpipes adjacent. There are two shrub borders (V and W) each with a standard specimen tree. The boundaries (G) are fenced with chain link but are supplemented with interwoven wood panels (O and X) at each end of the terrace and connecting path.

---

### Key

| | | | |
|---|---|---|---|
| A | Incinerator | O | Screening fence |
| B | Shed | P | Fuel bunkers |
| C | Vegetable garden | Q | Grass slope |
| D | Standpipes | R | Mixed shrubs |
| E | Service path | S | Boundary hedging |
| F | Sloping pathway | T | Rockery |
| G | Boundary fence in chain link | U | Hedge screen to vegetable garden |
| H | Low wall and mowing strip | V | Shrubbery and tree |
| I | Alpines | W | Shrubbery and tree |
| J | Prostrate conifer | X | Screening fence |
| K | Pond | Y | Lawn |
| L | Soakaway drain | Z | Garage with water and electricity connected |
| M | Three flower tubs | | |
| N | Refuse containers | | |

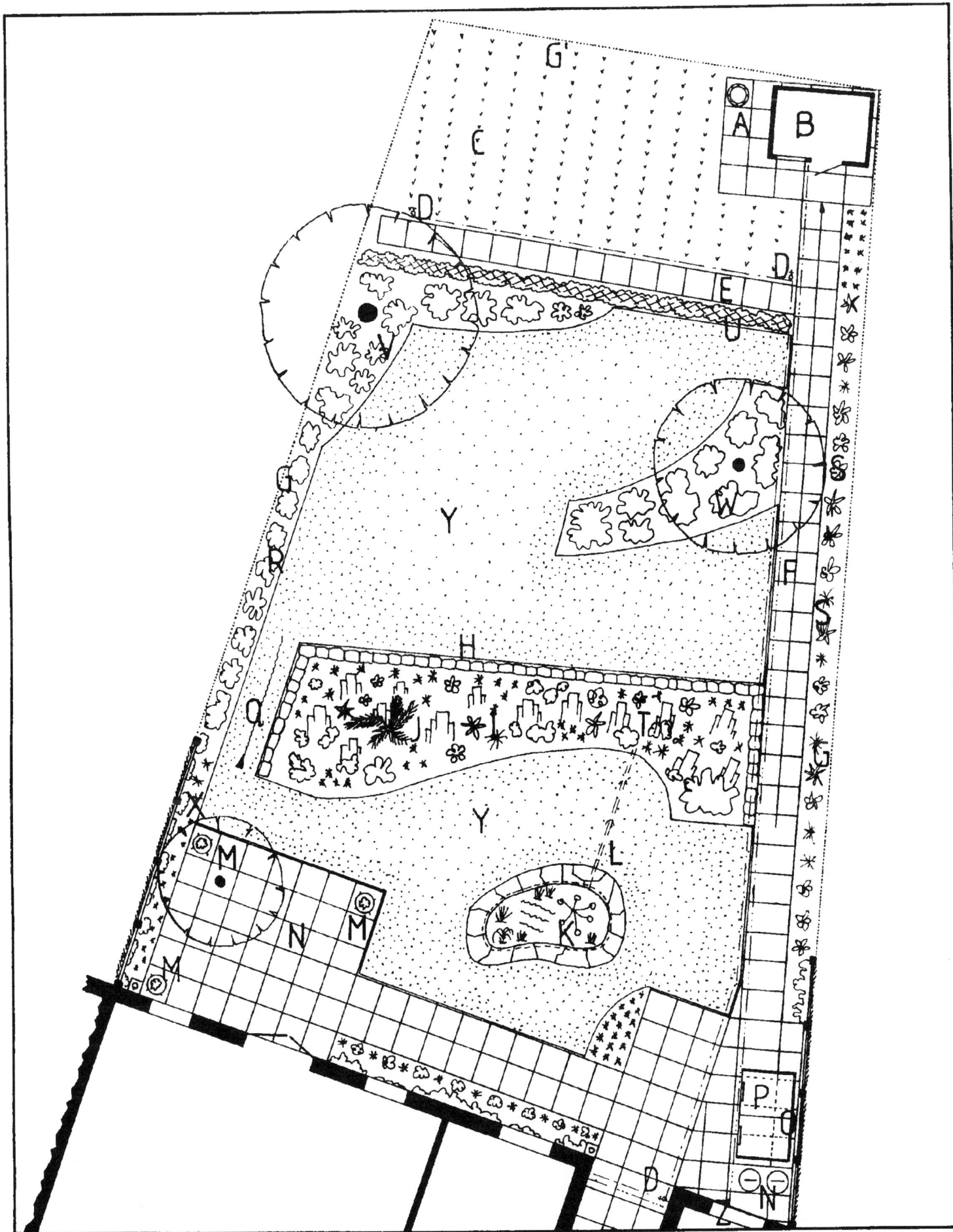

SCALE  1:100

## Paving and steps

This house has a low-level garage (N) with asphalt roof and a sloped drive (M) which has electric cable below the surface to combat icy conditions. Because of this the front garden paving has had to be sloped in places, supplemented by flights of steps (K). There is a level portion of the path (O) to accommodate a seat and flower tubs, all of which are backed with a brick retaining wall with weepholes.

The lawn (W) in the front is screened by a continuous belt (Z) of evergreen shrubs such as one of the berberis species. A central pathway (I) connects with the front terrace (H) embellished by flowering tubs (S) and borders. In the corner of the terrace is a water butt (R) to conserve rain-water. Because of limited space there is only a small vegetable garden (B) mainly for salad growing. At one end of this is the incinerator/compost zone. In the other there is a shed (F), fuel bunkers (E) and refuse containers (D). Should an oil storage tank be required, space is available in part of the terrace (G).

---

**Key**

| | | | |
|---|---|---|---|
| A | Incinerator/compost zone | N | Garage at lower level |
| B | Raised borders with low wall and weepholes for vegetables, and standpipe | O | Path gently sloped towards garage and steps |
| C | High wall with some low open joints for drainage | P | Levelled paved area with seat |
| D | Refuse containers | Q | Raised border of mixed shrubs with low brick retaining wall and weepholes |
| E | Fuel bunkers | R | Water butt with tap and overflow into bed |
| F | Shed with electricity and water | | |
| G | Paved area, space allocated for oil tank or washing line if required | S | Flower tubs |
| | | T | Flower tubs |
| H | Terrace to front door | U | Formal brick-edged planting bed |
| I | Paved approach path with border on side of garage | V | Formal brick-edged border for shrub and tree planting. Bricks reinforced in corner to allow for tree root expansion |
| J | Steps | | |
| K | Steps | W | Lawns |
| L | Long border full of mixed evergreen shrubs | X | Entrance gates with capped brick pillars |
| M | Garage slope with underground cable heating in case of icy conditions | Y | Brick retaining wall with weepholes |
| | | Z | Thick hedge of *Viburnum lauristinus* |

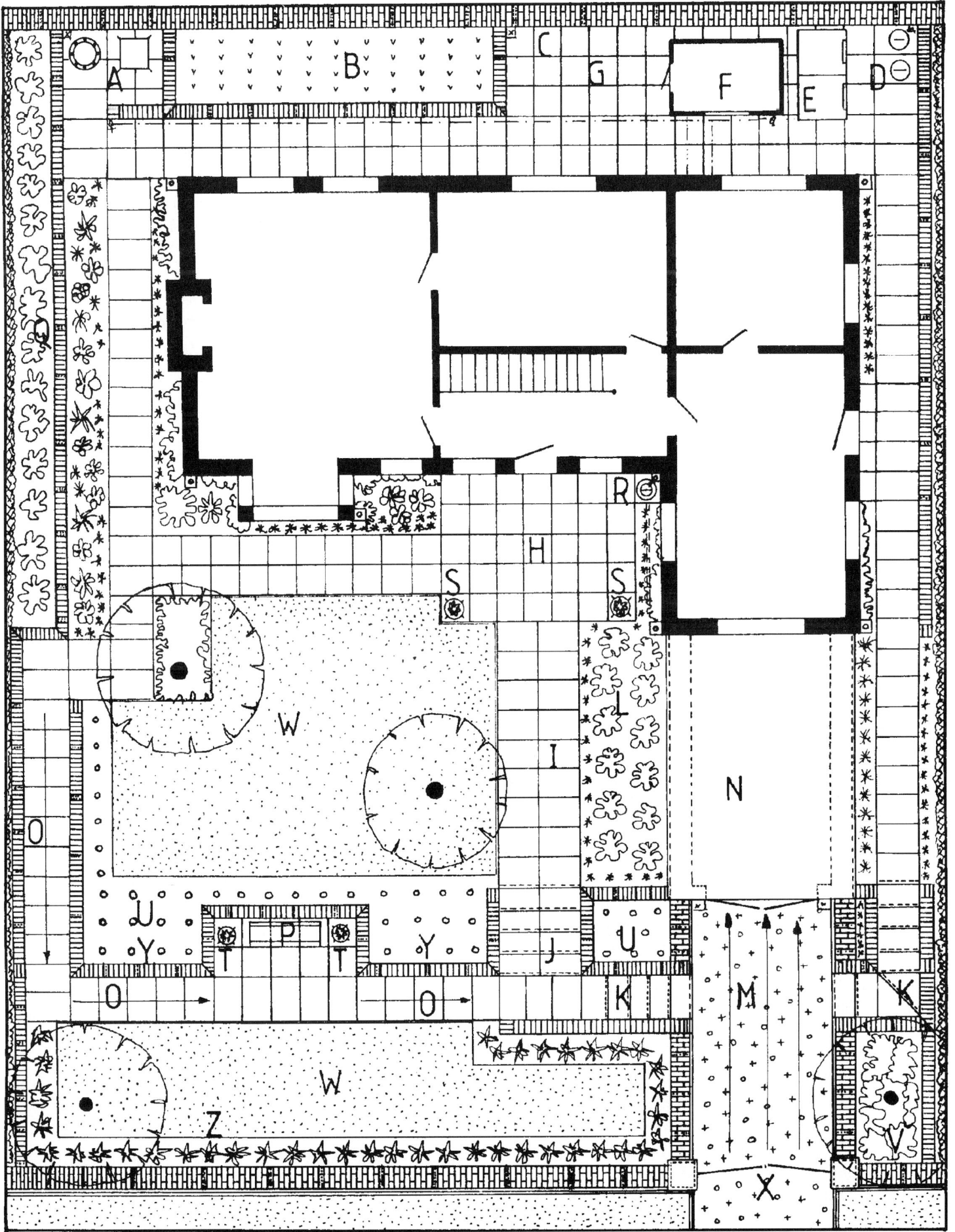

SCALE 1:100

## A secluded terrace

This semi-detached bungalow is built on a corner and therefore subject to traffic noise and the gaze of passers-by. A secluded terrace (F) has been constructed adjacent to the French windows. There is a small, well screened lawn (V) with a pond (H) surrounded by crazy paving. By the back door is the service area in concrete (K) with refuse container (J) and fuel bunkers (I).

Because of limited space there is only a small vegetable garden (A) screened by hedge (Z) with standpipe (Q). A further standpipe is situated by the concrete washdown area (C). The house is surrounded by 900mm pathways (M) and an approach pathway (R) to the front door from access gate (T). In the front garden are two equal-sized beds of standard roses (S) and two specimen conifers (E). The main lawn (V) is broken up by two dissimilar-sized shrub/tree borders (O and P). The whole property, adjacent to the pavement, has a low brick wall (W) with assorted shrubs (U) and a few trees.

---

## Key

A  Vegetable garden with access paths
B  Garage with electricity and water installed
C  Sloping concrete washdown towards pavement and gates
D  Side path to garage: extended paving to allow car passenger/driver to alight
E  Twin specimen *Cupressus fletcheri*
F  Terrace
G  Twin flower tubs
H  Rectangular pond with crazy paving surround and adjacent tap
I  Fuel bunkers
J  Refuse container
K  Concrete service area
L  Hedge to screen quiet area
M  Access path around house
N  Narrow long border for formal edging of bedding plants

O  Smaller shrub border with mixed trees
P  Larger shrub border with mixed trees
Q  Standpipe
R  Approach path to front door in slabs 900mm × 600mm
S  Twin borders of standard roses
T  Entrance gate between brick pillars
U  Perimeter border of mixed shrubs and occasional trees
V  Lawn
W  Perimeter low brick wall with bricks on edge as headers
X  Trellis-topped panel fence screen and windbreak
Y  Border around house containing mixed flowers and wall shrubs
Z  Thick hedge as windbreak and screen to vegetable garden

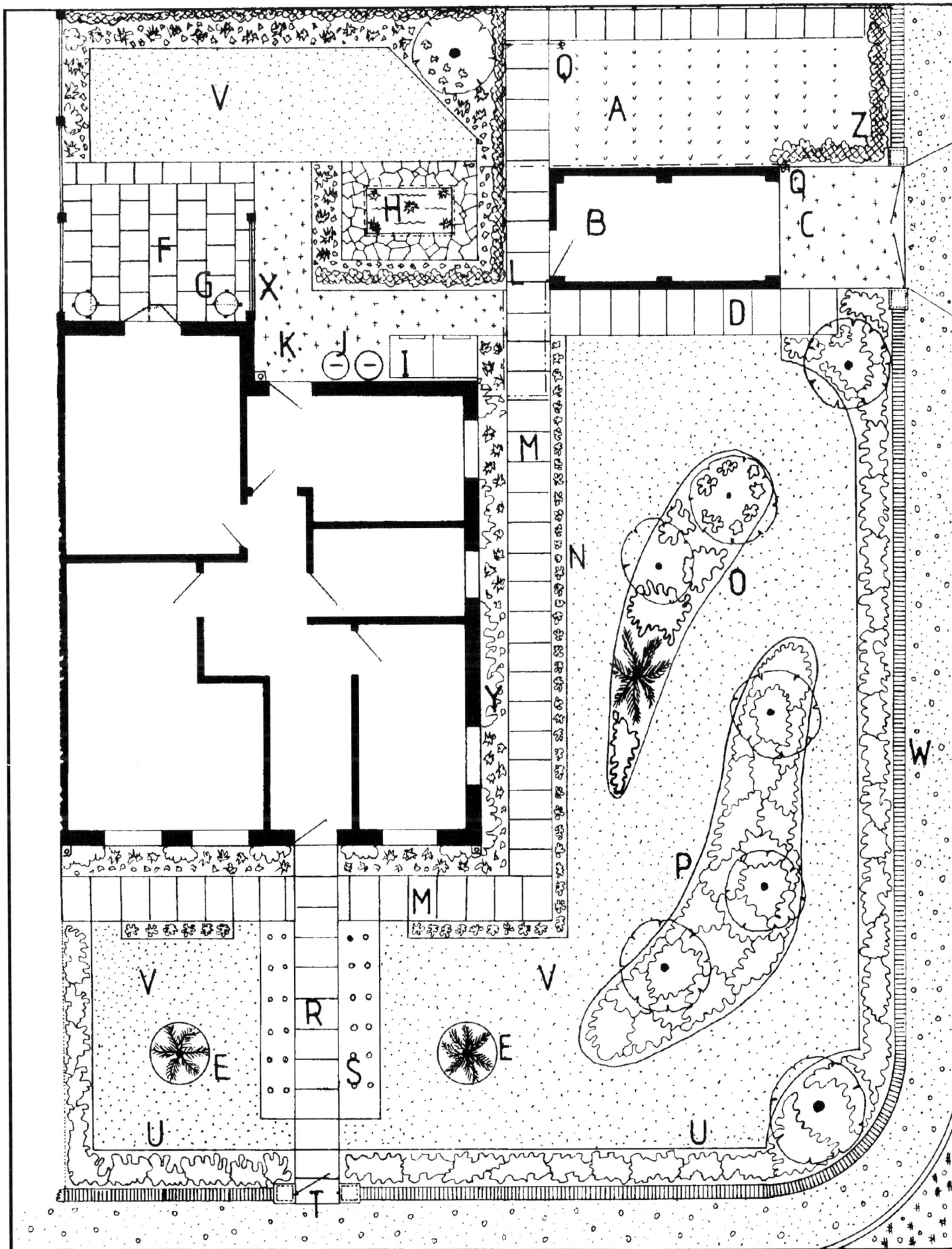

V

Q

A

Z

Q

B

C

L

D

F

H

G

X

K

J

I

M

N

O

W

P

M

V

V

R

E

S

E

U

U

T

SCALE 1:100

## Formal rose garden on clay soil

The garden of this house is situated on clay soil and therefore it offers the chance to plant all kinds of roses (W and E) and banks of species roses in border (V). There are two terraces constructed of stone paving from which there are steps (K and L) leading down to a very impressive brick on edge path with lawns either side. At the bottom of this path is a sundial feature with four identical square beds filled with roses. In one of the terraces there is a large rectangular pond with central fountain and with pockets of marginal aquatics in each corner. A triangular step also leads down to the stepping-stone path (T) at the end of which is a seat having a view at right angles of the sundial (G) and herbaceous border (B). Space (A) gives an opportunity for composting, etc.

To enclose the formal garden there is a curved hedge which provides a good backdrop. Various trees (C and X) in that vicinity provide a change from formality.

---

### Key

| | | | |
|---|---|---|---|
| A | Zone for compost/manure | M | Triangular step down to lawn |
| B | Herbaceous border, plants in clumps of three, four or five to give greater impact | N | Wall shrubs against brick wall set between brick pillars with stone caps |
| C | Curved hedge with trees and a shrubbery | O | Earth-filled brick bed |
| D | Wide pathway, bricks laid on edge, basketweave pattern | P | Wall shrubs against brick wall |
| | | Q | Rectangular pond with fountain and overflow pipe to weephole in wall |
| E | Four square beds of roses formally planted | R | Marginal aquatics in pond corners |
| F | Garden seat at right angles to main brick path | S | Side gate between brick pillars and associated brick wall |
| G | Sundial | T | Curved path of stepping stones |
| H | Stone paving slabs in random pattern | U | Lawn |
| I | Rendered block wall supporting terrace edge | V | Massed shrub roses |
| J | Pockets of brick and occasional alpines | W | Large L-shaped borders filled with roses |
| K | Steps down to lower level from terrace (J) | X | Group of trees with rough grass and bulbs planted round them |
| L | Steps down to lower level from terrace (H) | Y | Long brick wall bordering terrace |
| | | Z | Boundary hedge |

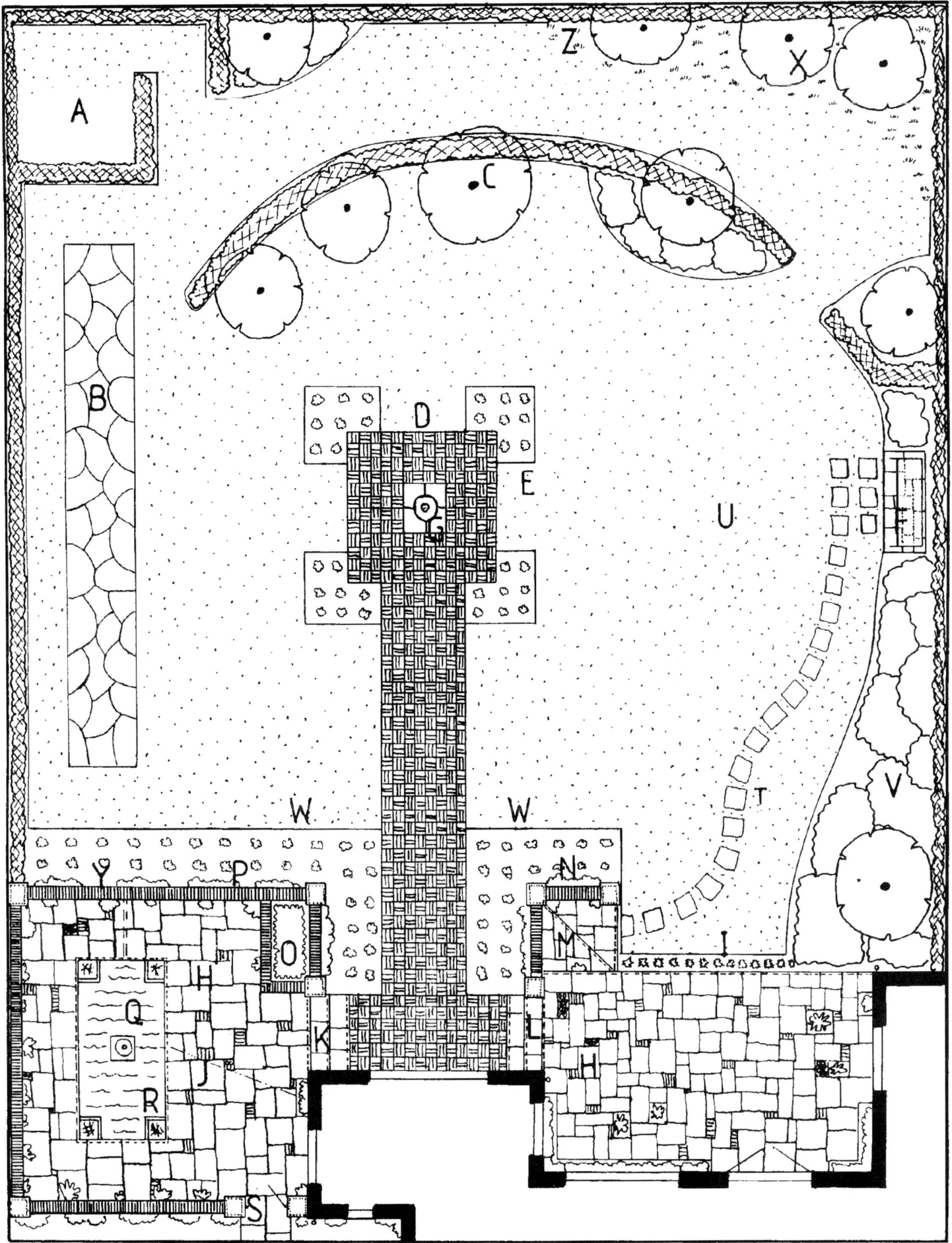

A

Z

X

C

B

D

E

U

F

G

W    W    N

Y    P    T    V

O

I

H    K    M

Q    J

R

S

H

SCALE 1:100

## A loggia and barbecue

This detached dwelling has, within its design, a tile-covered loggia (D) and, nearby, a barbecue (Z) on the terrace which, like the ornamental path (J) is constructed of random-sized paving with occasional brick inserts and pockets for alpines. It should be noted that by the wall shrubs alongside the house the paving has been sawn to give a serrated finish. There is a service path (R) connecting the garage drive, with washdown facilities, to the functional area comprising a shed (A) with electricity connected, fuel bunkers (B) and refuse container (C) together with standpipes. There is space for an oil tank if required, near the refuse containers.

Intentionally, because of the work factor, there is no vegetable garden. Zone (F) allows for incinerator, etc., and has a connecting path (H). Around the perimeter (T) there is hedging, and opposite the paving (J) there are extensive borders of shrubs (V and Y) with ornamental trees and two conifers of the 'Lawson' type (X and W). In the lawn (P) there is a shrub bed (R) with one tree. To view the house and terrace, etc, there is a seat (Q) on a small section of crazy paving.

| Key | | | |
|---|---|---|---|
| A | Shed | N | Drive with washdown gully and standpipe |
| B | Fuel bunkers | | |
| C | Refuse containers | O | Entrance gates with brick capped pillars |
| D | Loggia | P | Lawn |
| E | Bird bath | Q | Seat |
| F | Incinerator/compost zone | R | Shrub border with tree |
| G | Hedge screening incinerator/compost zone | S | Front hedge |
| | | T | Boundary hedge |
| H | Pathway | U | Ornamental crab tree |
| I | Main terrace | V | Mixed shrub border |
| J | Side terrace | W | Conifer |
| K | Terrace by front door | X | Conifer |
| L | Square wooden flower box | Y | Mixed shrub border with standard trees |
| M | Garage | Z | Barbecue area (note standpipe nearby) |

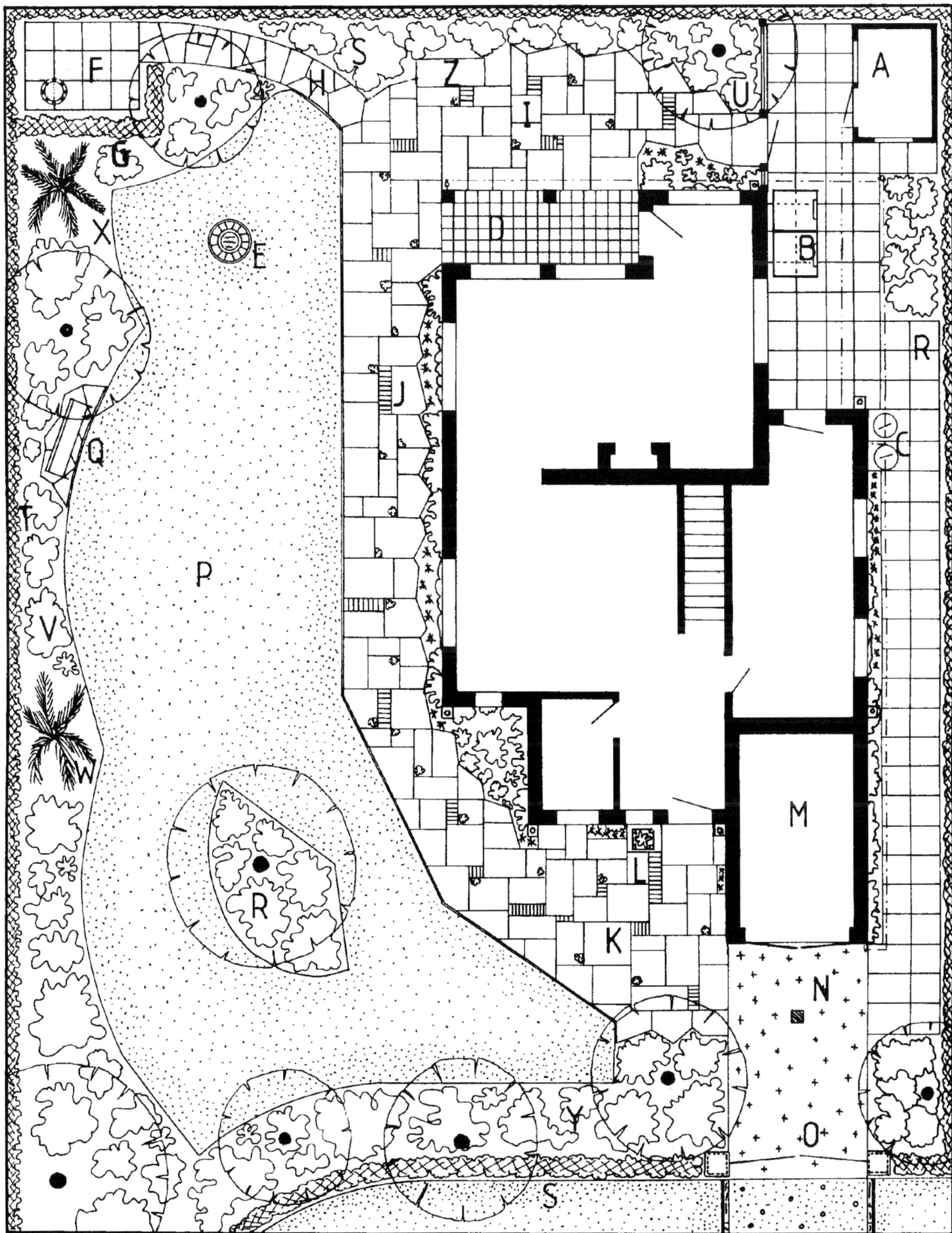

SCALE 1:100

## Two plots in one

This design concerns two adjacent building plots owned by the same person(s), equally divided by a central hedge (J) with a wide connecting archway (I). The garden has been designed as a whole but half could be sold in the future as a building plot.

The principal garden has four long, obliquely viewed, herbaceous borders (D) set geometrically symmetrical within the lawn (Y). The terrace near the house has two formal planting beds in the two corners (P). There is a bird table (X) at one end. Electricity (V) and water (W) have been installed and there are four standpipes (C). A single path (E) with a small area for a seat (F) goes from the terrace to the kitchen garden (B). Between this path and boundary hedge (G) there is a long mixed shrubbery (H). Next to the kitchen garden is a shed (A) and zone for composting and/or incinerator (Z) both of which are screened by a hedge. The functional area, i.e. fuel bunkers, refuse containers, etc., is not shown on this plan.

In the other half of the garden there is a large rectangular pool with a paved surround (T) with countersunk beds for aquatic plants (R and S). In the centre of the pool are three ornamental fountains (Q). At the other end of this garden is a circular centrepiece feature of paving and circles of brick on edge (M) in the centre of which is a large bird bath (L). To view all this there is a large seat on paving (N) with trees and shrubs (O) either side. On the flanks of this lawn (Y) there are three very large intensively planted rose borders (K).

| **Key** | | | |
|---|---|---|---|
| A | Shed | N | Seat |
| B | Kitchen garden | O | Trees and shrubs |
| C | Standpipes | P | Formal bedding area |
| D | Herbaceous border | Q | Three fountains (electricity supply not shown) |
| E | Pathways | | |
| F | Seat base | R | Marginal aquatic borders |
| G | Boundary hedges | S | Corner beds for aquatic plants |
| H | Mixed shrubbery | T | Paved surround to pool |
| I | Wide connecting arch | U | Overflow pipe |
| J | Central dividing hedge | V | Electricity supply |
| K | Rose borders | W | Water supply |
| L | Bird bath | X | Bird table |
| M | Circular paving and brick on edge with plant pockets | Y | Lawns |
| | | Z | Incinerator/composting zone |

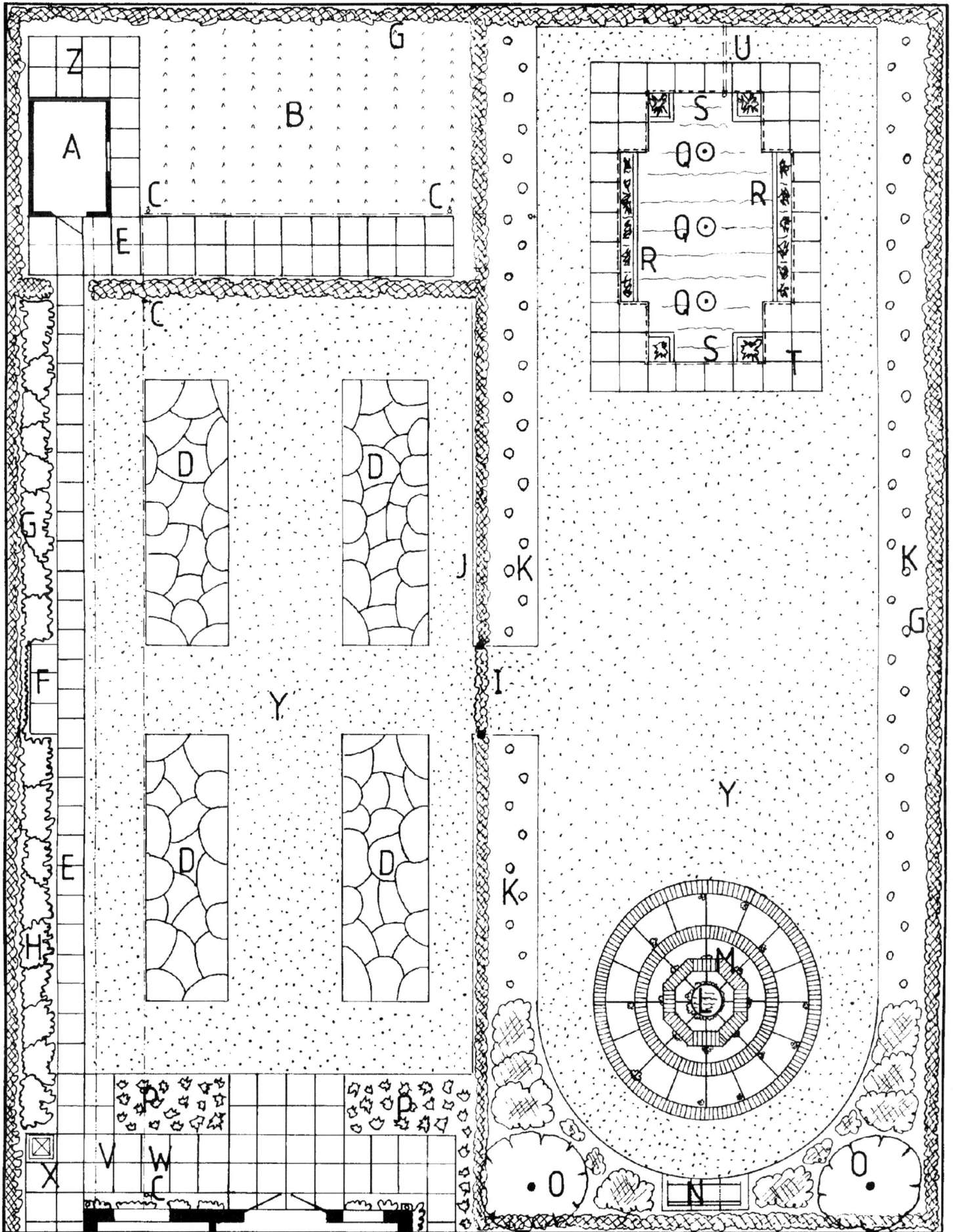

SCALE 1:100

## Dealing with a long driveway

This semi-detached bungalow is one of several located next to the turning area at the end of a cul-de-sac. As a result of this and the shape of the plot, the single garage (A) has had to be set right back with its approach formed by two lengths of in-situ concrete with grass in between (B). Nearer to the garage the central paving in front of the garage is flanked by two areas of paving to allow car passengers to alight on to a firm surface (C). The functional area (D) is for fuel bunkers, oil tank, and refuse containers. The front door has a quarry tiled entrance with a curved brick on edge surround (E) leading on to the pathway (F). The vegetable and soft fruit gardens (J and I) are served by various non-slip paths (G) with adjacent standpipes (H). One path leads down to a brick wall screened incinerator zone on concrete (K).

The garden is well planted with trees and shrubs (X, Y and P) and, around the dwelling, with formal planting and wall shrubs (Z). Between the trees (O and N) there is an area of crazy paving (M). It has a broken edge by the shrubbery, and a circular area around tree (N) for sitting in the shade. There is also a kidney-shaped pool (L) to provide a feature in that part of the garden.

| **Key** | | | |
|---|---|---|---|
| A | Garage | O | Standard specimen tree |
| B | Drive to garage | P | Mixed shrub border |
| C | Concrete slabs next to drive | Q | Lawns |
| D | Area for fuel bunkers, oil tank and refuse container | R | Rose border |
| E | Tiled entrance to front door | S | Specimen half-standard tree, e.g., *Prunus autumnalis* |
| F | Side pathway | T | Gated entrance to functional area |
| G | Service paths to kitchen garden | U | Curved brick wall with brick on edge and capped brick pillars |
| H | Standpipes | V | Formal wrought iron gates |
| I | Vegetable garden | W | Entrance to drive edged with bedded and haunched granite setts |
| J | Soft fruit garden | X | Mixed shrub border |
| K | Zone for incinerator | Y | Mixed shrub border with hedge behind |
| L | Pool | Z | Flower border with wall shrubs |
| M | Crazy paving | | |
| N | Shade tree and paving | | |

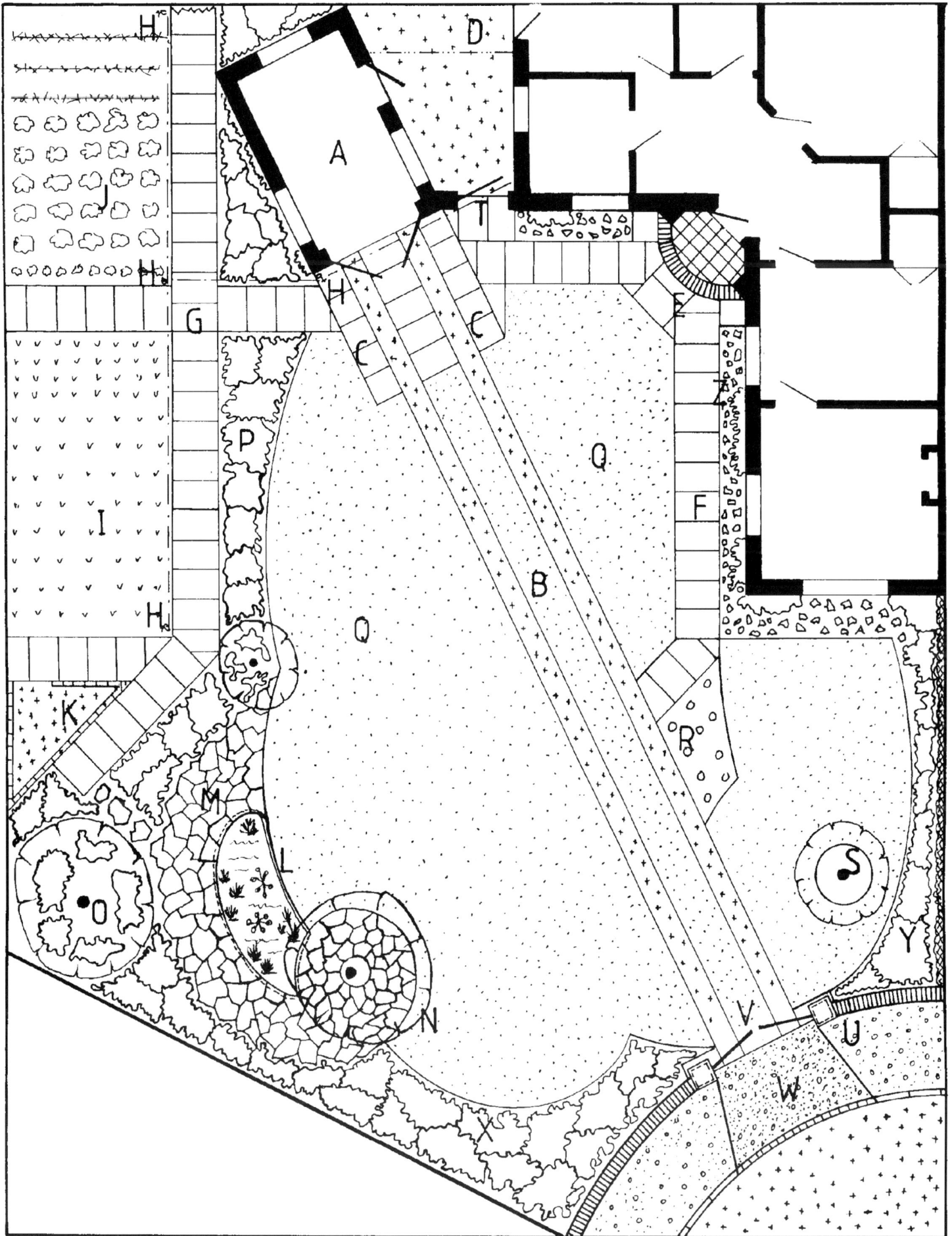

71

SCALE 1:100

## Garden near a railway embankment

This small detached house has been built on reasonably levelled ground adjacent to an old railway line where there is a well consolidated embankment (C). On it is growing a self-sown willow tree (B). It is possible that there will be foxes and rabbits on this deserted site. Strong fencing with rabbit wire will be desirable and it is hoped that both neighbours will do the same.

To screen derelict parts of the embankment and other boundaries, a good clippable hedge of *Thuja lobbii* should be planted (A). There is an adjacent 150mm land drain (J) set in a deep trench to drain off rain-water in storm conditions, going to a soakaway (F). The vegetable (K) and soft fruit (M) gardens are divided into two plots with standpipes at each end of the central path (L). There is no incinerator as the property is in a smoke-free urban zone. Near the garage (T) there is a garden shed (N), both connected to electricity. A twin cold-frame (O) is nearby. The house is heated by gas. A small terrace (S) is screened with small beds and trellis (P and R).

---

### Key

| | |
|---|---|
| A | Belt of conifers – *Thuja lobbii* |
| B | Self-sown willow tree |
| C | Old grassed-over embankment |
| D | Terrace with cobble infills |
| E | Partial brick wall with coping |
| F | Large soakaway, capped over, under terrace |
| G | Stepping stones in a curve, countersunk in lawn |
| H | Lawn |
| I | Refuse containers |
| J | Toe drain near base of bank some 750mm deep with falls towards terrace |
| K | Vegetable garden |
| L | Service path to vegetable and soft fruit garden |
| M | Soft fruit, e.g. loganberries, blackberries, red, black and white currants, gooseberries, raspberries, etc. |
| N | Garden shed |
| O | Cold-frames |
| P | L-shaped bed with trellis and hedge screen for terrace |
| Q | Hedge screen to vegetable garden |
| R | Small border with trellis and hedge screen |
| S | Terrace |
| T | Garage |
| U | Garage drive |
| V | Paved area around front door |
| W | Palisade fencing painted white |
| X | Pavement |
| Y | Specimen tree in curved shrub border |
| Z | Standpipes |

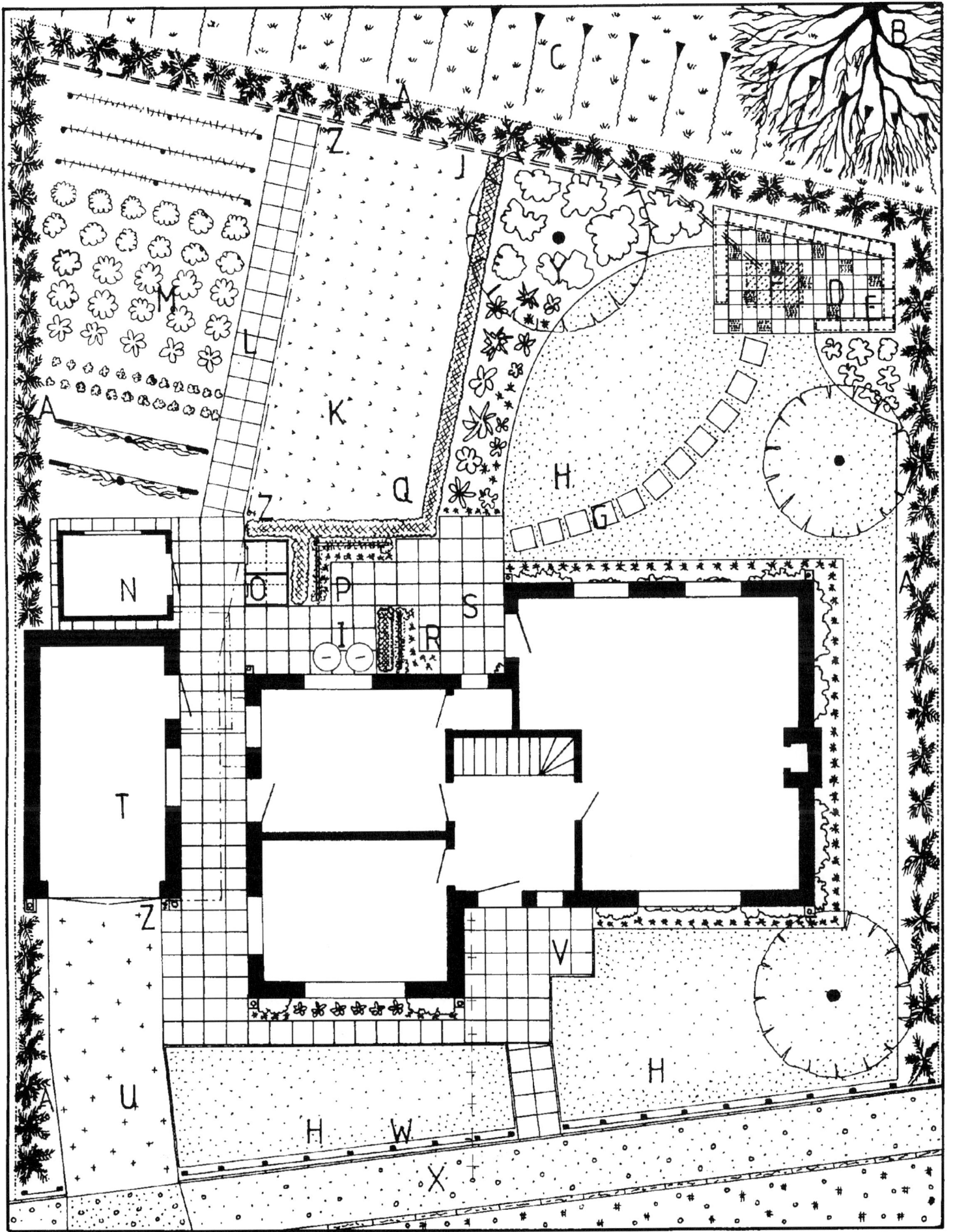

SCALE 1:100

## Vegetables and flowering trees

This garden has an intensive area devoted to vegetables, soft fruit, and greenhouse growing, supported by watering standpipes, with a service area comprising a compost bay, incinerator and shed which is supplied with electricity.

The formal garden is slightly lower than the terrace, hence steps at (M), wall at (L), and ramped path at (G). The irregular-shaped terrace (J) is sheltered while the seat (I) with adjacent tubs, gives an opportunity to view the pond complex (S) and the rockery (V).

Greater emphasis is given to mixed shrub planting with the occasional standard trees such as crab-apple, almond, flowering cherry, mountain ash, etc. If there are children, laburnum should be avoided because of the poisonous seeds.

The lawn has intentionally been designed with many curves to promote greater interest and an opportunity for height-graded shrub planting. There is a connecting path between the lawn and shed area. Note the mowing strip along wall (L) etc., so that the mower does not hit the brickwork, and draping alpines.

## Key

A   Compost area with interwoven panel screen
B   Incinerator
C   Garden shed
D   Fruit cage
E   Water standpipe
F   Electricity supply to garden shed workshop and greenhouse (heating and lighting)
G   Two ramped paths to facilitate mower, wheelbarrow and roller movement
H   Raised border with weepholes filled with screening shrubs and alpines growing in brickwork pockets
I   Garden seat with adjacent tubs
J   Paved area
K   Curved edging to paved area, bricks on edge, with mowing strip
L   Brick wall with mowing strip (in-situ cement) at base of wall, alpines growing in brickwork pockets
M   Flight of steps with mowing strip

N   Non-slip paving to pattern with cobble infill, with adequate crossfall
O   Garage
P   Coke and coal bunkers adjacent to outside tap
Q   Water standpipe for greenhouse
R   Screening hedge with path on to lawn adjacent to shed
S   Oval pond constructed in reinforced concrete with crazy paving surround and weeping willow
T   Screened service area with adjacent conifer and connecting path to lawn
U   Specimen fastigiate deciduous tree (dwarf growth)
V   Small intensive rockery with weeping flowering cherry
W   Brick boundary wall with top course of bricks on edge as headers
X   Long border of low-growing shrub roses
Y   Paving with alternate bonding
Z   Greenhouse

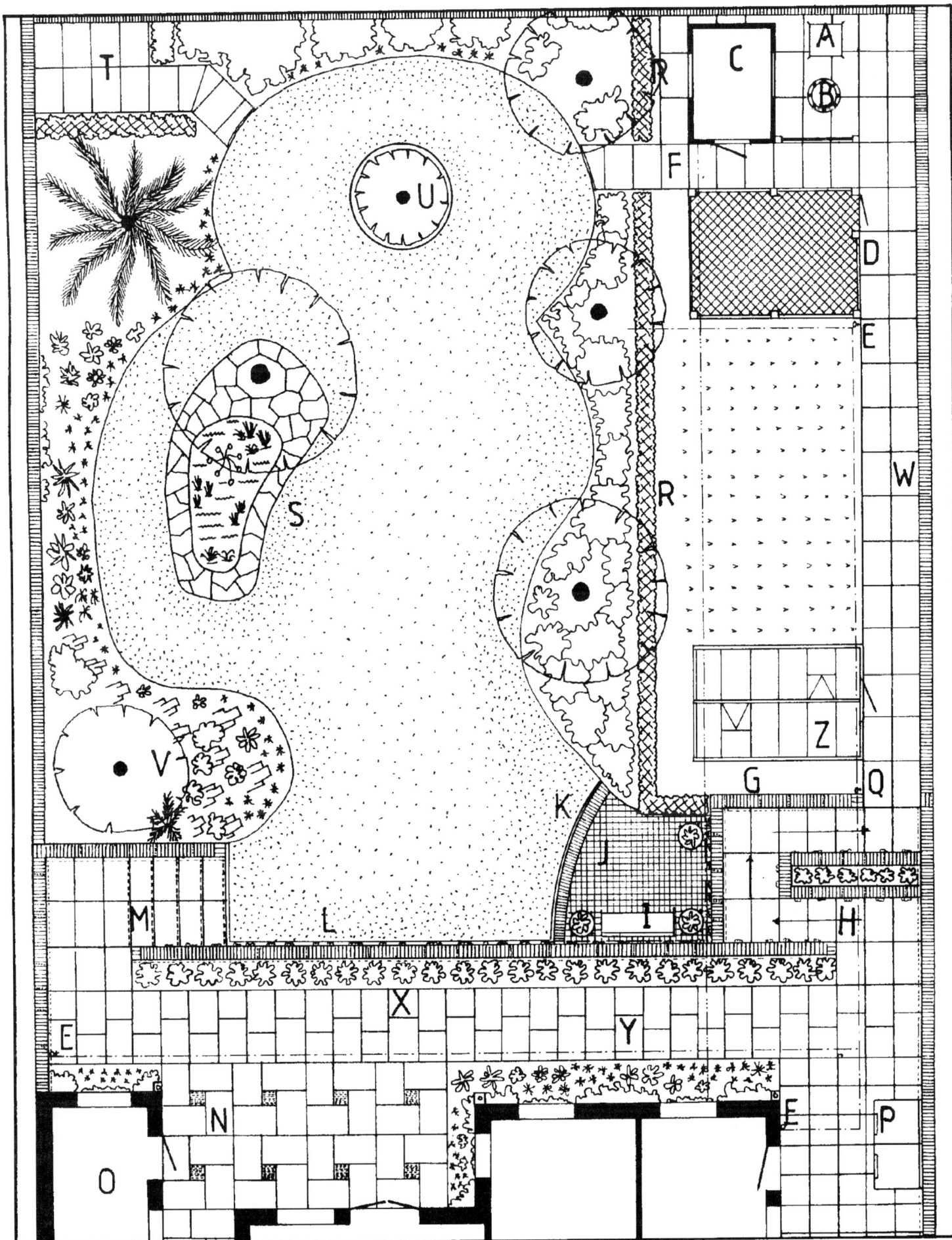

SCALE 1:100

## Large kitchen garden and fruit cage

About a quarter of this garden has been allocated to culinary purposes, i.e. a large intensively cropped vegetable and fruit garden irrigated by two water standpipes, one of which is for the fruit cage. The fruit cage has doors on two corners for easy access and is likely to be filled with strawberries, raspberries, currants, gooseberries, loganberries and blackberries. The whole is protected by an interwoven wood panel fence. A paved service area contains an incinerator, compost bay, and a small bed which can be used for plant propagation and/or manure stack. A double row of beech hedging screens the whole from the rest of the garden and access is under a wide pergola arch.

To give geometrical variation the lawn is curved with a parabolic-shaped bed with specimen trees as a focal point. There is a large conservatory with formal bedding around it. It should be noted that services, electricity to shed (I), water to vegetable garden (Z) and oil from house to storage tank (X), have been laid before landscaping. The socket for the large rotary washing line (Q) can be used for clothes drying or with a large umbrella for shade. A paved path has been laid near to the house window for easy cleaning access.

| Key | |
| --- | --- |
| A | Incinerator |
| B | Compost bay |
| C | Screen to service area |
| D | Non-slip functional slabs |
| E | Fruit cage – galvanised wire secured to permanent posts |
| F | Water tap for fruit cage |
| G | One of two access doors to fruit cage |
| H | Water tap for vegetables |
| I | Garden shed on timber bearers |
| J | Wide archway for roses |
| K | Beech hedge or similar to screen vegetable garden and act as backdrop to shrubbery |
| L | Conservatory |
| M | Specimen tree in parabolic-shaped border |
| N | Electricity supply from house and garage to shed |
| O | Bird table |
| P | Water supply to garden |
| Q | Rotary washing line adjacent to pathway |
| R | Formal pathway and small hard surface opposite conservatory doors |
| S | Rain-water gully with brick surround |
| T | Water tap with draining plug (winter protection) |
| U | Refuse containers |
| V | Oil tank |
| W | Coal and coke bunkers |
| X | Oil supply pipe well protected against accidental damage |
| Y | Interwoven panel fencing |
| Z | Vegetable garden with standard fruit trees on medium to dwarfing root stock |

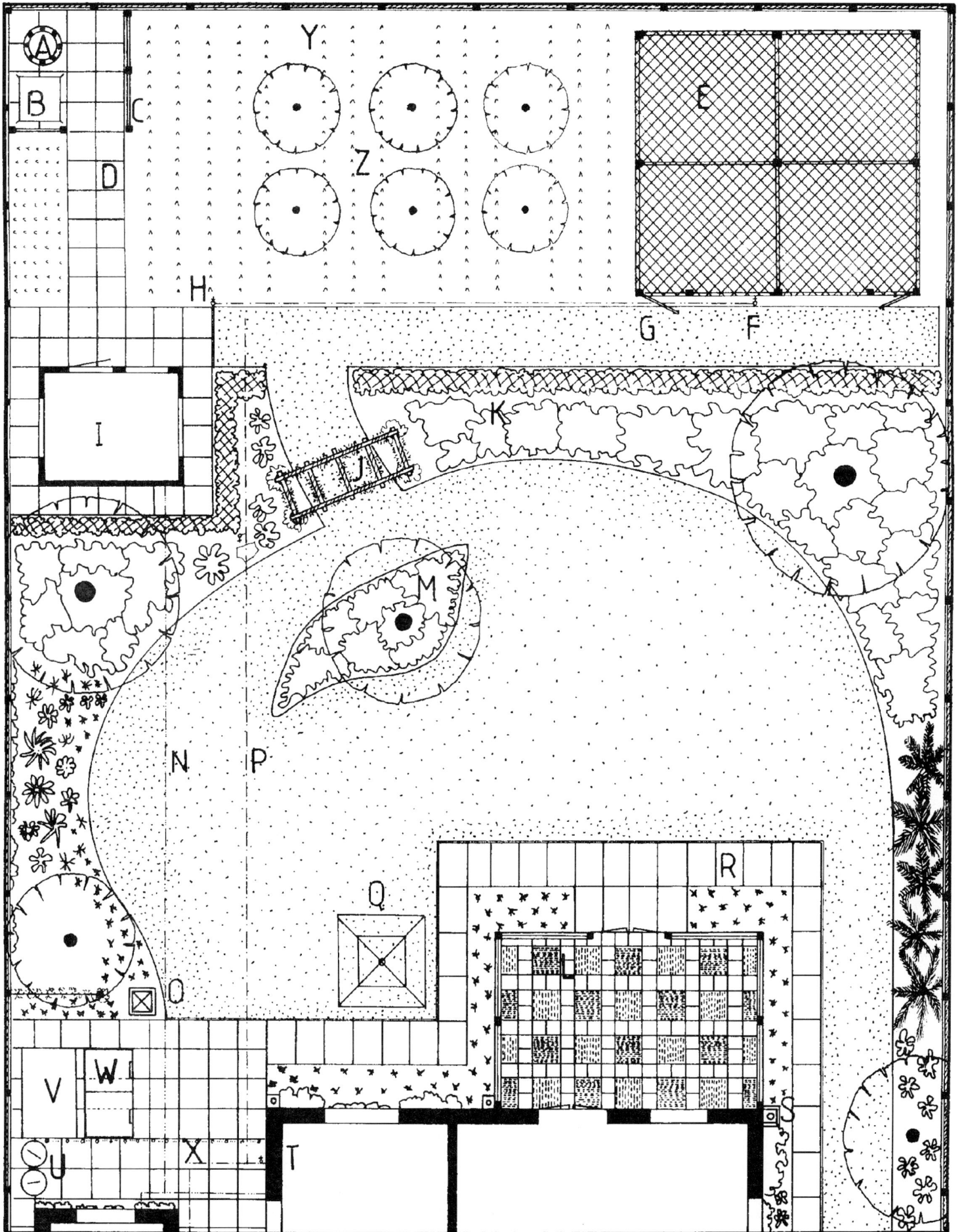

A

B

C

D

Y

Z

E

G   F

H

I

K

J

M

N   P

O

Q

R

V   W

U

X   T

S

SCALE 1: 100

## Sloping site with 'cut-and-fill'

This large bungalow has been built on a sloping site where there has had to be a 'cut-and-fill' operation hence the sloping grass banks (N) probably cut by hover mower, behind a perimeter wall. The property is surrounded by connecting pathways with shrubs, climbers and plants between these paths and the bungalow walls. The L-shaped lawn (U) has four ornamental trees planted but carefully positioned so that views will not be prejudiced. The garage (K), built on the lower level, must have a thick waterproof membrane on the outside of the wall next to the bed (J).

The vegetable garden (F) is well screened, having a standpipe in the corner. Note: the grass path adjacent to it is the same width as the paved path so that if the grass becomes too worn it can be exchanged with an extension of the 900mm slabbing. A broad flight of steps (H) leads up to the front door with capped brick pillars (L) at the top. There is an option to fit gates to these if security or the possibility of animals entering require this to be done. A shallow brick wall (Z) approximately 300mm high retains the soil in the border where there is an assortment of planting (X and Y). Note the variation of bonding of the non-slip paving slabs around the property.

## Key

| | | | |
|---|---|---|---|
| A | Oil tank | M | Low brick boundary walls |
| B | Shed with electricity connected | N | Banking to adjust levels |
| C | Fuel bunkers | O | Perimeter hedging |
| D | Refuse containers | P | Side path steps, pillars and gate |
| E | Area for compost/incinerator | Q | Side path to service area |
| F | Vegetable garden | R | Bird table |
| G | Standpipe | S | Terrace |
| H | Flight of wide steps to front door and circulating pathways | T | Four ornamental trees in lawn |
| | | U | Lawn |
| I | Sloped brick walls adjacent to steps | V | Brick wall and pillars with timber fence inserts |
| J | Formal bedding of roses | | |
| K | Garage with outside waterproof membrane on garden side | W | Close boarded boundary fence |
| | | X | Climbing shrubs |
| L | Brick pillars with caps – option for a pair of gates | Y | Assorted shrubs |
| | | Z | Shallow brick wall adjacent to paved path |

SCALE 1:100

## An asymmetrical shape

This property has been built on gently sloping land running from the house in the direction of the vegetable garden (T). The plot is also asymmetrical in shape. The garden has been designed to be relatively simple and easy to maintain. In order to have a levelled area (W) there has been a cut-and-fill operation. Steps (J) lead down from the sloped lawn (X) to the levelled lawn. To hold back the earth there is a battered stone wall (P) reduced in height as required, with mowing strip and weepholes. In order to remove any ponding of water during wet weather there are two systems of land drains (M) with crossfalls leading towards soakaways (Y and Z). A further flight of steps (N) leads down and joins up again with the sloping lawn. Similarly there is a battered stone wall (O) with weepholes and mowing strip for the lower part of this plateau.

There is a small vegetable garden (T), mainly for summer crops, at the bottom of the garden screened by hedge (U) and tall shrubs with an ornamental conifer (V). A small area (S), screened by a similar hedge, has been formed for composting and the disposal of grass cuttings. The whole perimeter is fenced with chain link fencing (F) camouflaged by a thick hedge (G). Ornamental trees with differing flowering times have been planted (H, I, Q, R) with adjacent mixed shrubs and flowers in the borders.

Near to the house is a terrace (part shown) (A) surrounded by a low stone wall (C) and mowing strip (D) with a step down at (B).

---

### Key

| | | | |
|---|---|---|---|
| A | Chequerboard terrace with adequate crossfall for surface water | N | Steps down from levelled lawn |
| B | Wide steps from terrace to lawn | O | Retaining stone wall, weepholes and mowing strip |
| C | Low stone edging with weepholes and positions for alpines | P | Mowing strip |
| D | Mowing strip | Q | Ornamental tree and naturalising bulbs in long grass |
| E | Ornamental tree and shrubs | R | Ornamental tree and shrubs |
| F | Chain link boundary fencing | S | Composting area with hedge screen |
| G | Thick hedge | T | Vegetable garden |
| H | Ornamental tree, shrubs and herbaceous plants | U | Hedge screen |
| I | Ornamental tree | V | Shrub screen and ornamental conifer |
| J | Steps down to levelled lawn | W | Levelled lawn |
| K | Rockery | X | Sloping lawn |
| L | Alpine plants | Y | Soakaway pit with cover |
| M | Land drains | Z | Soakaway pit with cover |

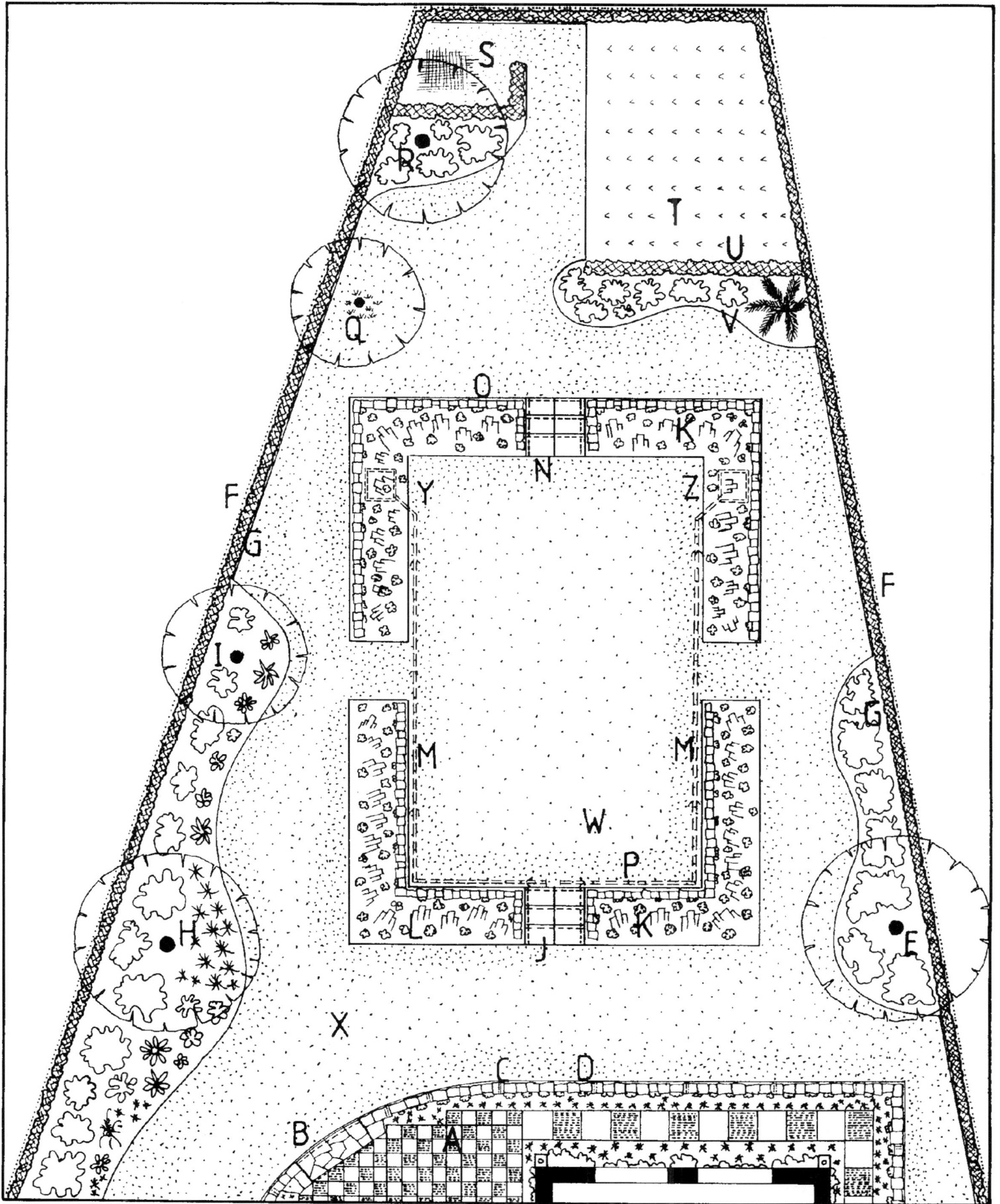

S

R

T

U

V

Q

O

K

F

N

Y

Z

G

I

F

M

M

G

W

P

H

E

X

C D

B

A

J

K

SCALE 1:100

## Gardening on two levels

The rear garden of this elegant property is constructed on two levels. The lower terrace (J) has small retaining walls (I) adjacent to the small formal beds. There is a lower curved step (K) and a further step (L) in order to reach step (M), a curved section of the path (D), which goes all round the garden including the higher level terrace (C) bordering the main rectangular lawn (H). In this lawn are ten different patterns (P) of paving around the specimen trees (O). It provides the owner with an opportunity to choose their preferen-ces. There is an area of small brick paving, herringbone pattern (B), at the top of the gar-den. In one corner of the terrace (B) is a sum-merhouse (A) supplied with electricity (S) and water (R).

In the other corner is a composting bay and incinerator (F) on a concrete slab and screened by walling. The whole garden is surrounded by capped brick walls (G) in front of which are masses of different shrubs (N). In the case of the border near the brick paving there is an emphasis on large bedding plants (T) with wall shrubs behind. There are standpipes (E) in both corners of the top of the garden.

---

**Key**

| | | | | |
|---|---|---|---|---|
| A | Summerhouse | | K | Lower flight of curved steps leading to long terrace |
| B | Brick area laid in herringbone pattern | | L | Middle step area |
| C | Top terrace random pattern with socket at the corner of one slab | | M | Top flight of curved steps with risers |
| D | Path of different sized slabs | | N | Mixed shrubs with graded height, vigour and spread |
| E | Standpipes | | O | Different kinds of specimen standard flowering trees |
| F | Incinerator/compost zone | | | |
| G | Thick brick wall with coping | | P | Different kinds of paving surrounds for trees |
| H | Lawn at a higher level to that of the terrace nearest house | | Q | Plant tubs |
| I | Low brick retaining wall, with weepholes, to take up difference in levels | | R | Water supply |
| | | | S | Electricity supply |
| J | Terrace, random pattern slabs | | T | Mixed border of wall shrubs and herbaceous plants |

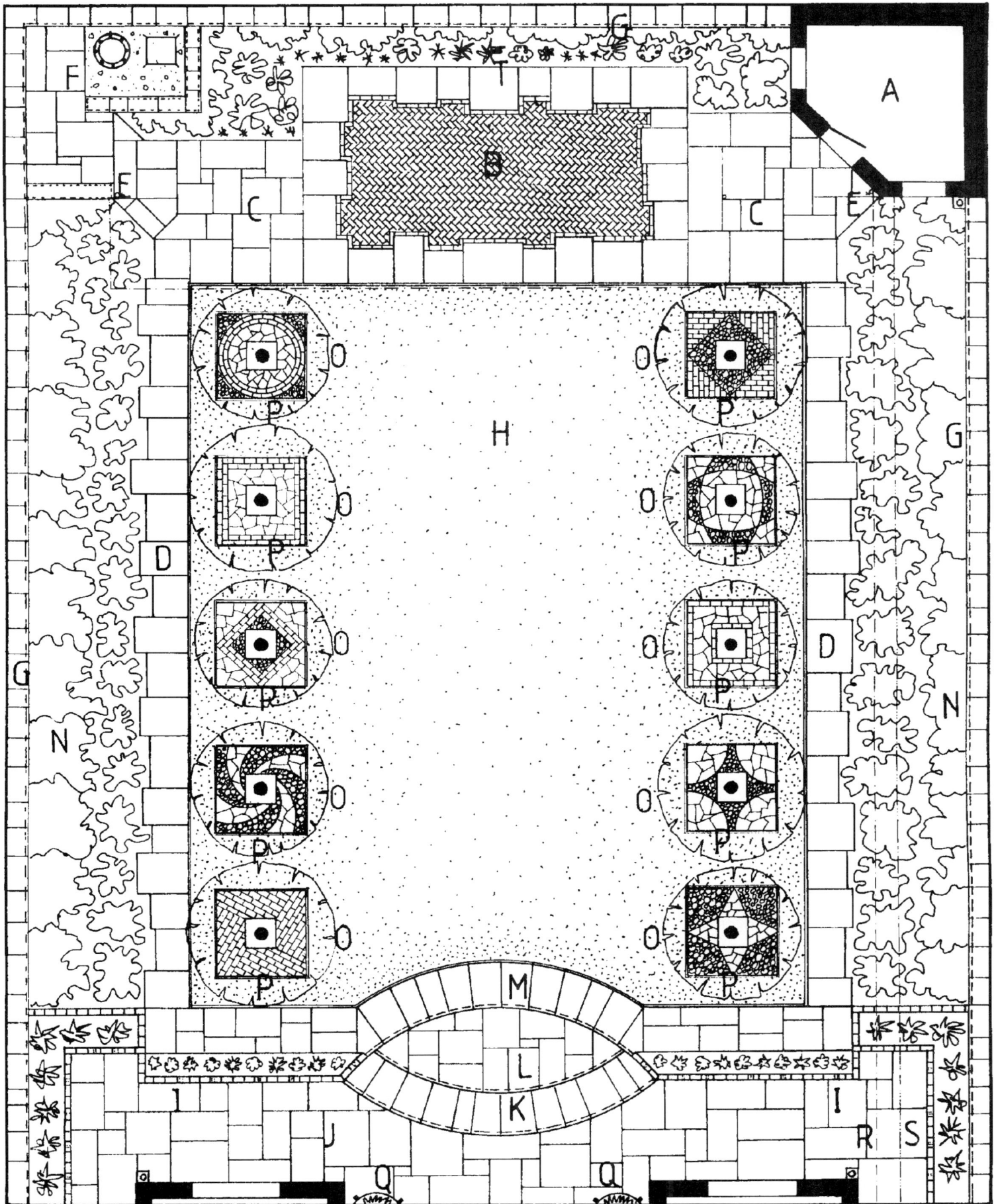

F

A

G

B

C

F

C

E

O

O

O

O

H

O

O

O

O

D

D

G

G

N

N

P

P

P

P

P

P

P

P

P

P

M

L

K

I

I

J

R

S

Q

Q

SCALE 1:100

## A central vista

The special feature of this garden is its central paved pathway (M) with overhead morticed tanalised timber beams (N) set upon strong reinforced brick columns which are thickly planted with climbing roses (O) with bush roses nearby. This achieves a magnificent vista from the main terrace area (P) opposite the French windows right through to the summerhouse (J). Around these features are curved borders of mixed trees and shrubs (I). A hedge (H) defines the separation of ornamental and kitchen gardens. The kitchen garden is divided between cane fruit (A), soft fruit (B), strawberries (C) and vegetables (D). Standpipes are located at (K). The functional area consists of an incinerator/composting zone (E), a garden shed (F) with connecting slab paths (W). Adjacent to the garage (G) are various flower borders to embellish the sides of the garage and refuse bin area.

---

**Key**

| | | | |
|---|---|---|---|
| A | Cane fruit – raspberries | M | Central paved pathway |
| B | Soft fruit – redcurrants, blackcurrants, gooseberries | N | Strong overhead tanalised beams morticed together on reinforced brick columns forming archway |
| C | Strawberries | | |
| D | Vegetable garden | O | Climbing roses with bush roses nearby |
| E | Incinerator/compost zone screened by fence | P | Patterned terrace of different colours |
| | | Q | Small end of terrace flower bed |
| F | Garden shed with electricity connected | R | Quadrant bed of low-growing shrubs |
| G | Garage | S | Fuel bunker |
| H | Hedge screen between kitchen and ornamental garden | T | Refuse container with brick wall screen |
| | | U | Flower border with trellis behind |
| I | Mixed shrub and tree borders around curved lawn | V | Boundary hedge |
| | | W | Connecting path between terrace and functional area |
| J | Summerhouse with paving surround and electricity connected | X | Electricity supply |
| | | Y | Water supply |
| K | Standpipe | Z | Side border of flowering shrubs |
| L | Lawn | | |

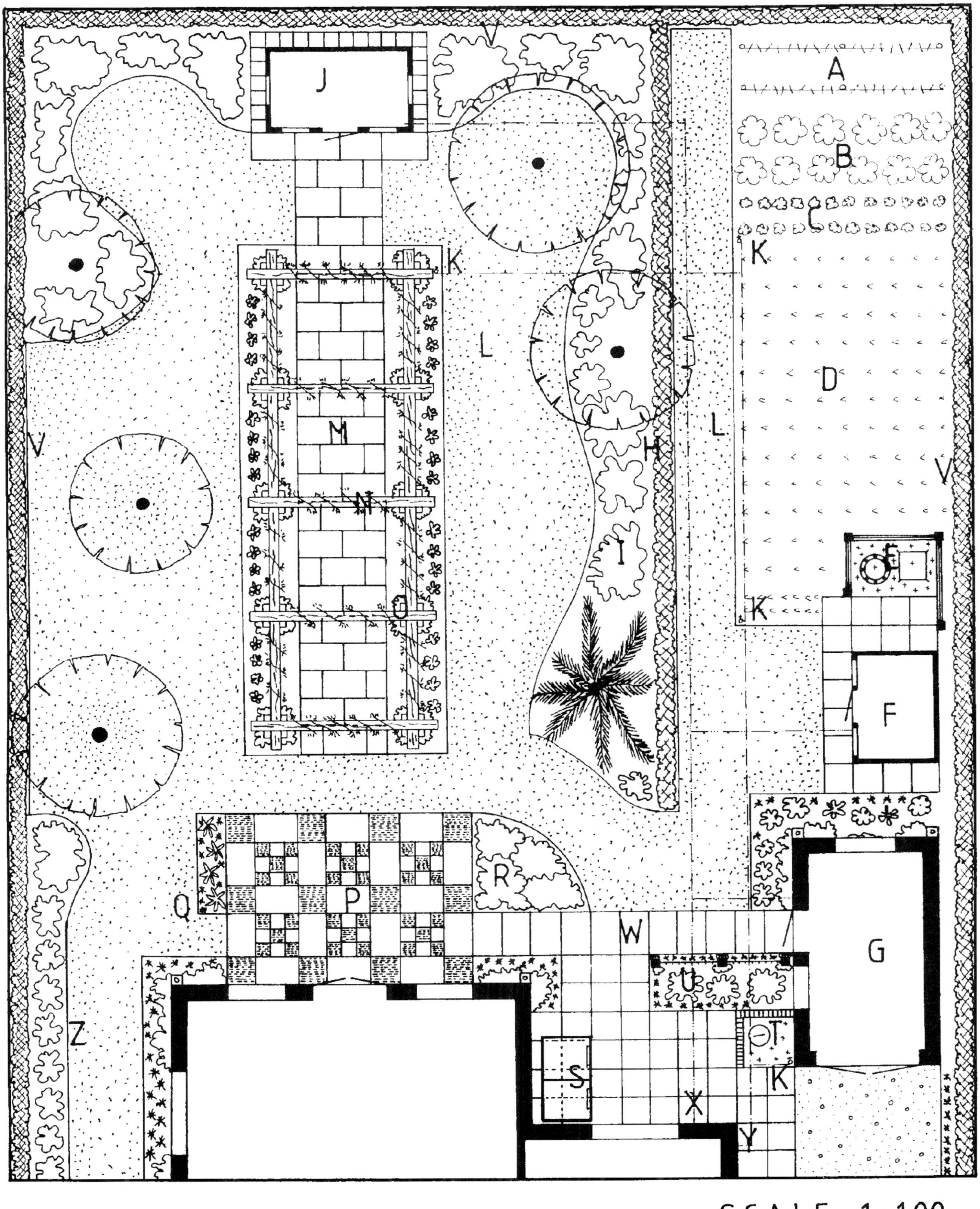

J

V

A

B

C

K

Z

V

K

L

M

N

O

L

H

I

K

D

V

K

E

F

Q

P

R

W

G

U

T

Z

S

X

K

Y

SCALE 1:100

## A circular lawn bordered by steps

This detached property is bordered entirely by interwoven wood panel fencing (G) upon which, adjacent to the rose border (F), climbing and rambler roses are grown (H). There is a long narrow vegetable garden (B) with path (C) and standpipes (D), leading to shed (A). To screen all this is a thick hedge (V). The lawn (K) which is almost circular, broken in line by a sitting out area (M), has within it a feature bird bath (J). Around the lawn is an extensively planted border (L) with mixed shrubs and trees, with a special weeping tree (W). To accommodate minor level differences and shallow slopes of grass there is stone edging with mowing strip (I). A grass path (Z) joins the main lawn with the kitchen garden.

Next to the main terrace (N) there are broad steps (X) down to the lawn, either side of which are large areas of mixed shrubs, heathers, etc. (U and T). At one end of the terrace there are quadrant-shaped steps (O) with an adjacent brick trough with plants (P) and standpipes.

**Key**

| | | | |
|---|---|---|---|
| A | Garden shed | O | Quadrant steps in crazy paving |
| B | Vegetable garden | P | Raised earth bricked bed |
| C | Access path to vegetable garden | Q | Wall shrubs and formal bedding |
| D | Standpipes | R | Bird table |
| E | Hedge screen to vegetable garden | S | Trellis screen to another paved area |
| F | Massed rose border | T | Mixed low-growing shrubs and heathers |
| G | Interwoven wood panel fence | | |
| H | Climbing and rambler roses | U | Mixed low-growing shrubs and heathers with Japanese azaleas if soil is acid |
| I | Stone edging with adjacent mowing strip | | |
| J | Central feature bird bath with a crazy paving surround with alpines | V | Background hedge separating kitchen and ornamental gardens |
| K | Main lawn | W | Special weeping standard tree |
| L | Mixed shrubbery and trees | X | Steps from terrace down to lawn |
| M | Sitting out area | Y | Well shaped dwarf prostrate conifer |
| N | Terrace with socket for garden umbrella | Z | Grass path from main lawn to kitchen garden |

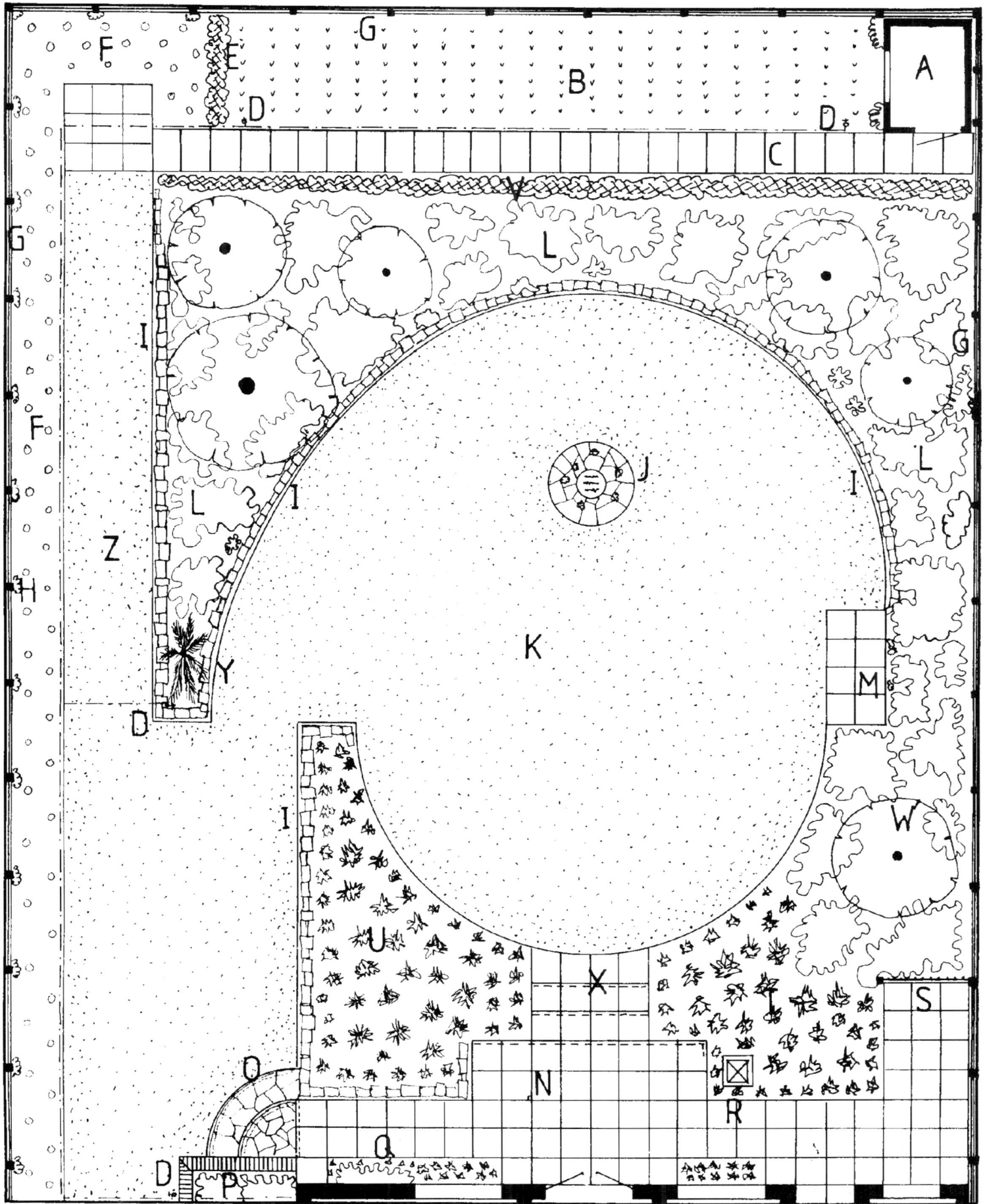

87

SCALE 1:100

## Perimeter problems: a shared drive

This semi-detached house has a shared concrete drive leading to a single garage with a party wall There is a small vegetable garden (E) set in a grass area, one side of which abuts the functional zone, consisting of a garden shed and incinerator bay. On the nearside there is an earth-filled brick trough in which there is a screening trellis. At one end of this trough there is a standpipe. The shed and garage are supplied with electricity. Between the shed and garage there is a narrow infill of in-situ concrete.

The whole back garden has a shared fence (Z) on the side opposite the drive (L). To give a perimeter interest there is a pergola (W) with a pergola archway (G). Adjacent to the drive are planted screening shrubs (U). In the corner of the main lawn is a paved area for garden furniture, which is bordered by a lavender hedge. By the French window there is a terrace and on one side of this is a high brick trough (R) to screen the bunkers (P) and refuse containers (Q). The kitchen door opens on to a lean-to greenhouse constructed on a low brick wall. There is a standpipe (Y) in the corner to provide water for propagating purposes and probably tomatoes in growing bags or pots in the summer. There is a side gate (T) to give access to the drive. A standard specimen tree such as an almond (M) is situated in the corner of the garden to give additional screening to the garage.

### Key

| | | | | |
|---|---|---|---|---|
| A | Incinerator | | N | Main lawn |
| B | Shed | | O | Terrace |
| C | Earth-filled brick trough | | P | Bunkers |
| D | Garage | | Q | Refuse container |
| E | Vegetable garden | | R | High brick trough |
| F | Grassed area | | S | Lean-to greenhouse |
| G | Pergola arch | | T | Side gate |
| H | Paved area | | U | Screening shrubs |
| I | Lavender hedge | | V | Climbing plants secured to fencing posts |
| J | Water supply | | W | Pergola |
| K | Electricity supply | | X | In-situ concrete |
| L | Drive | | Y | Standpipe |
| M | Formal specimen tree | | Z | Shared boundary fence |

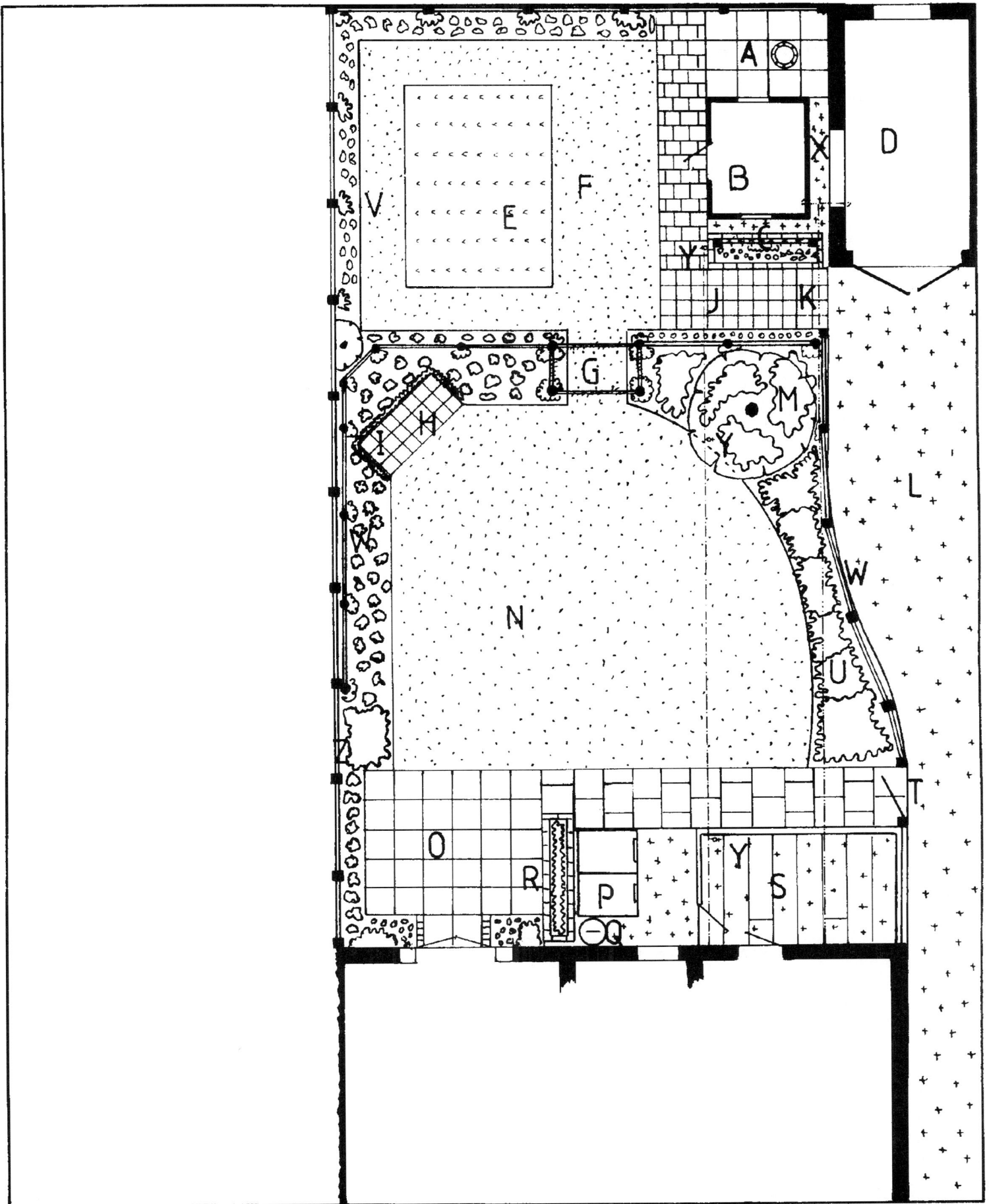

SCALE 1:100

## Paved areas and a beech hedge

This garden measures approximately 12m wide × 25m long and a great many features have been incorporated in the design. The terrace comprises 600mm × 600mm non-slip concrete slabs interspersed with cobble and granite sett inserts (R, S, T). There is a long plant border with strong foundations (U). Likewise at (Z) where the terrace leads on to a crazy paved area (quadrant) with curved brick steps (P) down on to a lower paved area in the corner of which is a large seat (Y). Being a semi-detached property there is a shared fence (J) on one boundary. On the opposite side there is a mixed copper and green beech hedge (X) both of which will go brown in winter.

A mixed paving path (O), curved in places, circles the lawn (N) and in one corner is a small formal pond (M) built from rendered concrete blocks. An aviary (I) is surrounded by cobbles, edged with brick, as it joins this path (O). A series of rose arches (G) gives a vista banked either side by blocks of bush roses (H). In the border (L) there are shrubs mixed with assorted low-growing herbaceous plants. The functional area consists of a compost bay (A), cold frame (B), shed (C) and access path (D). There are standpipes (E) around the garden, including the vegetable garden (F). From the back door there is a place for a refuse container (W) with steps down (V) to the paved area.

## Key

| | | | |
|---|---|---|---|
| A | Compost bay | N | Lawn |
| B | Cold frame | O | Pathway |
| C | Shed | P | Circular brick steps with crazy paving infill |
| D | Access path using slabs 900mm × 600mm | Q | Crazy paving |
| E | Standpipes | R | Granite setts |
| F | Vegetable garden | S | Cobbles |
| G | Rose arches | T | Non-slip 600mm × 600mm slabs |
| H | Bush roses | U | Long border for bedding plants similar to two borders by steps (Q) |
| I | Aviary | | |
| J | Shared fence | V | Steps down from back door |
| K | Washing-line pole set in concrete dolly | W | Refuse container |
| | | X | Thick hedge of beech |
| L | Mixed planting, shrubs, etc. | Y | Long seat |
| M | Small formal pond | Z | Foundations for edge of terrace |

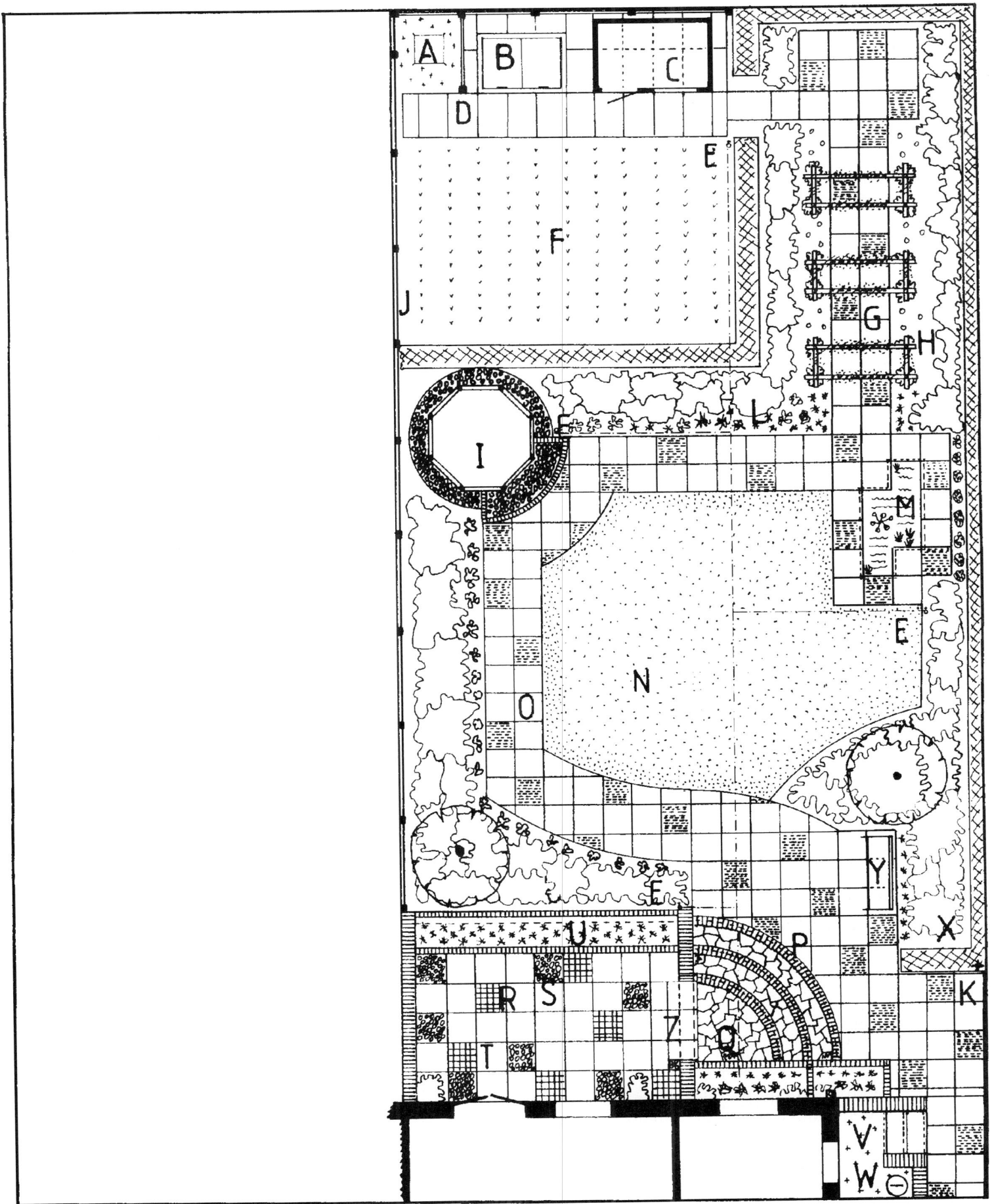

SCALE 1:100

## A corner plot

This end of terrace corner cottage is surrounded by 2m high brick walls (X) with rear entrance (R) leading on to a macadamised pavement (T). On one side there are street trees (U) which filter noise and dust from the highway. Internally there are several walls (Y) 1m high to separate various features. The vegetable garden (O) with standpipes (P) is in one corner adjacent to a small area used for salads and herbs (N). In the other corner there is a seat (Q) looking out over the rear terrace (Z) which is planted up with two large-leaved trees to give shade. Nearest to the cottage, leading up to the rotary washing line (H) is the functional area which contains fuel bunkers (D), refuse containers (E), sand-pit (F) and a bench (G), whilst on the other side of the wall is a terrace (A) with irregular-shaped rectangular plant beds. In that corner there is a pool (I) with marginal aquatics (K) with two stepping stone platforms (J). Terrace (A) is enhanced by a *Magnolia soulangeana* set in an area of granite setts and cobbles (L). The smaller chequer-board terrace (W) provides a good location for occasional garden furniture and an opportunity to view most of the ornamental and colourful garden.

## Key

| | |
|---|---|
| A | Main terrace |
| B | Vertical damp proof course or space between brick walls and house walls |
| C | Concrete service area |
| D | Fuel bunkers |
| E | Refuse containers |
| F | Sandpit play area |
| G | Bench |
| H | Rotary washing line |
| I | Square pool with waterlilies |
| J | Stepping stones on brick piers – fish-hides to provide shade |
| K | Various sized beds for marginal aquatics, i.e., water myosotis, marsh marigold, *Alisma plantago*, etc. |
| L | Specimen tree in cobble square with granite sett centrepiece, part open-jointed to allow rainwater access |
| M | Various rectangular beds of plants and low-growing shrubs |
| N | Smaller vegetable garden for salads and herbs screened by low wall |
| O | Main vegetable garden screened by low wall |
| P | Standpipes |
| Q | Secluded seat |
| R | Rear access |
| S | Bollards in pavement to prevent vehicular access with lamp post on corner |
| T | Macadam pathways |
| U | Street trees |
| V | Kerbstone |
| W | Chequer-board pattern section of paving (slab and granite setts) |
| X | Brick boundary wall approximately 2m high with bricks on edge as headers |
| Y | Brick wall some 1m high to divide garden into features |
| Z | End of garden terrace with occasional flower beds |

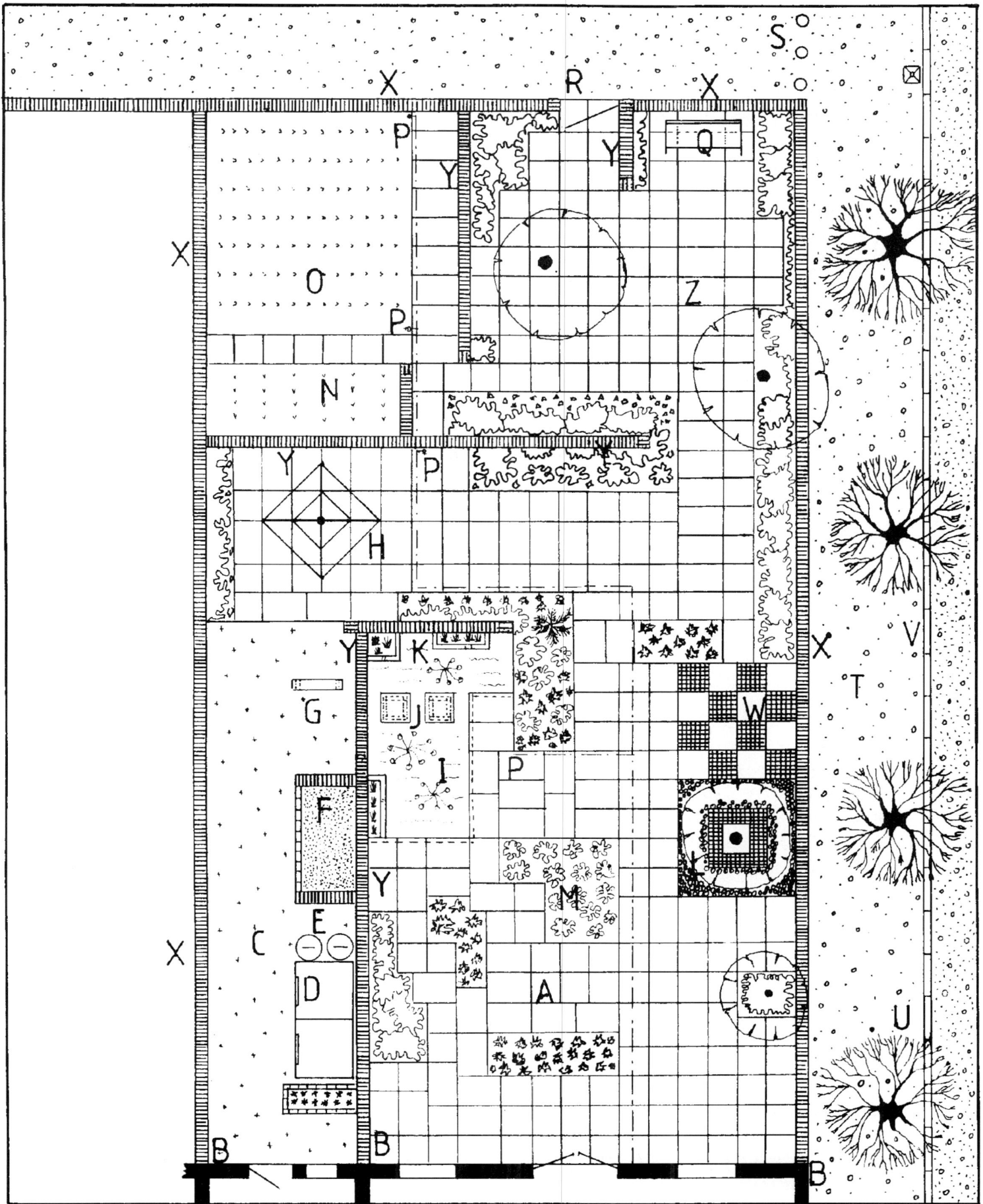

X R X

P
Y Y Q
O Z
P
N

Y P

H

Y K

G J
I P
F
Y
M
W
E
X C A
D

B B B

SCALE 1:100

## Curved borders – infill site

The garden of this house demonstrates the flowing curves of the shrub borders (P and Q). Trees are not planted in the lawn (F). There is gated access (K) at each end of the kitchen garden (M) as it connects with the lawn. This was an infill site with a field (A) at the bottom fenced off with chain link (J). On one side of the main garden is a neighbour's established garden (B) with bush roses and climbing roses with chain link fencing (J). In the far corner is the fourth neighbour's paddock in which is planted a conifer hedge (I). This is fenced off by post and rail (Z) and chain link fencing (J). There is an animal shelter (E) in it.

A service path (D) goes the whole length of the site with standpipes (G) nearby for kitchen garden (M) use. This path leads to a garden shed (N) screened by interwoven wood panel fence (H) and the incinerator/compost zone (L). In the longer border (P) there is an area of crazy paving (O) which is opposite the kidney-shaped border (R) with an ornamental tree and low-growing herbaceous plants. Nearer the house is a patterned terrace (S) which leads to a rotary washing line (T). Around the area of lawn (F) there is a continuation of the interwoven wood panel fencing (U) upon which are growing climbing plants to screen the fuel bunkers (V) and refuse containers (W). The border (X) gives an opportunity for mixed michaelmas daisies, lupins, delphiniums and dahlias. The water supply to the vegetable and soft fruit garden (M) comes from the kitchen (Y).

---

**Key**

| | | | |
|---|---|---|---|
| A | Field | N | Garden shed |
| B | Neighbour's planted-up garden | O | Crazy paving |
| C | Hedge | P | Long shrub border |
| D | Kitchen garden pathway | Q | Shrub border |
| E | Animal shelter | R | Kidney-shaped bed |
| F | Lawn | S | Terrace |
| G | Standpipe | T | Rotary washing line |
| H | Fence screen | U | Panel fence |
| I | Conifer tree belt | V | Fuel bunkers |
| J | Chain link fencing | W | Refuse containers |
| K | Access gates | X | Mixed herbaceous border |
| L | Incinerator/compost zone | Y | Kitchen and water supply pipe |
| M | Kitchen garden | Z | Post and rail fence |

A    J    O    L    K    N    E    Z    G    J    H    F    B    P    J    Q    D    M    J    C    K    G    J    F    T    X    S    V    W    G    Y

95

SCALE 1:100

## A feature pond

This small bungalow has been built on an irregular shaped plot and has an interwoven wood panel fence (S). The garden is divided into two sections. One is the functional vegetable/soft fruit garden (C) with access path (E) to two cold frames (B) and incinerator/composting/manure zone (A), having a concrete base. Alongside the path are two standpipes and a screening hedge (Y). Near to the garage (G) is a greenhouse (F) supplied with electricity, a rotary washing line area (H), refuse container (I), fuel bunkers (J) and oil storage tank (K). There is a creosoted sawn timber pergola arrangement (T) around (H, I, J and K) which allows for evergreen climbers such as *Lonicera halliana* and *Clematis armandii*.

Surface water drainage from downpipes (X) etc., connects with the garage drive wash-down gully (L) via inspection/rodding chamber with oil interceptor equipment (M) to go ultimately to a soakaway.

The pond (O) has a square slab surround with four marginal aquatic boxes in the corners. In the centre there is a large slab (N) on brick piers to form a fish hide as there are herons in the district. On top is a waterlily in a basket. An overflow (Q) to this pond is laid with butt-jointed drains to permit gradual seepage. There is a seat (R) opposite the pond and a sandpit (W) for children to play in near the end of the terrace (Z). The lawn (V) is edged with curved beds of trees and shrubs.

---

### Key

| | | | | |
|---|---|---|---|---|
| A | Incinerator/compost zone | | N | Fish hide |
| B | Cold frames | | O | Pond |
| C | Vegetable/soft fruit garden | | P | Pond surround |
| D | Standpipes | | Q | Overflow from pond |
| E | Service path | | R | Seat on paving slabs |
| F | Greenhouse | | S | Boundary fence |
| G | Garage | | T | Pergola screen |
| H | Drying area | | U | Mixed trees and shrubs |
| I | Refuse containers | | V | Lawn |
| J | Fuel bunkers | | W | Sandpit |
| K | Oil storage tank | | X | Rain water downpipes |
| L | Wash-down gully | | Y | Hedge screen |
| M | Inspection chamber with oil interceptor equipment | | Z | Terrace |

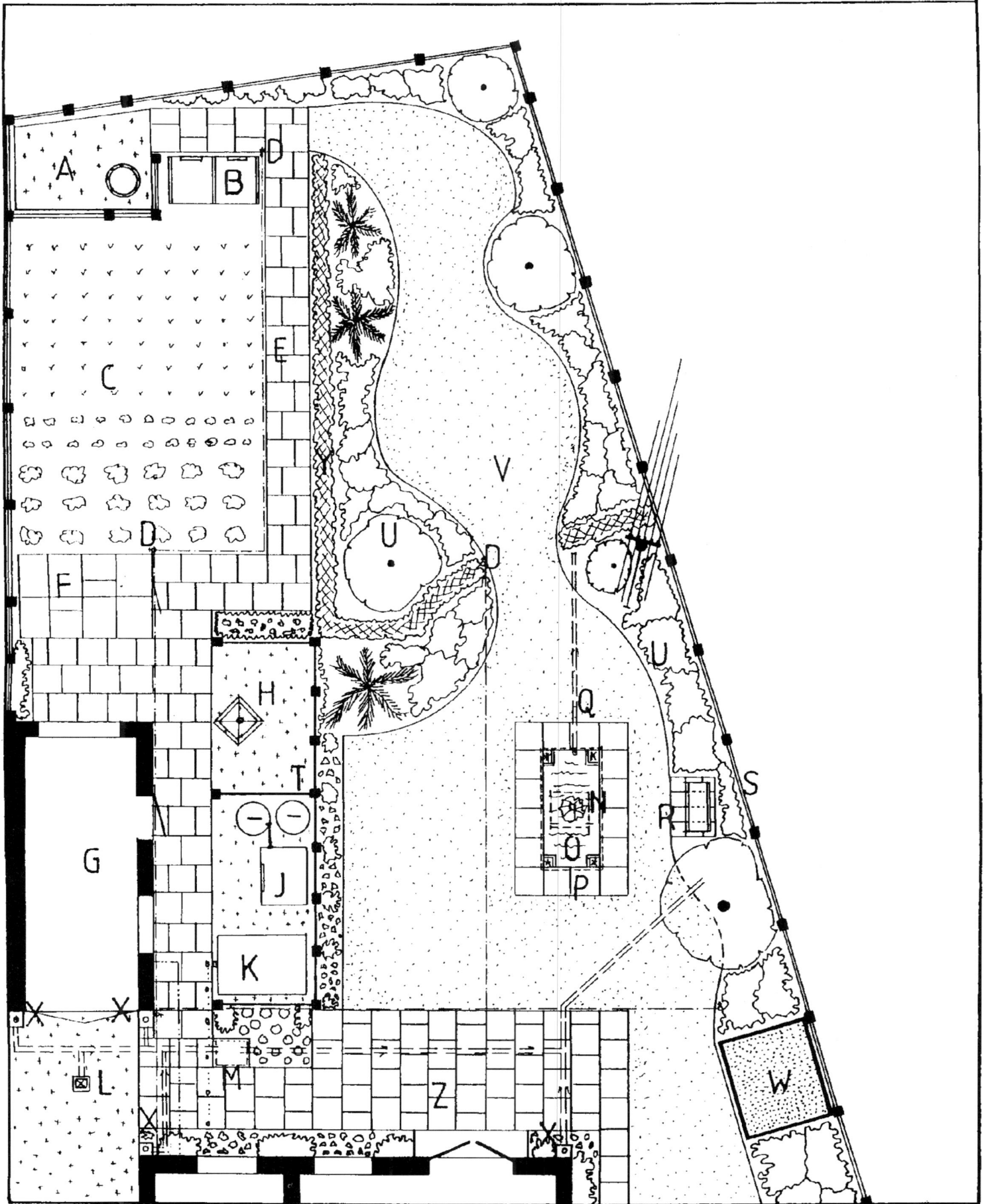

SCALE 1:100

## Mounded island bed

This property has a simple layout for the ornamental garden bordered by hedging (P), to diffuse the prevailing wind, and chain link fencing. There is a comprehensively planted soft fruit garden (T) and a larger vegetable garden (U) both with standpipes and divided by a 900mm access path of paving slabs. There is a large paved area (V) for a manure stack or composting, screened by trellis, the other side of which is a small greenhouse (W) with electricity connected.

On one side of the ornamental garden is a rose pergola system (J) joined to an archway (X) planted with honeysuckles. In the main lawn (K) is a narrow, shaped and mounded island bed (M) with one ornamental tree. By the terrace (A) there are large flower borders (C) between which is a flight of steps (B) from the terrace to the lawn (K). The paved area (H) between the shed (I) and fuel bunkers (E) has in it a socket for a rotary washing line. The half standard apple tree (Y) grown on a dwarfing root stock is of interest as it has different apple varieties grafted upon it.

---

### Key

| | |
|---|---|
| A | Main terrace |
| B | Steps from terrace to lawn |
| C | Slightly sloping beds with planting |
| D | Brick trough with plants |
| E | Fuel bunkers |
| F | Oil storage tank with trellis screen |
| G | Garage |
| H | Paved area with socket for rotary washing line |
| I | Shed with electricity connected |
| J | Pergola with climbing roses and rose bushes in border |
| K | Lawn |
| L | Long straight path |
| M | Mounded island bed with dwarf flowering tree |
| N | Seat on paved area |
| O | Tree and shrub border |
| P | Perimeter hedge |
| Q | Dividing hedge between ornamental and kitchen gardens |
| R | Grass path by kitchen garden |
| S | Massed mixed shrubs |
| T | Soft fruit garden with standpipe containing raspberries, loganberries, blackberries, gooseberries, and red, white and blackcurrants |
| U | Vegetable garden with standpipes |
| V | Area for stacking manure/compost |
| W | Small greenhouse with electricity connected |
| X | Archway with mixed honeysuckles |
| Y | Fruit tree |
| Z | Wall shrubs |

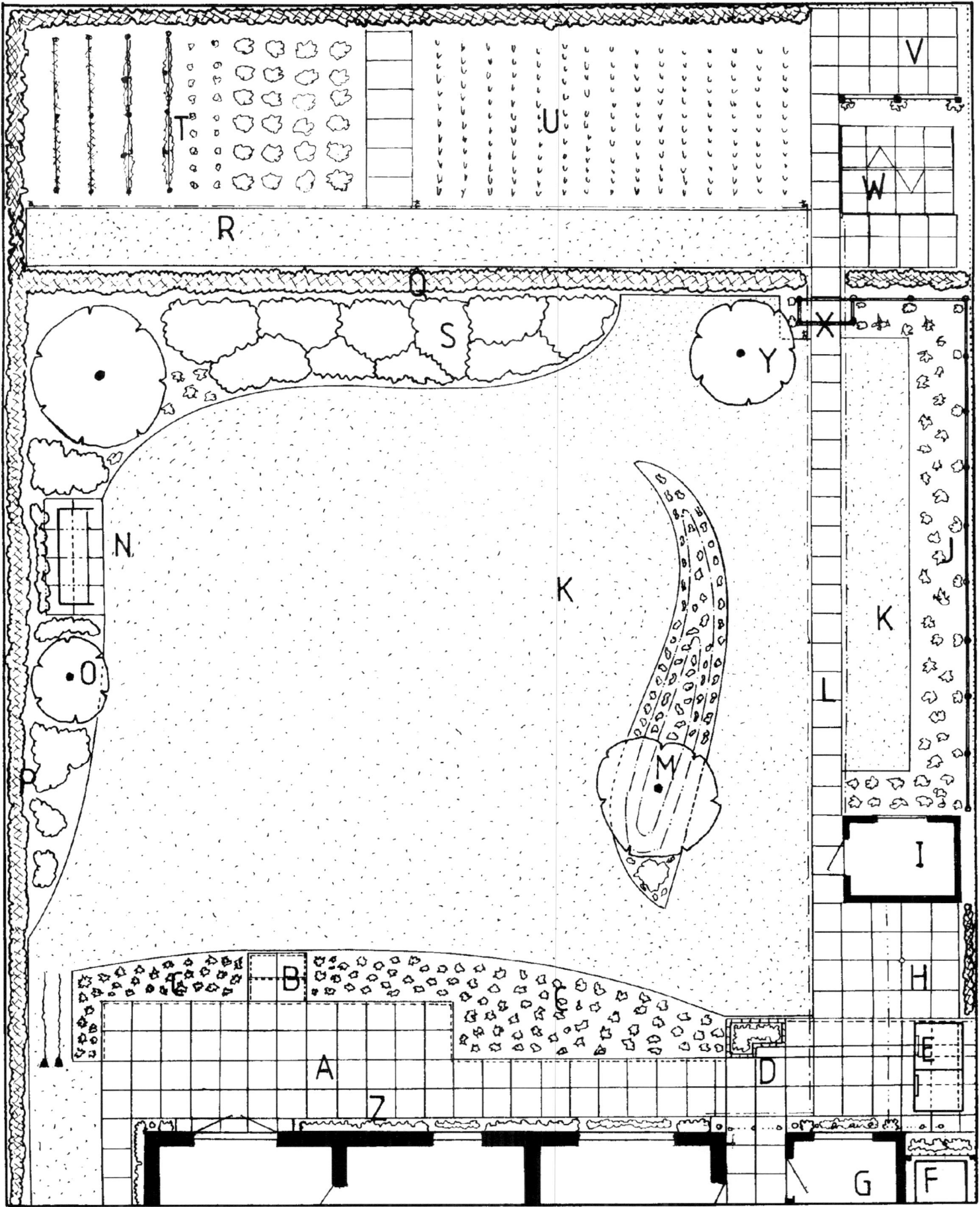

SCALE 1:100

# House set back in its garden

This house has been set back in the plot and, as a result, the rear garden is quite small. There is space for a vegetable garden (E) with a service path (C) and standpipe (B). To screen it there is an interwoven wood panel fence (D) and a hedge at right-angles to it. There is a long shrub border and two trees next to a rectangular lawn. Opposite the French windows is a terrace of chequer-board design (J) and a bird table (K). Next to the path from this terrace to the front garden is a long mixed shrubbery (W), at the back of which is the boundary fence constructed of chain link (M).

Either side of the front door are two flower tubs (S). The service area has an oil tank (G) and a shed (F) to which an electricity supply has been installed in the garage (O). The approach to the service area, where there are also the refuse containers (N), has a low brick wall and side gate (Z). The garage drive (P) has two small areas of paving slabs (Q) either side which allow car passengers to alight on a hard surface. On one side of the drive is a formal bed of standard roses (Y). Opposite this is another large mixed shrubbery (R). The front has been interestingly designed with recesses for the garage drive and main pathway gates (X and U). The trees and shrubs there are planted between the lawns (I) and the brick wall (V).

## Key

| | | | |
|---|---|---|---|
| A | Incinerator | N | Refuse containers |
| B | Standpipes | O | Garage |
| C | Service path to vegetable garden | P | Drive |
| D | Interwoven wood panel fence | Q | Paving |
| E | Vegetable garden | R | Shrubbery |
| F | Garden shed | S | Flower tubs by front door |
| G | Oil tank | T | Pathway from road to front door |
| H | Washing line posts | U | Gate to pathway |
| I | Lawns | V | Brick wall with capping |
| J | Terrace | W | Shrubbery |
| K | Bird table | X | Gates to garage drive |
| L | Shrubbery | Y | Border of standard roses |
| M | Chain link boundary fence | Z | Gate and low brick wall |

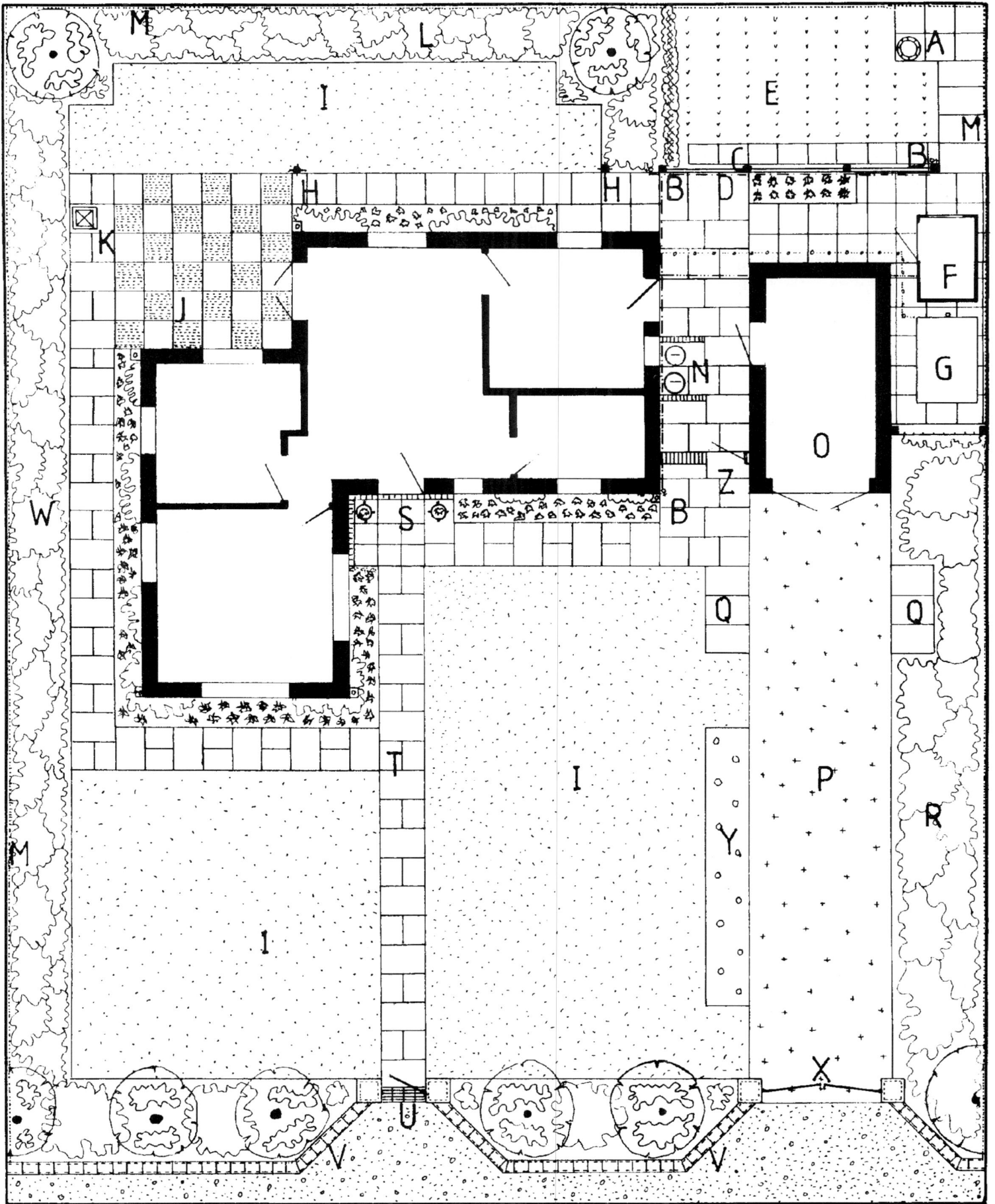

M

L

I

A

E

M

C

B

H

H

B

D

K

F

J

G

N

W

O

S

B

Z

M

Q

Q

T

I

P

R

Y

I

X

U

V

V

SCALE 1:100

## A wide plot

This house is situated in a plot broader than it is long and, as a result, most of the functional area is on one side by the back door and this includes a vegetable/fruit garden. The pathway from the garage hard-standing comprises 600mm × 900mm non-slip slabs with alternate bonding. Electricity is laid on to the garden shed and water is connected to the corner of the garage (R), the vegetable garden (P) and the ornamental garden (G).

In one corner there is a crazy paving path leading to an incinerator and compost bay, screened by an evergreen hedge such as *Viburnum lauristinus* (D). There is a secluded terrace (F) with an overhead arbour system which is splayed out and covered with a multitude of mixed large-flowered clematis growing adjacent to wiring. The clematis attach themselves by twisted leaf stalks (petioles). The pathway nearby and the terrace are constructed of special moulded slabs to give a different appearance.

---

### Key

| | | | |
|---|---|---|---|
| A | Incinerator | N | Shed |
| B | Compost bay | O | Vegetable/soft fruit garden |
| C | Access path in crazy paving | P | Standpipe |
| D | Thick evergreen hedge pruned but not clipped to provide winter flowering | Q | Electricity cable below ground |
| | | R | Water pipe to standpipe for wash-down area |
| E | One of these areas has columnar Cupressus such as *Allumi*, *Lawson*, *Lutea*, or *de Boskoop* | S | Side path |
| | | T | Concrete wash-down with gentle fall to twin gates |
| F | Terrace with area for planting climbers | | |
| G | Standpipe | U | Well-shaped specimen dwarf tree |
| H | Terrace using precast concrete discs | V | Garage |
| I | Lawn | W | Paving to front door |
| J | Long spinescent hedge such as *Berberis thunbergii* | X | Close-boarded fence with strong posts |
| | | Y | Mixed ornamental trees and flowering shrubs |
| K | Square wooden tub for columnar bay tree | Z | One or two specimen flowering cherry trees such as *Prunus hisakura* and *autumnalis* |
| L | Coal/coke bunkers | | |
| M | Refuse container | | |

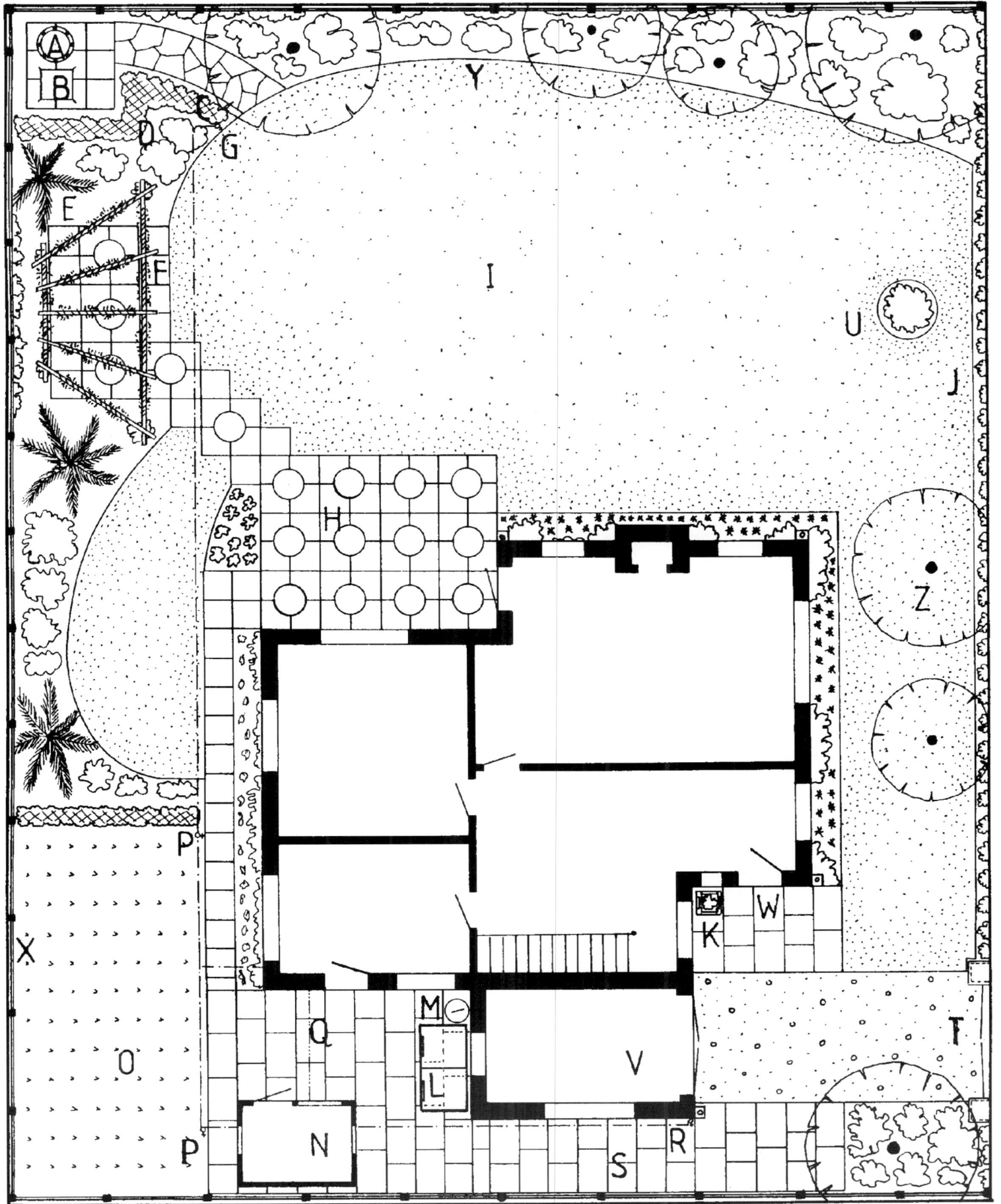

103

SCALE 1:100

**Play area with mixed planting**

The ornamental garden of this property is divided into two as the vegetable garden is reached by going through the gate (U). The smaller part is devoted to a play area for children, i.e., hammock and see-saw plus rough grass for toys and ball games. A hedge, some 1.25m high, is a screen and a buffer. The rest of the garden is a plantsman's paradise since it is partitioned by winding paths of crazy paving countersunk to the lawn levels. The paths lead to focal points such as the pond (F), the bird table (N), the old tree (O) and the kidney-shaped contoured bed (P) edged with stone (Q).

There are ample opportunities for climbing plants on the perimeter fencing, such as *Clematis tangutica*, honeysuckle (*Lonicera belgica* or *tellmanniana*), *Jasminum officinale*, *Solanum crispum*, etc. By very careful planting arrangements there is a feeling of discovery at every curve of the paths. Because trees and shrubs predominate over formal bedding, maintenance is reduced.

---

**Key**

| | | | |
|---|---|---|---|
| A | Children's see-saw | N | Bird table |
| B | Hard-wearing grass (with rye grass) probably rotascythed because of undulations caused by toys | O | Existing oak tree |
| | | P | Contoured bed full of assorted heathers (plenty of acid peat worked into soil) |
| C | Hammock | Q | Stone edging to bed |
| D | Grass left to grow longer | R | Horizontal wiring approximately 250mm apart upon which to train and tie in climbers |
| E | Hedgerow | | |
| F | Circular pond with marginal aquatic and oxygenating plants with short-stemmed waterlily | S | Close boarded fence |
| | | T | Cedar, *Atlantica glauca* |
| G | Overhead archway | U | Garden gate |
| H | Terrace constructed of crazy paving with planting pockets | V | Mixed large shrubs with occasional trees, not laburnum (seeds are poisonous) |
| I | Formal well shaped weeping cherry tree | | |
| J | Water butt and tap | W | Mountain ash tree, *Sorbus aucuparia* |
| K | French window leading to brick paving, herringbone pattern | X | Oak tree |
| | | Y | Bird cherry tree, *Prunus padus* 'Waterii' |
| L | Lawn close-mown by cylinder mower | | |
| M | Brick paving | Z | Himalayan birch, *Betula jacquemontii* |

SCALE 1:100

## Open plan garden

This semi-detached property has been built on a slightly mounded plot thus requiring the drive to the garage (A) to be graded, e.g., (B) slight fall with central gully for wash-down facility, (C) a gentle slope and (D) almost level to allow for inward swing of the pair of gates. The property is also partially open-plan hence the boundary fence between the front gardens is post and chain. In the main lawn (E) are two specimen standard flowering trees (K and L), both with their own circular earth border. Around the lawn are mixed shrubberies (M and N) with another half-standard upright growing tree (M) so that the branches will not obstruct the passage of a car. The frontage has a brick wall with pillars and close-boarded fence (H) outside which is a grass verge (J) next to the pavement. Between the lawn and that fence is a belt of suitable conifers (H).

There is a small front terrace (O) by the front door and this leads round the side of the house to where there are fuel bunkers (R) and a refuse container (Q). The property is connected to mains gas. Next to the garage there is a garden shed (F) both of which are connected to electricity. There is a long terrace pathway (S) ending with a flower trough. Brick walls (U and V) allow the ground levels to be maintained with a slope (W) down to the vegetable garden (Y) and mixed shrubbery (X). The rear of the property is fenced with chain link (Z). There is a flower bed in one corner (T). Note the two drainage gullies nearby (S). There are standpipes for water (G), for the vegetable garden, garage and front garden. If composting is required then it will have to be in one corner of the vegetable garden.

---

**Key**

| | | | | |
|---|---|---|---|---|
| A | Garage | N | Mixed shrubs and plants |
| B | Part of drive | O | Front terrace and pathway |
| C | Sloped part of drive | P | Side path |
| D | Level part of drive | Q | Refuse containers |
| E | Lawns | R | Fuel bunkers |
| F | Garden shed | S | Terrace with large flower trough |
| G | Standpipe | T | Rectangular flower bed |
| H | Close boarded fence between brick pillars and brick wall beneath | U | Brick retaining wall |
| | | V | Brick retaining wall |
| I | Conifer belt | W | Slope down from terrace pathway to lower level path |
| J | Grass verge | | |
| K | Ornamental tree | X | Mixed shrubbery |
| L | Ornamental tree | Y | Vegetable garden |
| M | Ornamental tree with upright habit | Z | Chain link fence |

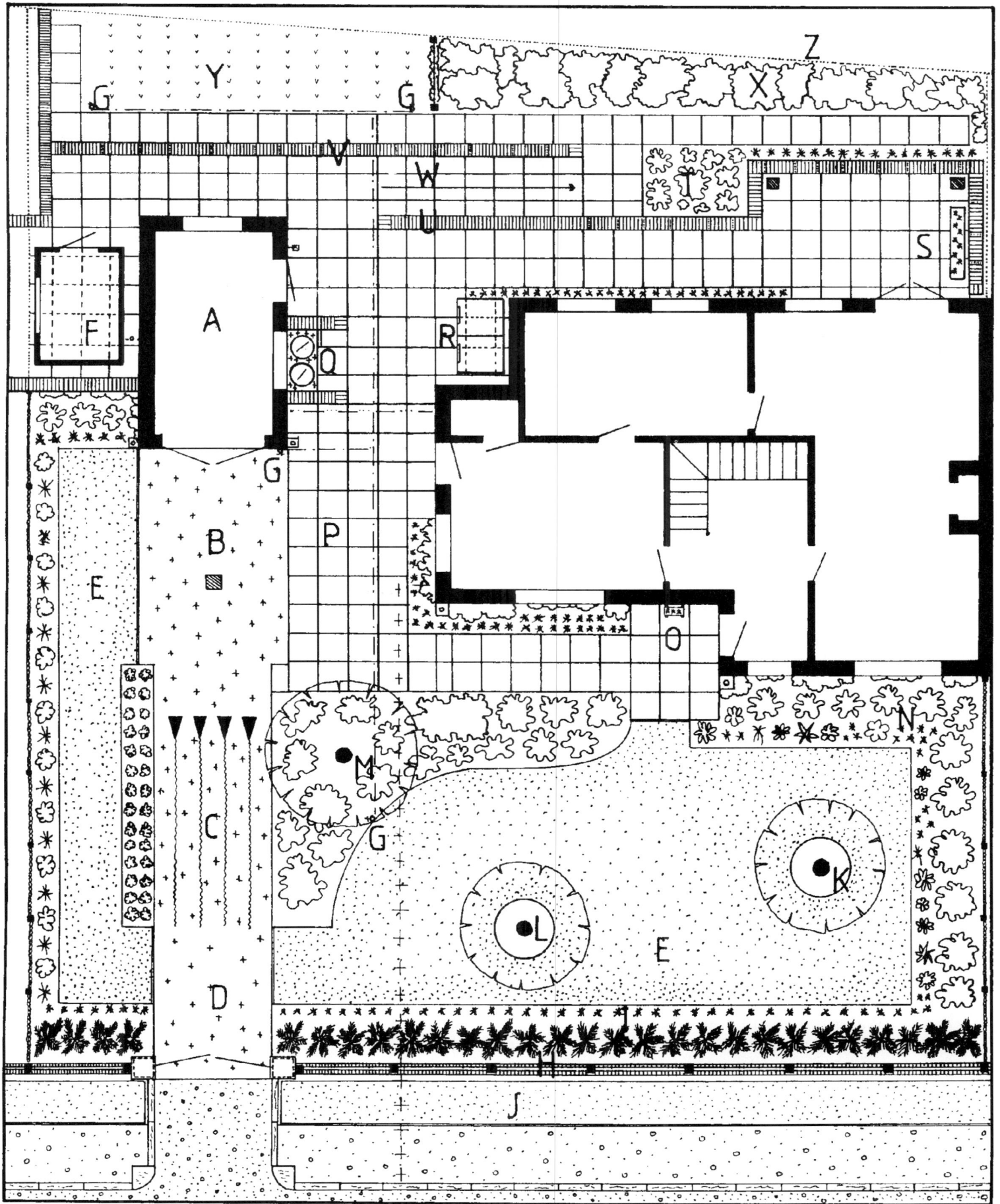

107

SCALE 1:100

## Low-maintenance garden

This garden has been designed to reduce the amount of work required to maintain it. There is a larger proportion of crazy paving paths, some at right angles, but the curved pathway with an overhead archway provides variation and an interesting feature leading up to the summerhouse.

There is only a small kitchen garden and composting area, both screened by beech hedging serviced by a path of non-slip concrete slabs. In juxtaposition to the curved pathway is a garden seat situated on an irregular-shaped area of paving. Near to the house there is a paved terrace with pond and bird table to provide interest. At (T) there is an extensive pergola system to provide a screen and windbreak. The specimen tree at (C) gives balance to the composition. The summerhouse, supplied with electricity, gives a long distance backdrop to the whole garden.

**Key**

| | | | |
|---|---|---|---|
| A | Summerhouse | M | Lawn |
| B | Garden seat on small irregular-shaped paved area | N | Rectangular pond |
| | | O | Overflow pipe from pond to soakaway in corner of border |
| C | Close planted shrub border with specimen tree | P | Bird table |
| D | Sundial as feature point | Q | Standpipe |
| E | Lawn | R | Crazy paving path |
| F | Kitchen garden | S | Standpipe |
| G | Water pipe from house to standpipes | T | Pergola system |
| H | Compost bay | U | Beech hedging as screen |
| I | Curved crazy paving path | V | Incinerator |
| J | Pergola archway along path | W | Edging plants such as aubretia, alpine phlox, campanula |
| K | Transition from crazy paving to regular non-slip concrete slabs | X | Specimen conifer |
| L | Electricity supply from house to summerhouse | Y | Formal bedding with wall shrubs |
| | | Z | Terrace adjacent to French windows |

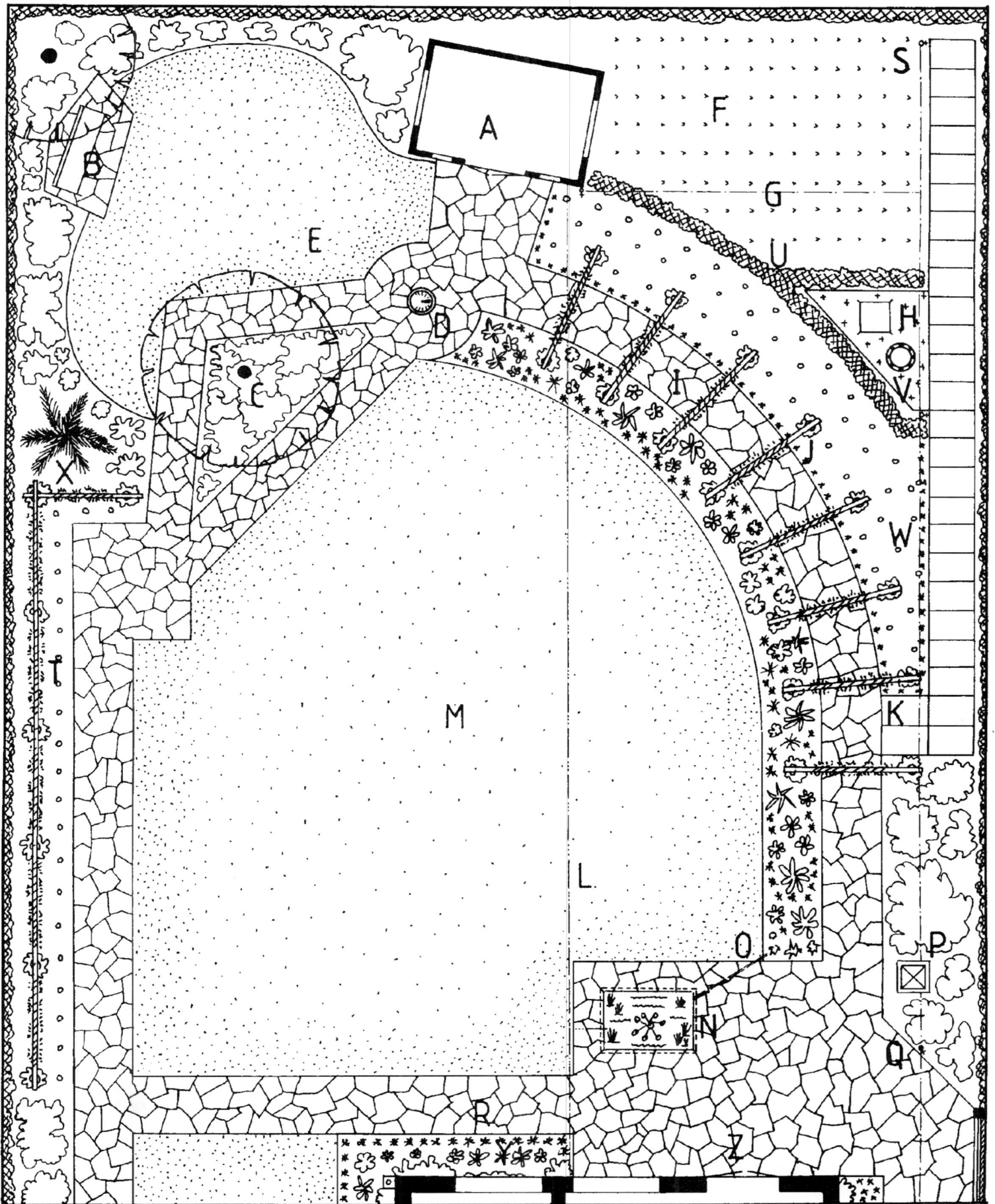

A

S

F

B

G

U

E

D

H

V

C

I

X

J

W

t

M

K

L

O

P

N

Q

R

Z

SCALE 1:100

## Tricky levels

The garden of this property, bordered by post and wire fence (I) and privet hedge (J) has been a difficult one to design from the point of view of levels. The ground falls away from the house and terrace, hence steps at (P) and cemented stone walling (K) with pockets for alpines (Q). The path (H) follows these contours to about halfway when it marries up with the lawn (W) after which it rises again to the vegetable/fruit garden (B & C). The lawn is banked to take this into account (F) with brick steps at (E). In the corner is a thatched summerhouse (D) adjacent to which are specimen trees (S, R, & U).

The vegetable garden (B) and soft fruit garden (C) have standpipes (T) in the corners and they are screened by a beech hedge (G) likewise the incinerator (A). There is also a conical Cupressus to screen the incinerator, together with flowering crab tree at (Z). Nearer the terrace (L) there is another specimen tree, e.g., flowering cherry (Y). The terrace has good surface water drainage with gullies at (O). The fuel bins (N) are screened from the house and French windows by a small planted bed with timber screen behind. The beds around the house are planted with flowering shrubs and some climbers to soften the corners. The shrubs under the window must be dwarf.

## Key

| | | | |
|---|---|---|---|
| A | Incinerator | N | Fuel bunkers |
| B | Vegetable garden | O | Drainage gullies |
| C | Soft fruit garden | P | Steps |
| D | Summerhouse | Q | Alpines |
| E | Steps | R | Specimen tree, e.g., snake bark acer |
| F | Banking of ground to adjust levels | S | Specimen tree, e.g., turkey oak |
| G | Beech hedge | T | Standpipes |
| H | Functional pathway | U | Specimen tree, e.g., *Liquidambar* |
| I | Post and wire fence | V | Massed flowering shrubs – dwarf types so as not to impede view from terrace |
| J | Hedge such as privet | | |
| K | Stone walling | W | Lawn |
| L | Terrace | X | Water butt |
| M | Refuse containers screened by brick wall enclosure | Y | Specimen tree, e.g., flowering cherry |
| | | Z | Specimen tree, e.g., crab apple |

SCALE 1:100

## Difficult surface water drainage

This semi-detached dwelling with shared garage entrance has been constructed on a site which was lower than road and pavement levels hence the slopes down to the garage and side entrance. The disposal of surface water drainage is therefore a factor. At (S) there is a gully with dirt trap when car-washing is required. This is connected to a surface water drain which then connects up with the rain-water downpipe. Also there are gullies set in the front pathway where an adequate crossfall is paramount, all leading to a large soakaway (A).

Retaining walls of different heights take up the adjustment in finished levels, e.g. (O) and (U). The kitchen garden with watering facilities is screened by a pergola system with interconnecting section of draped coir rope upon which are grown roses with assorted shrubs between it and the lawn.

A feature of this garden is a formal pond with central fountain connected to a submersible water pump. Location of this is immediately opposite the French windows and at right angles to a seat set on a paved area. Suitably placed stepping stones connect the pond feature to the house terrace.

---

### Key

| | |
|---|---|
| A | Soakaway |
| B | Incinerator |
| C | Water standpipe |
| D | Paved pathway |
| E | Post with interconnecting coir rope for rose screen and display |
| F | Octagonal pond – central fountain with paved surround. Provision for lilies and oxygenating plants |
| G | Garden seat |
| H | Stepping stones countersunk in grass |
| I | Lawn |
| J | Bunkers for coal and coke |
| K | Small garden shed including planted trellis screen on one side |
| L | Refuse containers next to kitchen door |
| M | Trellis screen at the end of a low-planted border with wall shrubs |

| | |
|---|---|
| N | Grating on gully for surface water disposal |
| O | Plant borders with low edging |
| P | Plant trough under window |
| Q | Hedge screen |
| R | Dense shrubbery |
| S | Gully for car-washing with connections to house rain-water downpipes |
| T | Gradual slope from road towards garage |
| U | Retaining wall – adjacent pathways having adequate crossfalls |
| V | Electric (armoured) cable from house to fountain pump threaded through galvanised conduit pipe |
| W | Side gate with gentle sloping path |
| X | Boundary hedge |
| Y | Vegetable garden |
| Z | Small borders for bedding plants |

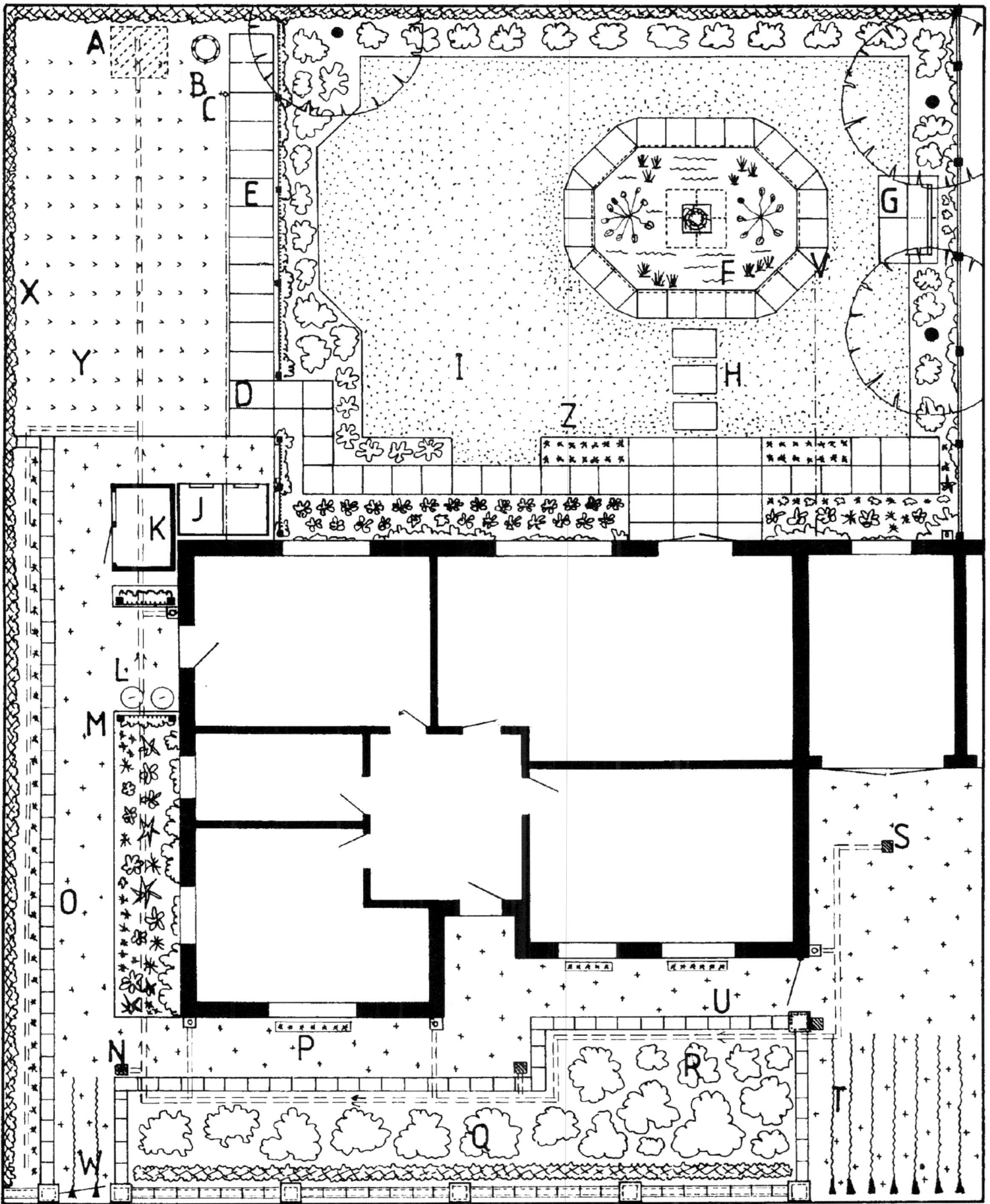

A

B
C

O

E

X

Y

D

G

F

V

I

H

Z

K

J

L

M

S

O

U

N

P

R

T

Q

W

113

SCALE   1:100

## A hammerhead driveway

This well appointed detached house is situated more or less in the centre of the plot. In the front there are wrought iron double gates hung from brick pillars. The drive, hammerhead in design, allows adequate parking and turning, being edged with either brick or stone. Next to these low edging walls there is a mowing strip to prevent damage to a mower. Adjacent to the garage is a concreted elliptical pond, planted with lilies and oxygenators such as *Elodea* or *Fontinalis antepyretica*. It has a backdrop of rocks and plants and a crazy paving surround.

It is embellished with a weeping birch tree, *Betula youngii*.

To give interest and privacy to the rear garden there are two brick gated arches (K and I). To give variation of interest the paving path (W) has slabs set at a 45° orientation. The kitchen garden is well supplied with standpipes. There is also another gated archway at (I) to keep dogs in the functional service area near the back door. Either side of the front door are two mophead bay trees in large tubs. The oil tank (H) is screened by a trellis upon which is growing an evergreen honeysuckle, *Lonicera halliana*.

**Key**

| | | | |
|---|---|---|---|
| A | Brick wall and gated archway | O | Small retaining wall away from garage |
| B | Compost bay | P | Rockery |
| C | Incinerator | Q | Elliptical pond |
| D | Vegetable garden | R | Crazy paving surround |
| E | Paved area and socket for garden umbrella or rotary washing line | S | Entrance gates |
| | | T | Oil pipe |
| F | Coke/coal bunkers | U | Water supply |
| G | Refuse container | V | Paved entrance (with step) with two bay trees |
| H | Oil tank | | |
| I | Gated archway | W | Paving slabs at 45° orientation |
| J | Trellis screen to oil tank | X | Brick wall with occasional buttresses for additional strength |
| K | Wall and gated archway | | |
| L | Driveway edging | Y | Garden seat resting on slabs in the shade of a neighbouring tree |
| M | Drive | | |
| N | Garage/logstore | Z | Lawn |

A B C D E F G H I J K L M N O P Q R S T U V W X Y Z

SCALE 1:100

## Three interlinked ponds

This garden has been designed especially for those who are interested in ponds, waterfalls and aquatic life. There are opportunities for many types of marginal and submerged plants, including oxygenators. Various kinds of fish, such as Koi carp, freshwater mussels and snails can be introduced while adjacent plants can be hosts to dragonflies and damsel flies. These three ponds, at varying levels, have interconnecting lipstones and an abundance of large well placed rocks with suitable alpines, ferns and mosses. A pump has been installed to circulate water, (P) to (N). Note: there is a top-up pipe connection to counter water evaporation in the summer. In winter an overflow pipe (Z) takes care of excessive rainfall. The type of lily planted in boxes will be determined by the larger pond depth. Because of this major feature the site has had to be adjusted to suitable levels.

Paved areas (G, H) and (F, E) have slopes and, to take up these differentials in levels, steps with risers at (T) and stone walling with 15° batter (G, F) and walling adjacent to the sloped pathways. The bisecting pathway rises again at (M) to a sitting out area (J), with seat (I) giving an excellent view of the pond complex in juxtaposition to the lawn and small terrace (V). Random sizes of paving adjacent to stone edging (Y) are set in, countersunk to the lawn, this paving being bedded down in a cement mixture on a concrete foundation. This design is best suited to a gently sloping site.

## Key

| | | | |
|---|---|---|---|
| A | Garden shed | O | Waterlilies |
| B | Kitchen garden | P | Pit containing water circulating pump |
| C | Standpipe | Q | Lipstone giving waterfall effect |
| D | Level pathway | R | Edging stones bedded preferably on concrete – impossible to be quite secure if butyl sheeting is used |
| E | Highest end of sloped pathway | | |
| F | Lowest point of sloped pathway | | |
| G | Lowest end of steeper sloped pathway | | |
| H | Highest end of steeper sloped pathway | S | Overhanging rock |
| I | Garden seat | T | Steps downward from higher to lower lawns |
| J | Small sitting out area between trees with backdrop of shrubs | | |
| | | U | Stone edging to sloping path |
| K | Evergreen hedge | V | Small terrace by French window |
| L | Beech hedge | W | Crazy paving |
| M | Steps with risers leading to sitting out area | X | Marginal paving to lawn |
| | | Y | Stone edging with pockets for alpines |
| N | Outfall for circulating water | Z | Overflow drain pipe to soakaway |

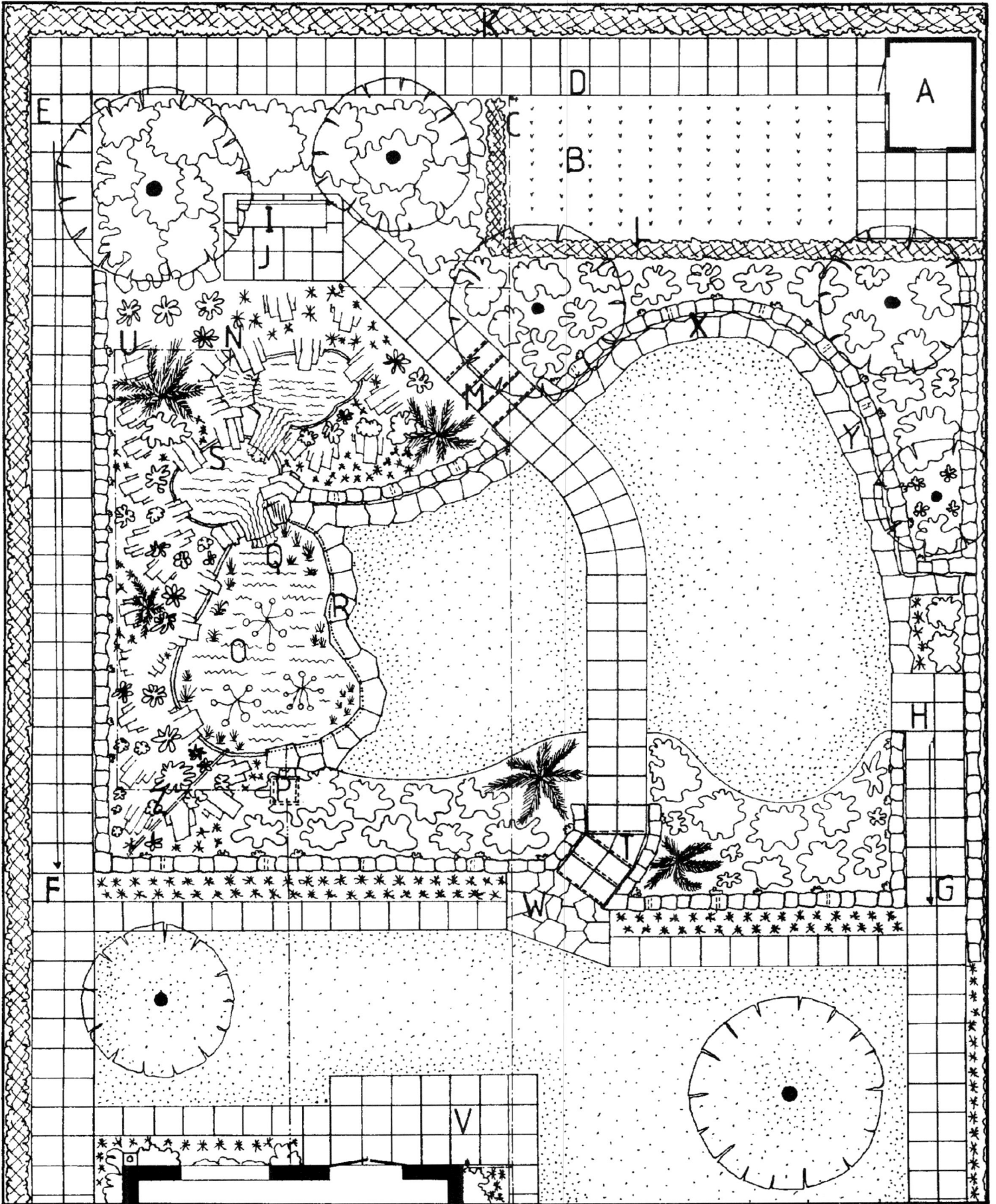

SCALE 1:100

## Urban walled garden

This urban house (note pavement and lamp post) has been built as an infill between two large gardens within local planning approval, hence its unusual shape and the accompanying design difficulties.

As the whole garden is relatively small and a decision has been made not to have a vegetable garden but to give each area its own features, thoughtful new planting of suitable trees and assorted shrubs takes precedence. Because of the comparatively high brick walls there are frequent opportunities for colourful wall shrubs. Deciduous shrubs in some of the borders can be mixed with sympathetic herbaceous plants.

It is essential to make this garden easy to look after with borders of suitable width for hoeing and other cultivations.

## Key

| | | | |
|---|---|---|---|
| A | Garage with rear access door on to pathway | O | Water butt with tap high enough off ground for watering-can access |
| B | Small garden shed | P | Incinerator area with brick wall screen |
| C | Coke and coal bunkers | Q | Evergreen shrubs |
| D | Refuse containers | R | Sitting area constructed of tiles and cobbles |
| E | Concrete path | S | Narrow border with wall shrubs |
| F | Small flower borders under windows | T | Corner of border for specimen bulbs, e.g., Nerines |
| G | Side access gate | U | Plant tubs |
| H | Border with rockery and associated alpine plants | V | Lawn |
| I | Sundial with small stone plinth | W | Paved threshold with brick risers to main door |
| J | Brick walling with slab top | X | Neighbouring garden with large existing tree |
| K | Bird table | Y | One of many specimen trees |
| L | Brick plant troughs | Z | Concrete edging as upstand between path and border |
| M | Terrace using chequer-board design and materials | | |
| N | Bird bath | | |

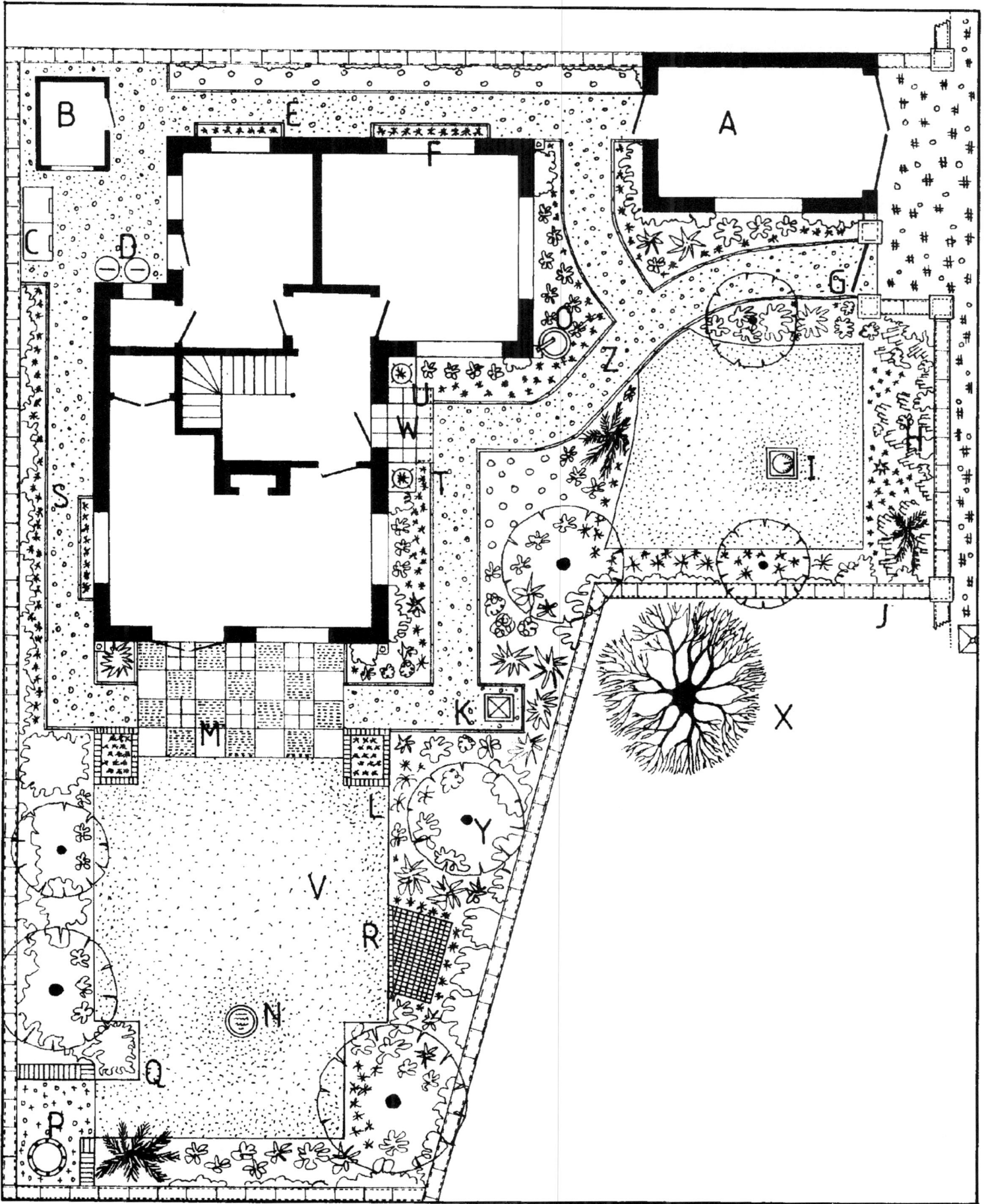

B

A

C

D

E

F

G

S

Z

H

I

J

U

W

T

X

K

M

L

Y

V

R

N

Q

P

SCALE 1:100

## Plot for a partially disabled gardener

The garden of this property has been intentionally designed for partially disabled gardeners, i.e., easy pathways and gently sloping ramps (J, H, Q). There are many raised earth borders for growing plants and shrubs. The borders are constructed with faced concrete blocks with many open joints for alpine plants, and weepholes. There are several standpipes (Y) for easy watering and in the lawn (W) there is a seat and table on paving slabs (I). All round these raised areas (E, K, L, M, T) there are mowing strips.

The lawn area (W) is at a slightly lower level than the rest of the garden, which has a chain link boundary fence (B). There is no kitchen garden, only a small bed for herbs (O) near the kitchen door. Around part of the perimeter are espalier fruit trees (F) and cordons (C) both secured to straining wires between strong posts. The terrace (U) is constructed of crazy paving with a seat at one end. At the other end is a gentle ramp (V) with small steps adjacent.

**Key**

| | | | |
|---|---|---|---|
| A | Shed | M | Square earth border with half standard tree and plants |
| B | Chain link boundary fence | N | L-shaped earth border with plants |
| C | Fruit tree cordons – apples, pears, etc. | O | Planting bed of mixed herbs |
| D | Pathway in 600mm × 600mm non-slip slabs | P | Garage drive with wash-down facility and gully |
| E | Raised planting border with mixed dwarf shrubs | Q | Gently sloping concrete ramp with rough surface |
| F | Espalier trees, plums, etc. | R | Fuel bunkers |
| G | Small standard flowering trees with shrubs below | S | Refuse containers hidden by low walling |
| H | Gently sloping concrete ramp with rough surface | T | Side earth border with planting |
| I | Seat and table on paving slabs | U | Crazy paving terrace with seat at one end |
| J | Gently sloping concrete ramp with rough surface | V | Gently sloping ramp in crazy paving with small adjacent steps |
| K | Square earth border with half standard tree and plants | W | Lawn |
| L | Square earth border with half standard tree and plants | X | Water butt with tap |
| | | Y | Standpipes |
| | | Z | Pre-cast concrete garage |

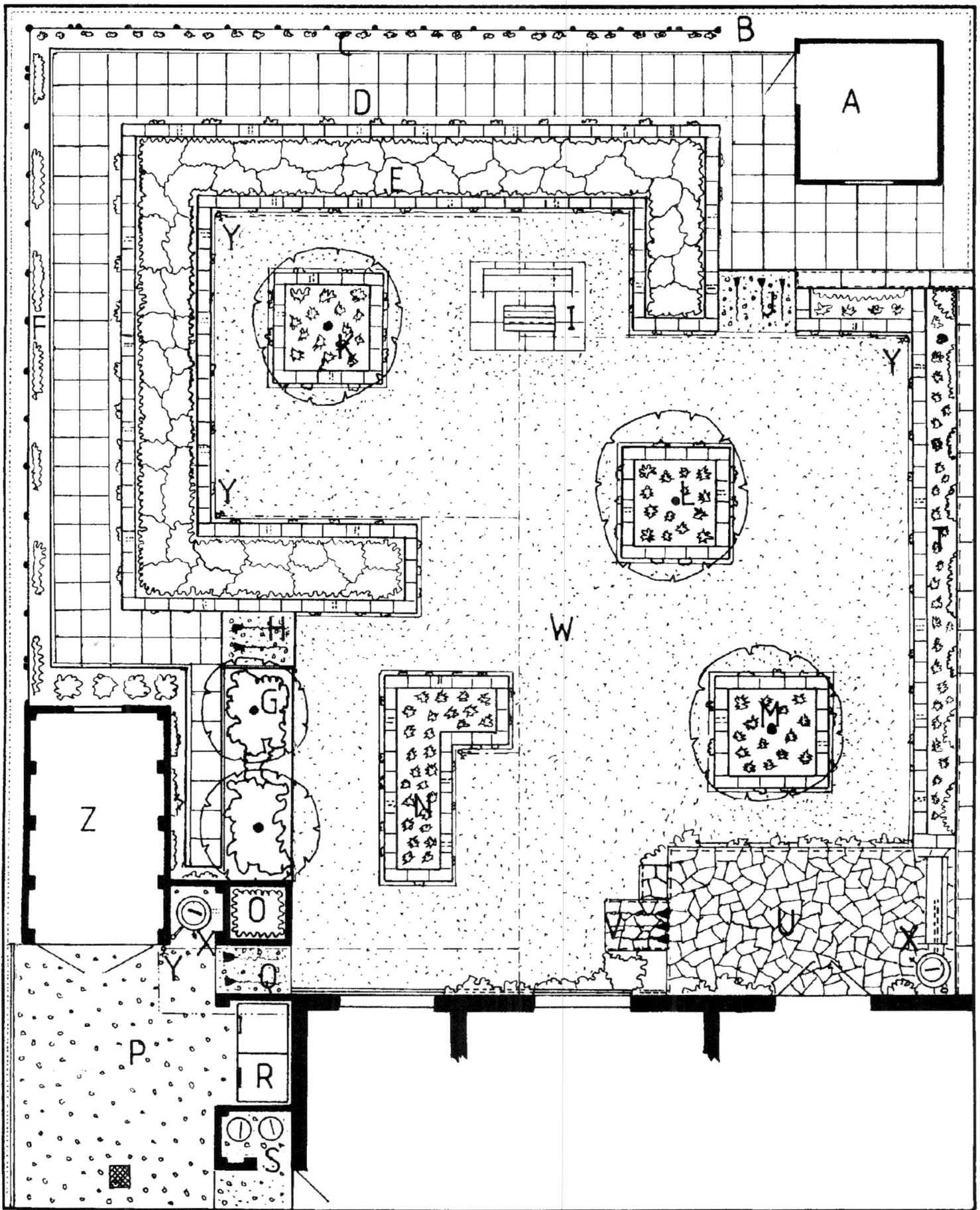

SCALE 1:100

## Large front garden

This fairly large bungalow is set well back from the road with the drive (R) widening from the gates (V) as it approaches the single garage (I). Between the garage and the bungalow there is a side gate opening on to the functional area which consists of fuel bunkers (B), a small shed with electricity (A), refuse container bay (C), incinerator/composting area (D) and small raised bed for culinary herbs (E). The service path (H) goes on past the vegetable garden (Y) with standpipes (F) to a small secluded garden (G) where there can be peace and privacy.

The bungalow has a continuous border of shrubs and climbers growing on wall trellis (J and U). In the front garden of the house there are two flowering tubs on the paved area by the main door (K) with a small expanse of paving (Q) leading to the drive via a curved pathway (N) of countersunk paving slabs. Either side of this are two dissimilar areas of lawn (O) with occasional trees (P). There are two raised planting borders (L and S) contained in a low stone wall with mowing strips where the walls abut the lawn. The front garden is demarcated by interwoven wood panel fencing (X) in front of which are mixed shrubs (M, W and Z).

---

**Key**

| | | | | |
|---|---|---|---|---|
| A | Shed with electricity connected | | N | Curved pathway in lawn |
| B | Fuel bunkers | | O | Lawn |
| C | Refuse containers | | P | Trees |
| D | Incinerator/composting zone with fence screen | | Q | Paving |
| | | | R | Drive |
| E | Raised border for herbs | | S | Raised planting border |
| F | Standpipes | | T | Path connecting drive to front door |
| G | Secluded garden | | U | Mixed shrubs and herbaceous plants |
| H | Service path | | | |
| I | Garage with electricity connected | | V | Double entrance gates |
| J | Shrub border around dwelling | | W | Mixed shrub border |
| K | Front door and flower tubs | | X | Interwoven wood panel fence |
| L | Raised planting border | | Y | Vegetable garden |
| M | Mixed shrub border and trees | | Z | Mixed shrubs |

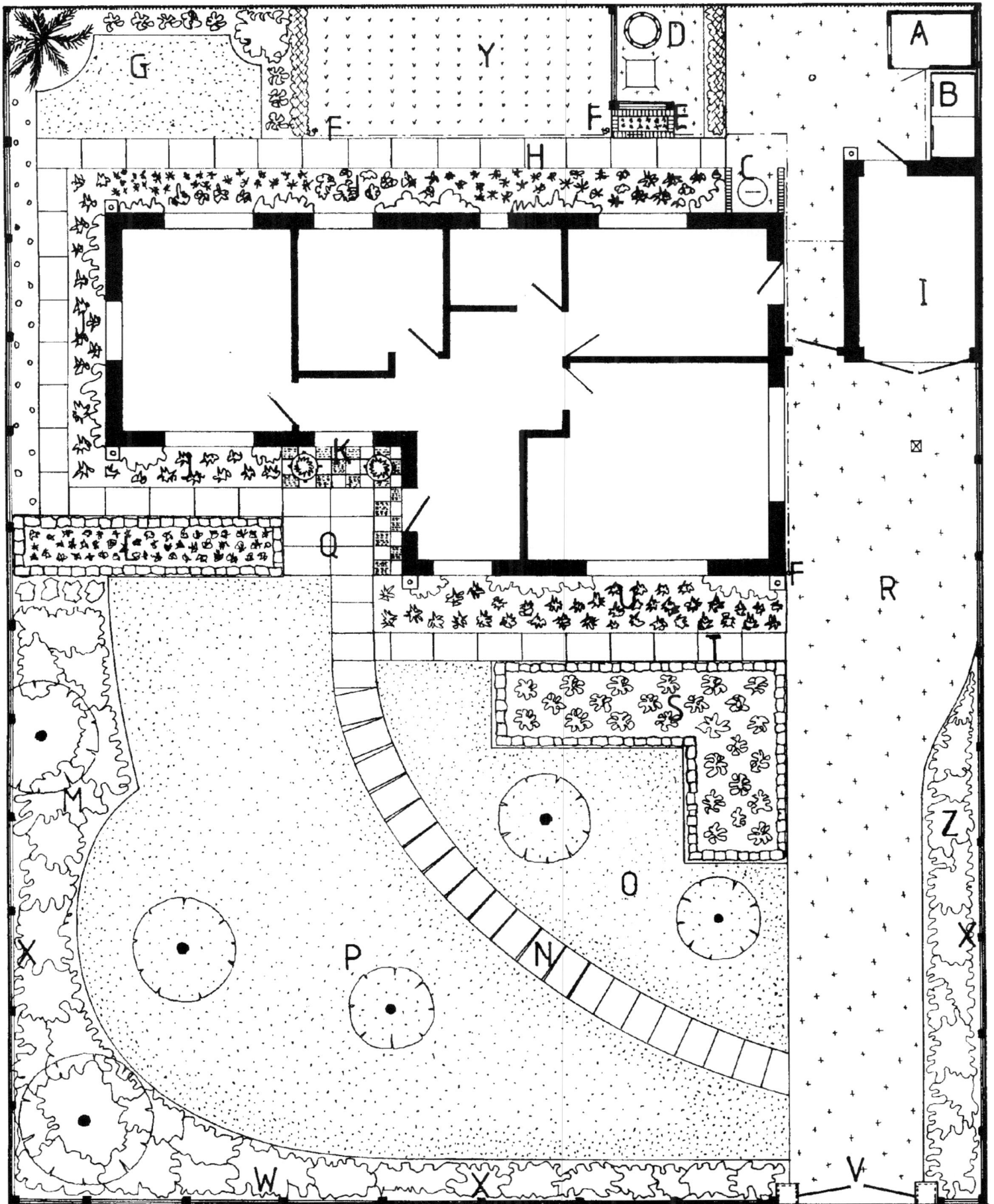

SCALE 1:100

## Terrace with alpines

The rear garden of this property has a large terrace (T) with plant pockets between a large rockery (U) and areas of alpines and associated stepping stones (Q and J). Another feature is the lower-level crazy paving area (L) with bird bath (K) and steps down to it (N).

There is a service path (B) going to the vegetable garden (C) past the garden shed which has electricity connected. There are many standpipes (E), one of which is near the pool (I). There is a paved archway (F) to join the service path (B) with the lawn. A garden seat (H) on paving, backed by a rose pergola system (G), provides a focal point. All around the garden there are massed shrubs and trees (Z).

### Key

| | | | |
|---|---|---|---|
| A | Incinerator area | O | Small rectangular sitting out area with wall shrubs on house |
| B | Service path | | |
| C | Vegetable garden | P | Shallow earth-filled brick troughs for formal planting |
| D | Hedge screening vegetable garden and shed | | |
| | | Q | Meandering pathways of stepping stones among planted area |
| E | Standpipes | | |
| F | Pergola archway over connecting path from functional area to lawn | R | Assorted alpines |
| | | S | End section of lawn from front garden (not shown) |
| G | Pergola behind seat | | |
| H | Garden seat on crazy paving | T | Large expanse of crazy paving to form terrace, with plant pockets |
| I | Pool with crazy paving surround | | |
| J | Meandering path of stepping stones among planted area providing access for cultivation | U | Rockery |
| | | V | Heathers among rockery with adjoining Acer |
| K | Bird bath | W | Kidney-shaped shrubbery with ornamental tree in lawn |
| L | Low level area of crazy paving | | |
| M | Stone wall surround to crazy paving area | X | Circular shaped shrubbery with ornamental tree in lawn |
| N | Steps down to crazy paving area | Y | Boundary hedge |
| | | Z | Massed shrubs and mixed trees |

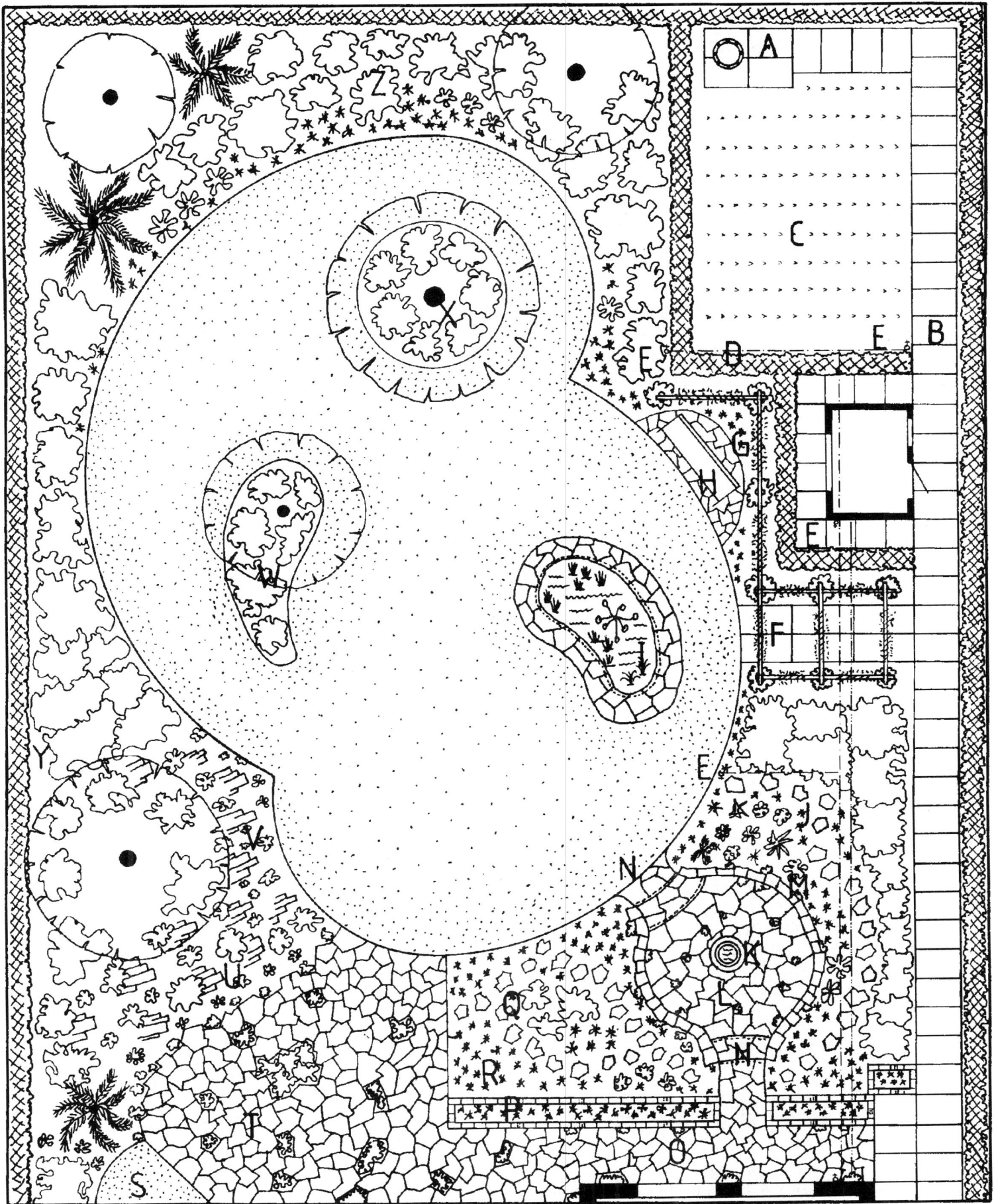

SCALE 1:100

## A front door at the back!

The garden of this property has an unusual landscape design in that the front door and tiled entrance (N) are in the rear garden so that the approaches have the best panoramic views. The semi-circular brick terrace (K) leads on to the lawn (Q) which has many shrub and tree borders (V) with curved edges. There are two individual borders (U and T) within it. Another unusual feature of the garden is the border (O) which has a series of stone-edged pockets for delicate alpines. The vegetable garden (B) and shed (A) have standpipes nearby and there is a hedge (X) separating them from the shrubbery. The shed is connected with electricity.

In this garden there is no fixed position for an incinerator (D) which can be moved around at will with stepping stones leading to it when the soil nearby is wet and soft. There are two side gates (H). Fuel bunkers (F) and refuse containers (G) are located near the kitchen door. In one corner of the house there is a water butt (I), overflow and tap, in case there is a water restriction in a dry summer. There are two washing line posts (W) allowing for the inclusion of low-growing plants under the lines even if there are drips.

## Key

| | | | |
|---|---|---|---|
| A | Garden shed | P | Bird bath with cobble surround countersunk in lawn |
| B | Vegetable garden | | |
| C | Standpipes | Q | Lawn with curved edges |
| D | Movable incinerator and stepping stones | R | Garage drive |
| | | S | Brick paving to front door |
| E | Broken concrete slab path | T | Curved shrub border with ornamental tree |
| F | Fuel bunkers | | |
| G | Refuse containers | U | Curved shrub border with large foliar tree, like *Acer osakazuki* |
| H | Side gates, one of which is attached to posts, and adjacent trellis | | |
| | | V | Mixed shrubs and trees on boundary backed by beech hedging |
| I | Water butt and overflow | | |
| J | Bird table | W | Washing line posts set in concrete dollies |
| K | Half-moon-shaped terrace in paving bricks | | |
| | | X | Hedge separating vegetable garden from shrub border |
| L | Brick on edge surround to terrace | | |
| M | Two identical flower tubs | Y | Plants and wall shrubs adjacent to house |
| N | Front door and tiled entrance | | |
| O | Large bed and rockery pockets in stone planted with assorted alpines | Z | Border planted with mixed flowers and low-growing shrubs |

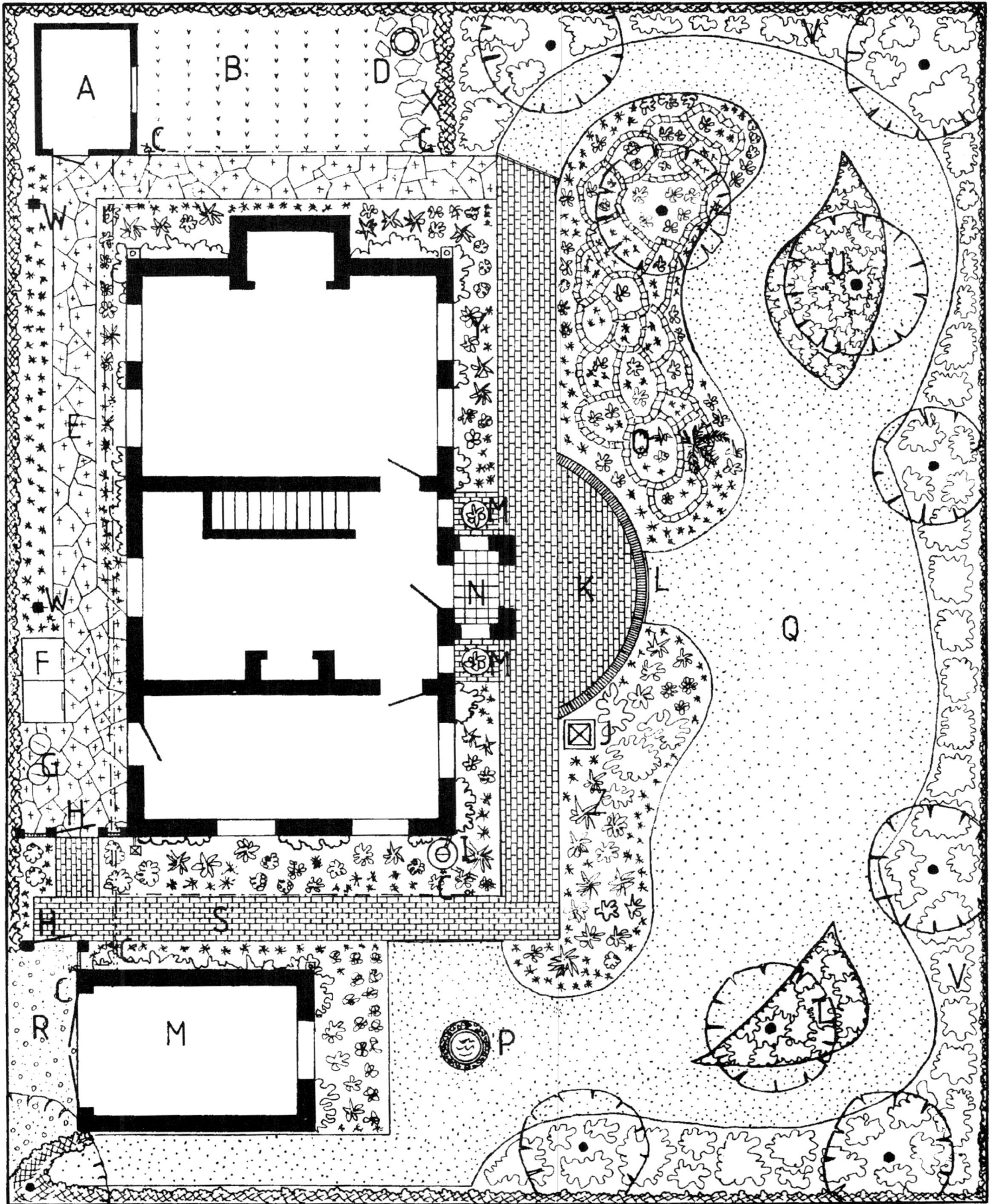

SCALE 1:100

## Walkway and feature pool

This small garden has two main features. Leading away from the house and terrace (A), which has a socket for a rotary washing line or garden umbrella, is a walkway (C) with overhead sawn timber pergola components (D) butting up against the high wall (H). On both sides of the walkway are climbing roses and a multitude of herbaceous plants (W) and it leads to some further paving with a brick screening wall (S) upon which is a large manger (E) full of hanging plants plus other plant pockets for climbers.

The second feature is a long rectangular pool (N) with waterlilies and submerged brick boxes containing marginal aquatics and oxygenating plants (O). It also has a fountain (P) connected to an electric pump which helps to oxygenate the water. On one side of the pool is a brick wall, and on the other paving is laid to an interesting serrated pattern in juxtaposition to that on the other side of the lawn (R).

The walkway and pool are connected by a curved path (X) separating the large lawn from the smaller one. Around the smaller one are various shrubs and trees (V and L) in the midst of which is an area for a seat (K). There is a brick wall (Y) which separates all that from the vegetable garden (G) which is serviced by a path (I) leading down to a shed (J) connected with electricity. There are various standpipes (T).

---

**Key**

| | | | |
|---|---|---|---|
| A | Terrace with socket in paving | O | Boxes for various water plants |
| B | Small raised brick bed with mowing strip next to lawn | P | Ornamental fountain |
| C | Walkway | Q | Brick edged planting bed over soakaway |
| D | Overhead pergola system | R | Lawn |
| E | Large manger secured to wall | S | Brick wall screening kitchen garden complex |
| F | Compost bay within brick wall enclosure | T | Standpipes |
| G | Vegetable garden | U | Overflow drain from pool to soakaway |
| H | High brick boundary wall | V | Mixed shrubs and trees |
| I | Service path by vegetable garden | W | Mixed herbaceous plants of different kinds |
| J | Garden shed | | |
| K | Area for seat | X | Curved connecting path |
| L | Mixed shrubbery and spreading conifer | Y | Brick wall separating kitchen garden from smaller ornamental garden |
| M | Quadrant shaped water feature with electric pump to circulate water | Z | Climbing *Hydrangea petiolaris* to cover brickwork |
| N | Long rectangular pool | | |

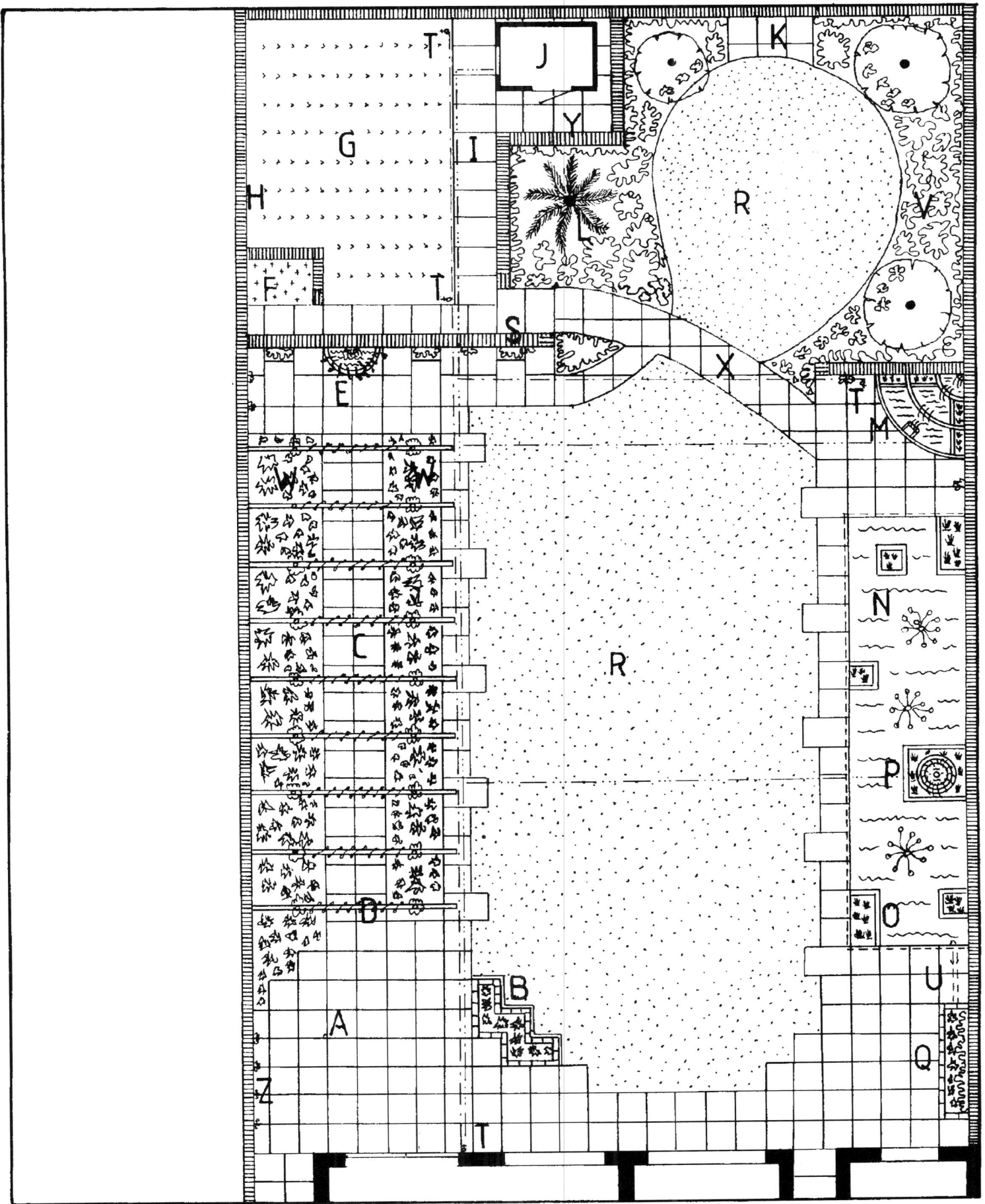

SCALE 1:100

## A modern house with a small garden

This two-storey property is of modern design, set in a small garden, the front and back being of similar size. Much of the front, however, must be functional, i.e., drive (P) and parking space. The borders around the house must be narrow and emphasis is given to wall shrubs to soften the severity of the corners of the house. From the macadamised drive there are two shallow steps up to the lawn, while the rest of the drive is edged with stone (L) and precast concrete edging which, in both cases, is bedded down in concrete and haunched to prevent the outside of the drive being broken away.

In the back garden there is a terrace (F) surrounded by shrubs and trees for shade. Stepping stones (G) are bedded in diagonally to link this terrace to the house. The vegetable garden, adequately screened with hedging, has two standpipes for watering.

**Key**

| | | | |
|---|---|---|---|
| A | Vegetable/soft fruit garden | O | Concrete slabs outside French windows |
| B | Garden shed | P | Drive |
| C | Compost bay | Q | Wall shrubs secured to wire and vine screw eye fixings |
| D | Coal/coke bunkers or oil tank | R | Low prostrate shrubs under window |
| E | Refuse container or wheelie bin | S | Concrete edging |
| F | Patterned terrace | T | Pathway in non-slip slabs |
| G | Slabs as stepping stones countersunk in lawn | U | Concrete hard-standing |
| H | Lawn | V | Walls with earth-fill between brick pillars and coping slabs |
| I | Interwoven panels with gravel boards secured to precast concrete posts | W | Pergola |
| J | Garage | X | Conifer screen – not *Cupressus leylandii* |
| K | Wash-down drain cover | Y | Paved area adjacent to front door |
| L | Stone edging | Z | Two metal poles set in concrete dollies for washing line |
| M | Pair of gates | | |
| N | Small raised border with stone surround and mowing strip – adjacent are two shallow steps | | |

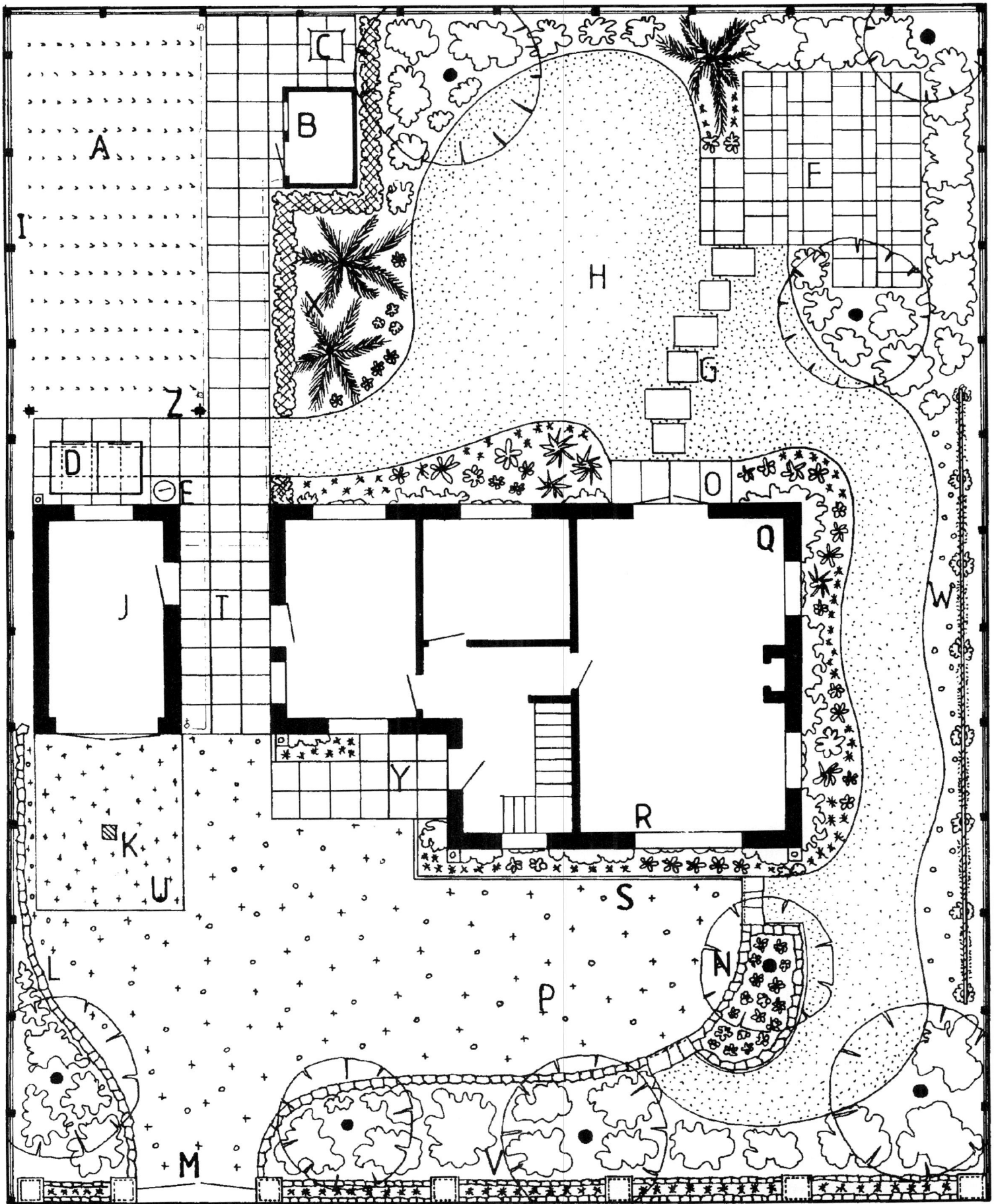

A

C

B

I

F

H

Z

G

D

E

O

Q

J

T

W

Y

R

K

U

S

L

N

P

M

V

131

SCALE 1:100

## A family garden

This small detached dwelling is ideal for a family with young children. The front and back gardens are securely divided by gates (G). Pathways (U) are wide enough for mobile toys and far enough away from windows which may be opened without the risk of injury to children. The back garden is divided into a functional area including a sandpit and a very large, strong, rotary clothes line. Water is laid on to the vegetable garden at standpipe (R). There is a children's play house at (A) and a seesaw (B). Both can be under surveillance, if required, with seats on the terrace (Q) or the paved area (V) in the corner of the lawn.

This dwelling has been built in an open plan development and there are connecting lawns to adjoining properties, with a few suitable trees planted to give some embellishment and privacy. The front lawn has a post and chain fence at the back edge of pavement. The kitchen garden is well screened by a pergola (Z). There are storage lockers (D) for various bulky toys and small bicycles.

---

## Key

| | | | |
|---|---|---|---|
| A | Children's play house | O | Refuse containers |
| B | Seesaw | P | Fuel bunkers |
| C | Shed | Q | Terrace by French windows |
| D | Storage lockers | R | Standpipes |
| E | Children's sandpit | S | Chequer-board design terrace to front door |
| F | Rotary washing line | | |
| G | Access gates | T | Soft fruit |
| H | Concrete drive | U | Access paths |
| I | Small pebbles between concrete | V | Paved area for chairs, etc. |
| J | Post and chain fence | W | Tree and shrub screen |
| K | Incinerator and compost bay | X | Close boarded fence around rear of property |
| L | Vegetable garden | | |
| M | Land drain from base of sandpit | Y | Lawns |
| N | Brick flower troughs on terrace | Z | Rose pergola |

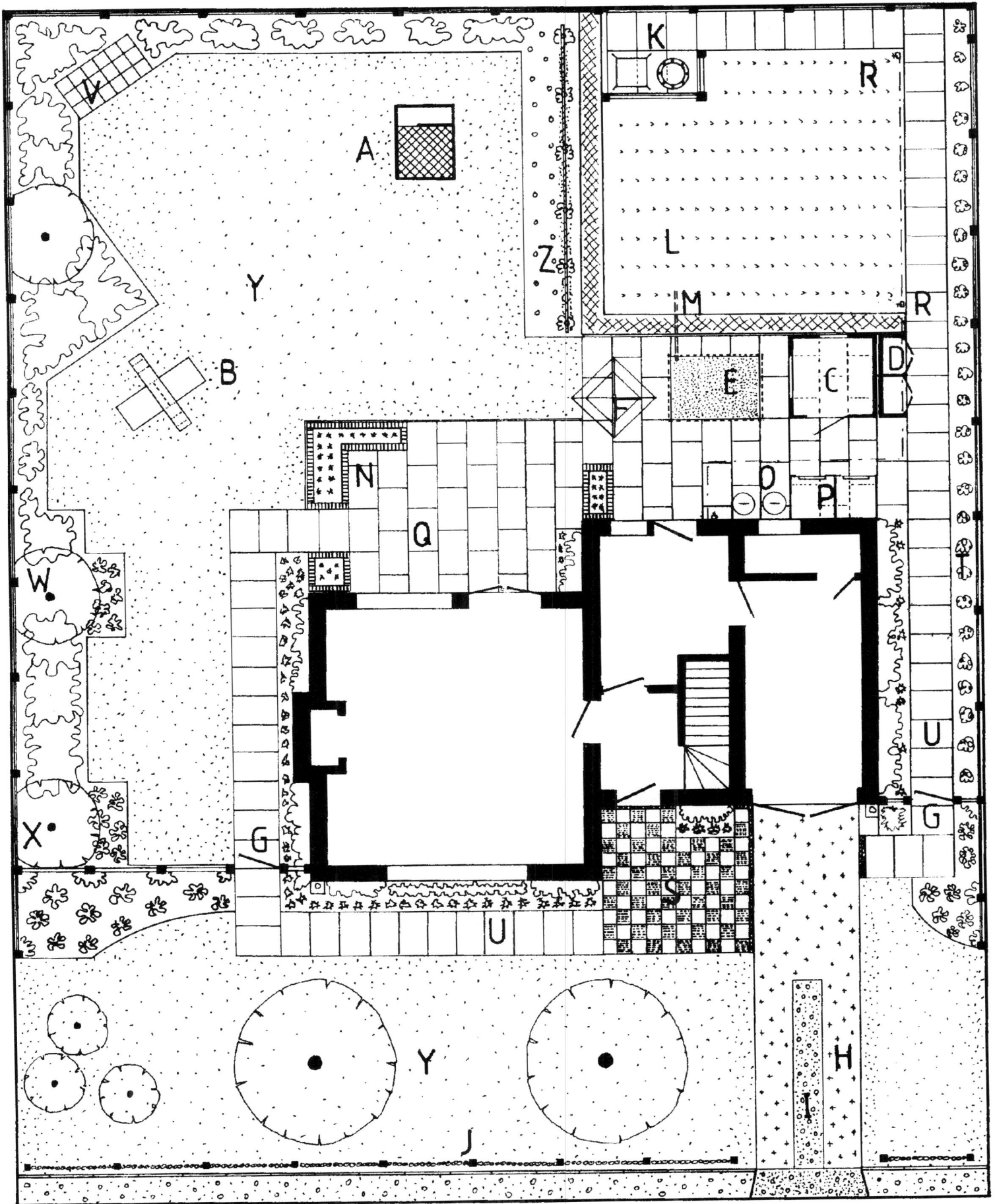

A  B  C  D  E  F  G  H  I  J  K  L  M  N  O  P  Q  R  S  U  V  W  X  Y  Z

SCALE 1:100

## Urban garden with screening

This is a corner plot in a typical urban situation where visual and acoustic screening are essential, plus the need to reduce dust and exhaust emissions from passing traffic. The kitchen garden has been sited in the far corner while the sitting out area (J) off the surrounding path is well screened from passers-by. The approach to the front door is enhanced by a tiled archway with gate (S).

Garden maintenance work has been limited to shrub borders and narrow, easily cultivated borders. Being a two-storey building, design perspective and balance in this type of location are of much importance.

**Key**

| | | | |
|---|---|---|---|
| A | Incinerator with connecting path | N | Pedestrian footpath |
| B | Interwoven panels with gravel boards secured to tanalised posts set in concrete dollies with pillar caps | O | Grass verge with kerbing to road |
| | | P | Existing roadside trees |
| | | Q | Lawn |
| C | Garden shed | R | Pillar supporting overhanging roof to front door |
| D | Electricity supply cable to shed | | |
| E | Protected oil supply pipe | S | Tiled archway with gate |
| F | Refuse containers | T | Ornamental tree with shrubs |
| G | Coal and coke bunkers | U | Screening trees with shrubs |
| H | Oil tank with screening | V | Bricks on edge entrance to lounge door |
| I | Wrought iron gate separating terrace area and vegetable garden | W | Path with water supply pipe alongside |
| | | X | Wall shrubs disguising rain-water downpipe |
| J | Patterned terrace using small paving slabs | | |
| | | Y | Low wall shrub under stairway window |
| K | Concrete block wall (option – painting) | Z | Extra paving slabs to connecting pathway to allow car passengers to alight on to a hard surface especially in wet weather |
| L | Twin brick wall with earth infill for planting | | |
| M | Brick pillars with coping stone | | |

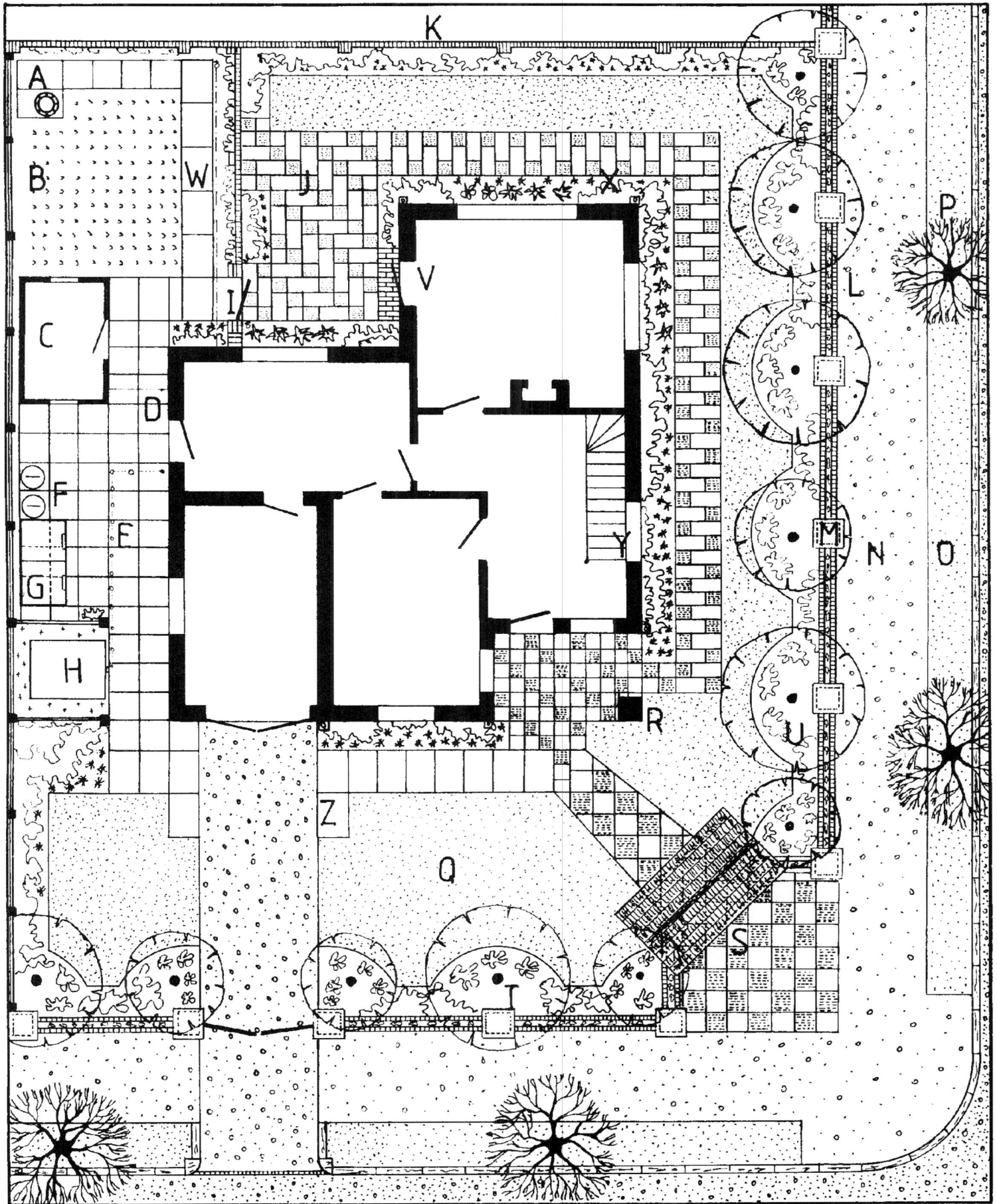

A

B W

J

X

V

C

I

D

F

F

G Y

H

R

M N O

P

L

U

Z

Q

S

135                    SCALE  1:100

## One-third functional, two-thirds ornamental

The garden of this property is divided up into one-third functional and two-thirds ornamental with a long straight slightly sloping path between them. The kitchen garden is further partitioned between an orchard garden (D) of top fruit in grass and the vegetable/soft fruit zone (E), the latter filled with cane fruit, soft fruit bushes, strawberries and mixed vegetables. There is a beech hedge between them for, if the bushes are clipped at the end of July/early August, the leaves are likely to go brown and stay on through the winter. Water is connected to standpipes (I). The small paved area for manure/compost (A) is screened by panels (B) and its approach screened by evergreen shrubs (C).

There is also a service area with fuel bunkers (F) and a propagating house (G) with water and electricity. These are screened by trellis topped panels and a conifer hedge of *Thuja lobbii*. In the ornamental garden there is a large terrace with small L-shaped beds and the occasional infill of a different kind of paving.

---

### Key

| | | | |
|---|---|---|---|
| A | Paved storage area for manure, etc. | N | Circular pond |
| B | Panel fence | O | Crazy paving surround |
| C | Evergreen shrubs | P | Level lawn with slope to adjust to lower lawn |
| D | Half-standard fruit trees on semi-dwarfing root stocks | Q | Long narrow gently sloping lawn |
| E | Vegetable/soft fruit garden | R | Posts set in concrete dollies supporting fence |
| F | Fuel bunkers | | |
| G | Propagating house connected to water and electricity supplies | S | Seat on paving |
| | | T | Tree and shrub border |
| H | Trellis-topped panel fence with herb border at the base | U | Stone edging |
| | | V | Mowing strip |
| I | Standpipes | W | Interwoven panel fence |
| J | Main terrace | X | Beech hedging |
| K | Small terrace, planting zones | Y | Pathway to manure storage area |
| L | Flight of shallow steps | Z | Ornamental flowering trees |
| M | Rockery to be viewed on two sides | | |

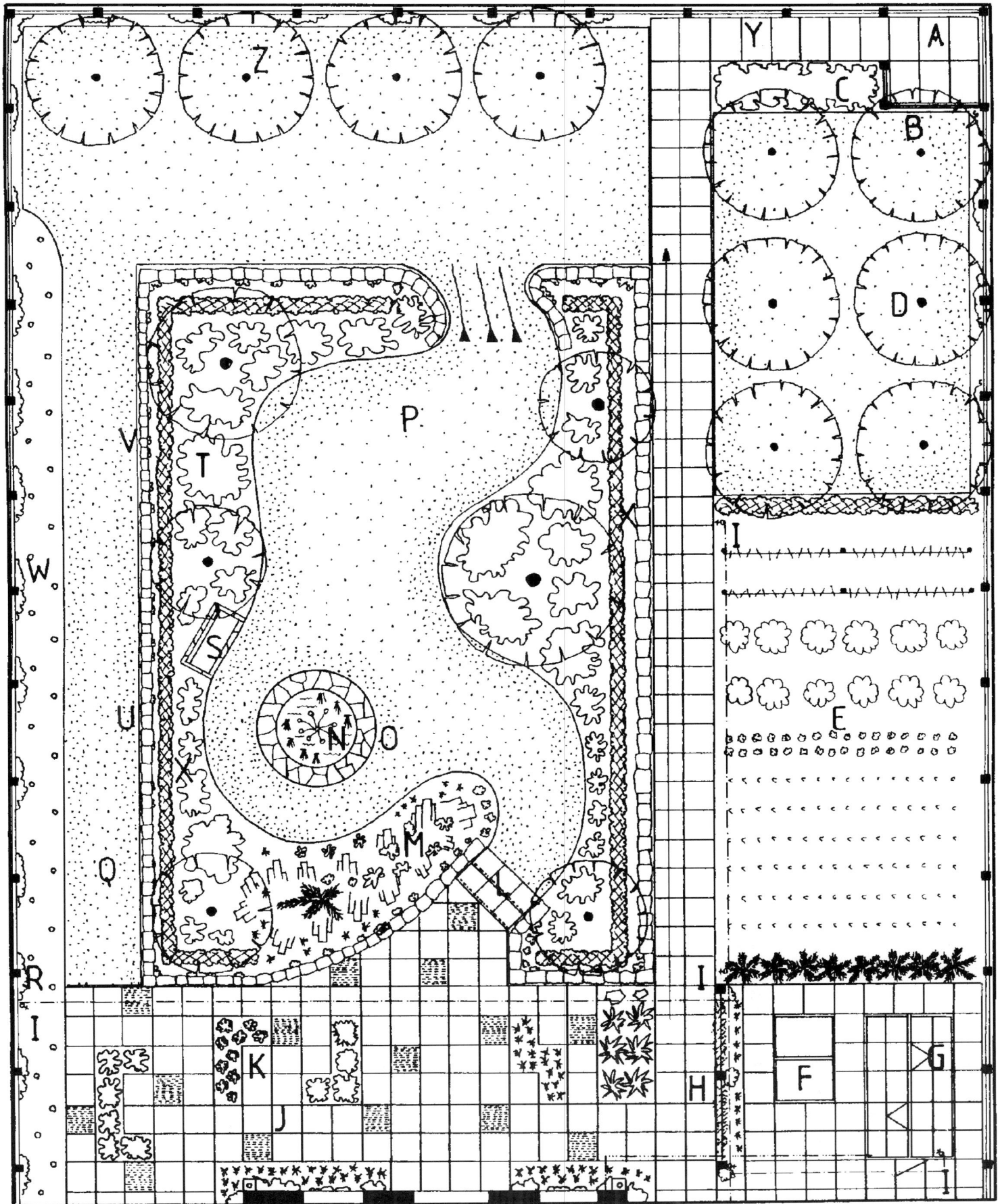

SCALE 1:100

## Patterns of paving on a large terrace

This large house has paved paths all around with an extensive terrace (R) at the end of which is a games room (A). There are two small lawns (U) with shrub and tree borders adjacent (Q, G). In the corner of the back garden there is a vegetable garden (L) with standpipes (K) with an adjoining path (M) and screening hedge (N). The drive (C) to garage (B) is curved with double gates (T) to the road. There is a well defined rockery with large rocks (E) by the front door with heathers and a small prostrate conifer.

There are very many kinds of patterns in the paving, shown to demonstrate the different arrangements that can be made using standard rectangular sizes. It would be up to the occupant to choose. Likewise the service area (S) has been left paved only for the occupier to decide what and where functional items should be situated (i.e., refuse containers, shed, fuel bins and oil tank).

**Key**

| | | | |
|---|---|---|---|
| A | Games room | N | Screening hedge |
| B | Garage | O | Kidney-shaped tree and shrub border |
| C | Drive | P | Semi-elliptical tree/shrub bed |
| D | Front terrace | Q | Large border of mixed shrubs and trees |
| E | Rockery with dwarf spreading conifer | R | Large formal terrace |
| F | Close-boarded fence | S | Service area with shed, oil tank, refuse container, intentionally not shown, to allow owner options |
| G | Tree and shrub screen | | |
| H | Side gate | T | Access gates to drive |
| I | Perimeter hedge | U | Lawns |
| J | Bird table | V | Narrow beds for bedding plants |
| K | Standpipe | W | Shrub bed |
| L | Vegetable garden | X | Wall shrubs |
| M | Service path adjacent to vegetable garden | Y | Mixed shrubs |
| | | Z | Rotary washing line |

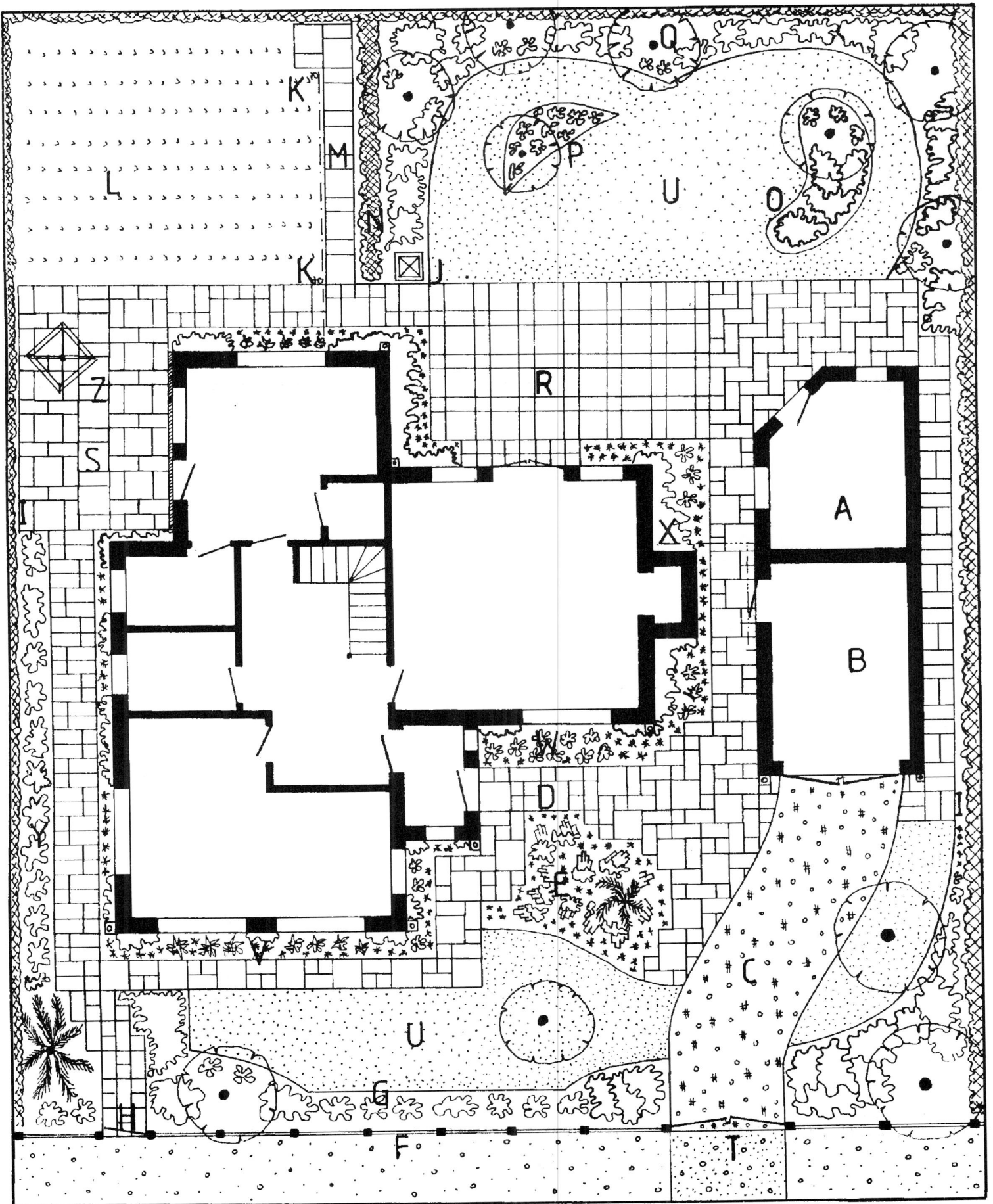

A

B

K

M

L

Q

P

U

O

J

K

N

K

Z

R

S

I

X

A

B

D

W

E

U

C

G

H

F

T

SCALE 1:100

## Crazy paving terrace

This large property has a garage (A) very near to the road with a short drive (F) and an entrance gate (E) nearby. From this area there is a winding crazy paving path (K) with stone edging (N) and various flower and shrub borders (Z) adjacent. The terrace (M) by the front door has upon it two large tubs (L) and a long seat. The functional area consists of an oil tank (B) and rotary washing line (C), refuse container (D) and fuel bunkers. Leading away from them through an arch (H) is a paved pathway to a terrace (I) at the rear of the house. To join this with the kitchen garden area (S) which has a central path (T) is a mixed slab and crazy paving pathway (J) with a large number of mixed shrubs (X) between that and the boundary hedge (Y). By the kitchen garden is a garden shed (V) with electricity connected and a triple compost/incinerator bay (W). There are standpipes (G). The kitchen garden is well screened by a tall hedge (Q) in front of which are three standard trees (P) and on the side of which are two formal rose beds (O) within the lawn area (R). There is a semi-circular plant border with dovecote (U).

---

**Key**

| | |
|---|---|
| A | Garage |
| B | Oil tank |
| C | Rotary washing line |
| D | Refuse container |
| E | Entrance gate |
| F | Garage drive |
| G | Standpipes |
| H | Timber archway over path |
| I | Terrace with socket in one trimmed paving slab for sun umbrella |
| J | Side path with house flower border adjacent |
| K | Crazy paving path |
| L | Large flower tubs either side of main entrance to house |
| M | Front terrace with steps down to crazy paving pathway |
| N | Stone edging to borders |
| O | Formal rose beds |
| P | Three identical standard flowering trees, e.g. *Prunus hisakura* |
| Q | Hedge screening vegetable garden |
| R | Lawn |
| S | Vegetable garden |
| T | Access path to vegetable garden |
| U | Semi-circular bed with plants and dovecote |
| V | Garden shed |
| W | Triple bays for compost and incinerator |
| X | Long mixed shrub border |
| Y | Boundary hedge |
| Z | Front shrub border |

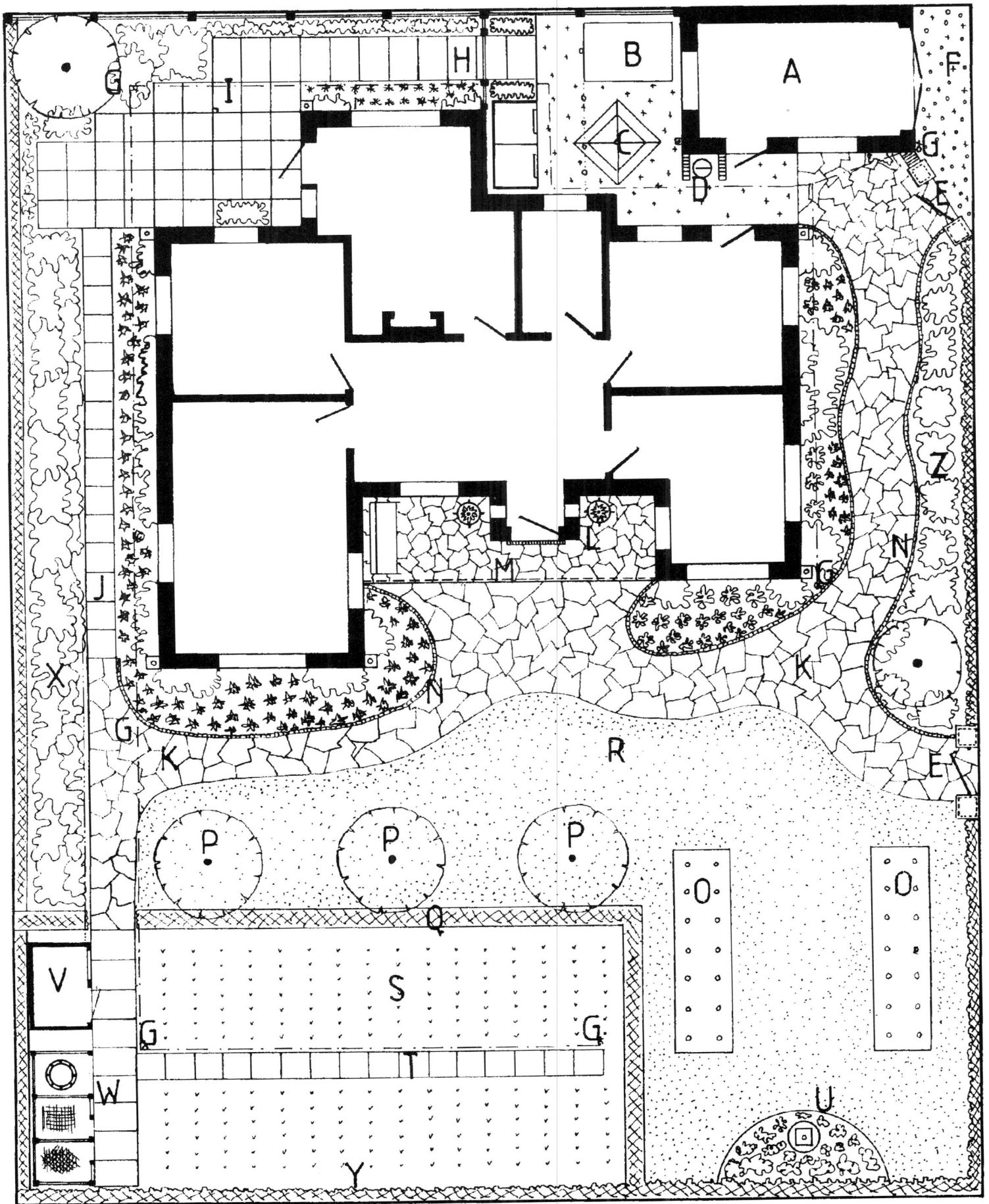

SCALE    1:100

## Garden for a partially sighted person

The garden of this property has been specially designed for a person who is partially sighted. Around the house there is a flat terrace (B) without any alpines or changes in level, such as cobble or brick, where there could be a risk of tripping. At each house corner there is an L-shaped shin rail to signify the nearness of the house and border plants. There is a revolving summerhouse (A) on the terrace which can be moved so that the sun can shine on the occupant. Nearby is a bird table (C) well secured to the ground to avoid being pushed over, and a table (D) for bird food preparation. Concrete slab stepping stones (H) meander to a seat (M) in the belt of mixed trees which include an aspen (*Populis tremula*) because of the rustling of the leaves, and those having interesting bark, i.e., snake bark acer. There are guiding shin rails (E) round much of the garden to prevent the risk of falling into the shrub borders (V) and ornamental flowering trees (R, S and T). There is a beautiful turkey oak (*Quercus cerris*) (Q) and a sweet gum (*Liquidambar*) (I) planted in the two central borders together with non-spinescent shrubs, i.e., not harmful to touch.

To provide scent there are two different pine trees at (L). There is a chalet (N) connecting to the path leading towards the seat (M). In the centre of the garden there is a special feature of a raised circular reinforced pool with waterlilies and other aquatic plants. In the centre is a fountain to give acoustic interest. Around it is paving (U) and behind it is a raised stone border (Y) with recess for a seat (O). Fragrant plants such as catmint, verbena, etc., fill this border while lavender is growing in the three flower boxes (J) near the summerhouse. These are backed by a brick wall.

**Key**

| | | | |
|---|---|---|---|
| A | Summerhouse | O | Recess for seat |
| B | Terrace | P | Lawn |
| C | Bird table | Q | Turkey oak |
| D | Table | R | Horse chestnut (scented) |
| E | Shin rails | S | *Sorbus essertauina* (scented) |
| F | L-shaped shin rails | T | *Malus floribunda* (scented) |
| G | Footpath alongside house | U | Circular paving |
| H | Meandering stepping stones to seat and chalet | V | Assorted non-spinescent flowering shrubs |
| I | *Liquidambar* tree | W | Pool with waterlilies and other aquatic plants |
| J | Flower boxes | | |
| K | Central path to pool | X | Reinforced circular wall with capping |
| L | Pine trees | Y | Stone wall |
| M | Seat on paving | Z | Various plantings including those which are fragrant and tactile, i.e., furry or leathery |
| N | Chalet | | |

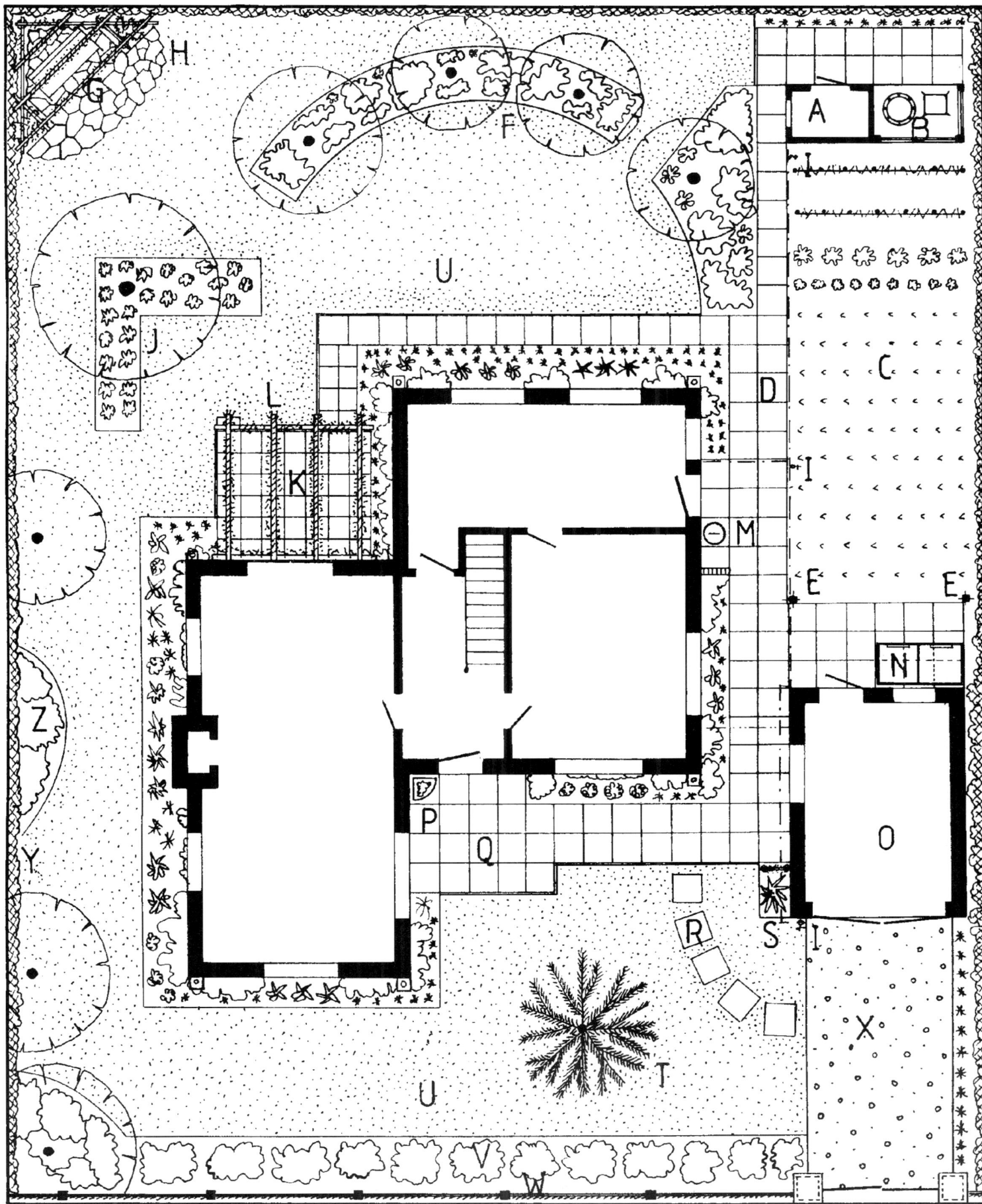

SCALE 1:100

## A woodland garden for a mobile home

This site for a caravan or mobile home is located in a woodland area, hence the surroundings are very verdant and a perfect place for peaceful seclusion. There is an approach road (B) leading to the concrete hard-standing (L). Water (E) and electricity (F) are connected via control boxes near the access path (I). The site is defined by post and wire fence (C). There is a telephone in the caravan connected to overhead wires (D). A hammock (R) is secured by ropes to two large trees. The sitting out area (S) is well screened by large clumps of indigenous berried shrubs (V), while by the bird table (M) in the shrubbery (N), there are massed gorse bushes (U) as a nesting area for birds. Two crossing paths (O) of countersunk crazy paving slabs are located in part of the lawn area (Y). Foul drainage has not been shown on this drawing.

### Key

| | | | |
|---|---|---|---|
| A | Box on post for mail and papers | M | Bird table |
| B | Macadam drive leading to concrete hard-standing on which the mobile home is placed | N | Mixed low-growing shrubs |
| | | O | Large pieces of crazy paving set in grass as stepping stones |
| C | Strutted corner posts for post and wire boundary fence | P | Lamp post |
| D | Telegraph post and wires | Q | Four flower tubs by jockey wheel |
| E | Underground water supply to control box | R | Hammock |
| | | S | Sitting out area, well screened |
| F | Underground electricity supply to control box | T | Stile over wire fence |
| | | U | Bold planting of gorse for nesting birds |
| G | Grass verge 100mm high, only occasionally mown | V | Massed shrubs bearing berries for birds including female holly |
| H | Irregular pathway made from rolled and slurried binding gravel | W | Rough grass with naturalising bulbs |
| I | Macadam pathway | X | Larch plantation giving opportunity for nesting boxes |
| J | Small plant border | |  |
| K | Step and two flower boxes | Y | Main lawn area |
| L | Concrete slab | Z | Narrow thick evergreen shrubbery as screen for sleeping quarters |

SCALE 1:100

## Mews house with a roof garden

This drawing shows a very old three storey corner house outside which is a cobbled roadway (B) with central gullies (A) forming part of a mews. Some of the old carriage sheds have been converted to garages for small cars. The roofs of the garages are asphalted and on these are lightweight easily maintained flower troughs (Z). At ground level are flower troughs (X), boxes (W), and tubs (D). At either side of the archway, protected by bollards (Y), are hanging baskets (E).

In the main garden there is a large fountain (F) in a paved area (G) with a pathway (H) leading to the lawn area. Along the pathway (H) are two identical seats (I) backed by flower borders. The lawn (K) has a small, elegant statue (J). The front door with stone steps (O) leads down to pathways (P) encompassing the lawn, with adjacent flower borders and wall shrubs. The whole garden is bordered by a high brick wall (T) with access gates (M) supported by brick pillars with caps (U).

### Key

| | | | |
|---|---|---|---|
| A | Centrally situated gullies | O | Rectangular stone steps to front door |
| B | Cobbled driveway | P | Paving surround to lawn, between which and the house walls are flower borders |
| C | Concrete with rough finish | | |
| D | Ornamental flower tubs | | |
| E | Hanging baskets | Q | Asphalted roofs to garages |
| F | Wide diameter fountain with electricity connected | R | Flower tubs of limited weight |
| | | S | Flower troughs and trellis to form screen |
| G | Random rectangular paving with small planting pockets | T | High brick wall with brick on edge |
| H | Pathway to fountain area | U | Brick pillars with stone caps |
| I | Two identical seats facing each other | V | Flower troughs |
| J | Small statue | W | Heavy plant containers leaving space for access to garage |
| K | Lawn | | |
| L | Bow windows overlooking garden | X | Heavy flower troughs |
| M | Wrought iron gates | Y | Bollards to protect corners of archway |
| N | Steps down from second floor of house on to garage roof | | |
| | | Z | Flower troughs of limited weight |

SCALE 1:100

## Riverside garden with slipway

This riverside dwelling has its own slipway (B) as part of the garage drive complex (L). Adjacent to this slipway is a small landing stage with securing bollard at one end and a lantern at the other end. A single bar barrier (C) indicates the beginning of the slope. Nearby is a shed cum workshop (A) for boat maintenance with water and electricity connected. The river bank (N) gives opportunities for naturalising bulbs and marginal aquatics such as meadowsweet, iris, flowering rush, etc. There is a low fence (D) to prevent young children wandering off. Garden furniture (F) is placed on the lawn (H). Alder trees (U) help to consolidate the bank in places as well as providing shade.

The dwelling itself has a long verandah (I) upon which flower troughs are placed. It has steps down (Y) to the lawn and there are steps down (J) from the interconnecting path (W) between the dwelling and the garage. There is an opportunity for formal bedding such as tulips and wallflowers in the long narrow bed (R) next to the fence (D) which also can give some protection from wind off the water. A curved bed enhances the rear of the garage with occasional wall shrubs.

---

### Key

| | |
|---|---|
| A | Shed/workshop for boat gear |
| B | Slipway in ribbed concrete |
| C | Single bar barrier gate |
| D | Wooden fence |
| E | Sitting out platform |
| F | Garden table and chairs |
| G | Flowering tubs resting on a paving slab |
| H | Lawn |
| I | Verandah with flower troughs |
| J | Steps from pathway to lawn |
| K | Garage |
| L | Garage drive |
| M | Landing stage |
| N | Marginal aquatics, rushes, etc., at the bottom of the river bank |
| O | Willow tree |
| P | Clumps of different dogwood – Cornus |
| Q | Rough lawn |
| R | Bed of formal bedding plants, tulips, etc. |
| S | Lantern on post |
| T | Mooring bollard with ring bolt |
| U | Alder trees |
| V | Specimen standard flowering tree |
| W | Paving from drive also connecting garage to main building |
| X | Riverside flat-roofed dwelling |
| Y | Steps down from verandah to lawn |
| Z | Existing trees – oak, maple, thorn, birch, etc. |

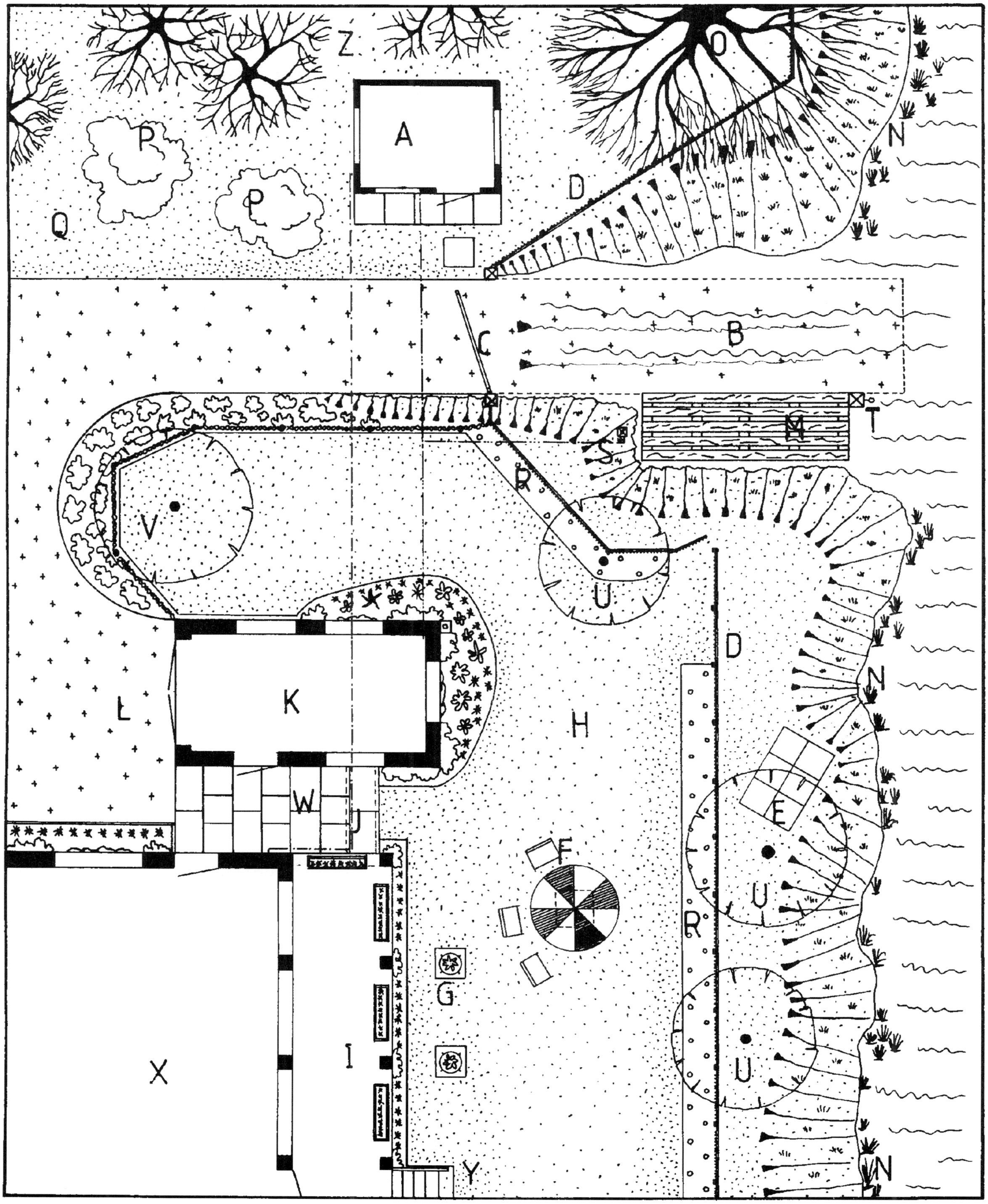

Z

O

P

P

A

N

Q

D

C

B

M

T

R

V

U

D

L

K

H

N

W

J

E

U

F

R

G

X

I

U

Y

N

SCALE 1:100

## Lakeside garden with terrace

This lakeside property has a long terrace (B) for sitting out in the summer. From this there are wide steps leading down to the main lawn. To allow for a difference in levels there are two rockeries either side giving an opportunity for varied alpine planting arrangements. Two curved paths of wide slabs as stepping stones lead down to the water's edge, in one case to a landing stage down to which are steps and a retaining wall with some open joints for drainage. The other path goes down, via steps, to a boat-house (shown on plan without a roof). Adjacent is a weeping willow (W).

There is a chalet (Q) with terrace (S) at the other end of the lawn with a large see-saw (O) and sandpit (R) for children to play, with a swing (Z) suitably suspended from the oak tree (T). There is also a flagstaff (M) adjacent to a flower bed by the landing stage. Electricity goes underground to the chalet via two lanterns (F). Well graded banking occurs all along the frontage of the water, strengthened by tanalised stakes in the vicinity of the boat-house. The water's edge allows for planting of marginal aquatic plants such as yellow flag iris, meadow-sweet, purple loosestrife, rushes, reedmace, etc., which provide a good habitat for dragon and damsel flies.

---

**Key**

| | | | |
|---|---|---|---|
| A | Broad steps to lawn | N | Steps down to landing stage |
| B | Long terrace | O | See-saw |
| C | Stepping stones curved path | P | Alder tree |
| D | Path to boat-house | Q | Chalet |
| E | Steps down to boat-house | R | Sandpit |
| F | Lanterns | S | Terrace with chequer-board pattern |
| G | Mooring bollard | T | Oak tree |
| H | Non-slip slabs | U | Rockeries |
| I | In-situ concrete with roughened finish | V | Two formal circular planting beds |
| J | Landing stage | W | Weeping willow |
| K | Fenders | X | Rowing boat |
| L | Life-belt | Y | Boat-house |
| M | Flagstaff | Z | Swing with suitable base |

153

SCALE 1:100

## Garden for a model railway enthusiast

This garden has been designed specifically for the model railway enthusiast. Signalling equipment has not been shown nor the necessary associated supply of electric cabling above or below ground level. The track has been shown but with only a section of sleepers detailed (U). In various suitable locations trees and shrubs have been planted (O, S, K, X, Y, M, P, etc.) but attention must be given to planting small-leafed trees because of removing leaves in the autumn, preferably by vacuuming equipment.

The grass areas (T) should be cut frequently by strimmer to enable rapid drying out of the clippings. To add interest, there is a small pool (I) with crazy paving surround (J), weeping tree, and standpipe. There are lengths of stepping stones (G) for access in wet grass conditions.

A signal box/shed (D) is located at suitable height to control operations and this is connected with electricity, and probably operated by radio.

**Key**

| | | | |
|---|---|---|---|
| A | Engine/carriage shed | N | Narrow bridge over track with stone sides |
| B | Seat | O | Clump of larch trees |
| C | Terrace with French windows | P | Clump of birch trees |
| D | Signal box | Q | Plants and wall shrubs next to house wall |
| E | Bridge over track | | |
| F | Station platforms | R | Side path |
| G | Stepping stones countersunk in grass | S | Clump of field maples |
| H | Bridge over track with stone sides | T | Grass area |
| I | Pool with aquatics | U | Track with sleepers |
| J | Weeping birch | V | Boundary hedge |
| K | Tunnel with massed low-growing shrubs | W | Crushed shingle as bedding for sleepers |
| | | X | Many small planting areas |
| L | Level crossing with gates | Y | Area of dwarf indigenous shrubs |
| M | Mounded area with trees | Z | Small planting area |

SCALE 1: 100

## Yew hedges and a swimming pool

This expensive property, which has a swimming pool complex (A) is totally bordered, and some internal hedges, by clipped yew (Y). There is a secluded garden (G) for those desiring some seclusion for sunbathing, etc. Two rectangular areas are for fruit (I) and vegetables (J). There is the spectacle of a long herbaceous border (K). In the middle of the lawn is a formal pond (L) with paved surround and electrically operated fountain with transformer.

On the other side of the main lawn there is an avenue of specimen standard trees (R). A curved terrace (M) with steps down to lawn (N) plus two pipe sockets for large sun umbrellas is next to the French windows. A contoured bed with trees and long grass for naturalising bulbs (Q) is situated in the front lawn adjacent to a curved border of mixed trees and shrubs (W). The drive has a wash-down gully (X) and is edged with a low stone wall. There is space for extra cars to park. The functional area comprises a greenhouse (T), refuse area (U), oil tank and fuel bunkers.

## Key

A  Swimming pool with paved surround and grass banking
B  Changing rooms, one with a fresh water tap for pool maintenance outside
C  Seat overlooking swimming pool
D  Springboard
E  Steps up to swimming pool
F  Summerhouse directly aligned with pond feature, terrace steps, French windows, standpipes
G  Secluded lawn with four ornamental trees with entrance through wrought iron gate secured to brick pillars
H  Area for grass cuttings, manure, etc.
I  Soft fruit garden – currants, gooseberries, strawberries and raspberries with standpipe
J  Vegetable garden with standpipe and two washing line poles
K  Thickly planted herbaceous border backed by well clipped yew hedge
L  Formal pond, electrically operated fountain with overflow. Four boxes of marginal aquatics

M  Curved terrace with two pipe sockets for large sun umbrellas
N  Formal steps down from terrace to lawn and steps at each end to pathways
O  Curved brick troughs with bedding plants
P  Earth-filled low brick pillars
Q  Contoured bed with trees and long grass for naturalising bulbs
R  Avenue of eight similar specimen trees
S  Lawns
T  Greenhouse with electricity connected
U  Service area with tap outside screening wall. Oil and fuel bunkers nearby
V  Paved entrance to front door with tubs full of flowering plants
W  Curved shrub and mixed trees border
X  Drive with wash-down gully, entrance gate, parking area, and low stone wall, part with mowing strip
Y  Clipped boundary hedges of English yew
Z  Lamp post to illuminate way for night-time bathing

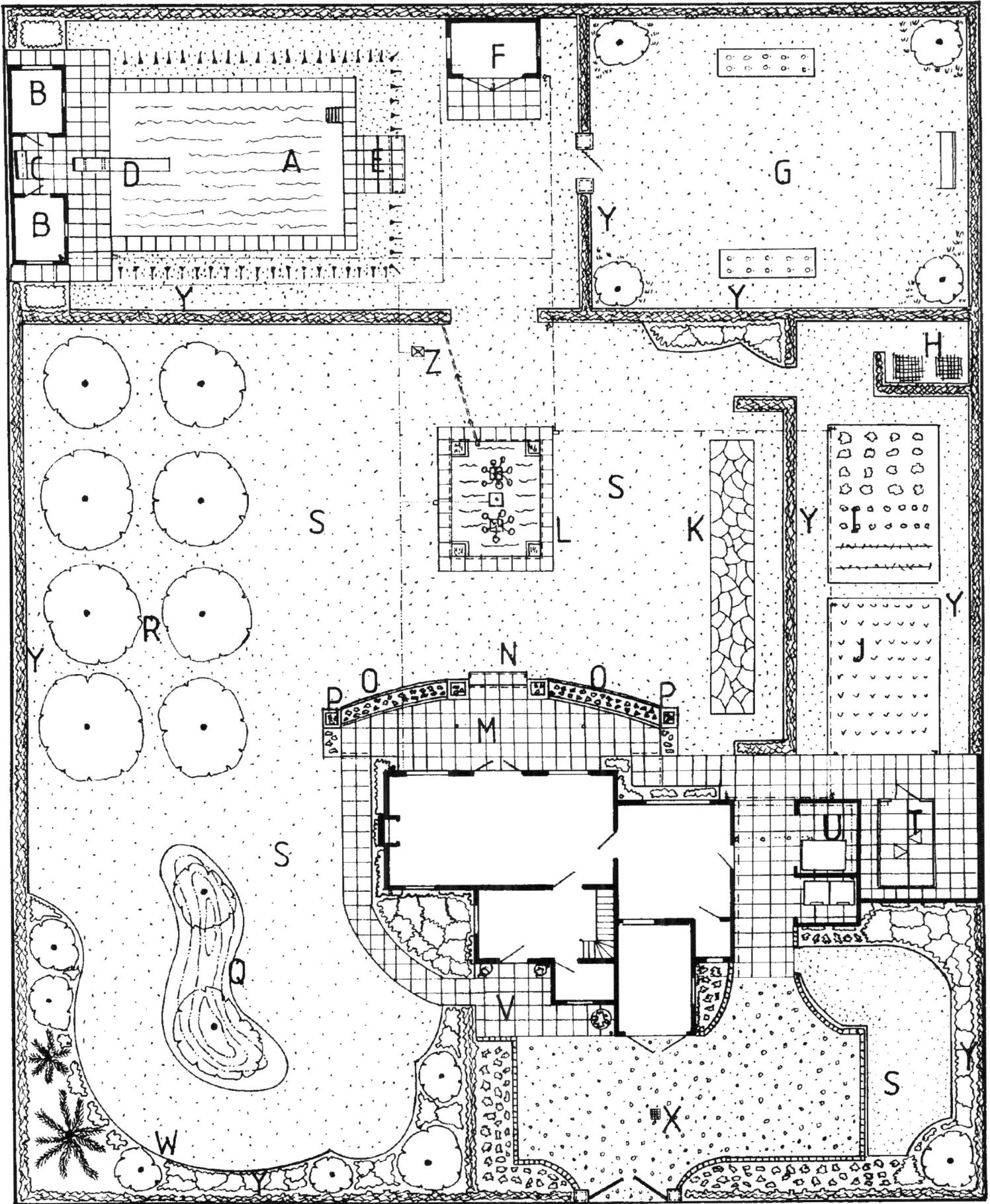

SCALE 1:200

## A peaceful orchard

One of the main features of this garden is that it is served by two accesses with ornamental gates, with the drive possibly surfaced with graded gravel leading to a large detached double garage. In front of the house the layout is formal while the back garden is more naturally developed with an archway and vista from the gate (U) through to the pond (Q) leading through the trees (N) to the focal point of a large bird bath (M).

Quiet solitude can be achieved by looking at the orchard especially in spring with masses of daffodils/narcissus /crocus, etc., from the seat (L). There are two long herbaceous borders (P) in a direct line giving an oblique viewing of them from the dining room adjacent to the lounge. From the kitchen door there is easy access to the kitchen garden and outbuildings well served by electricity and water.

### Key

| | | | |
|---|---|---|---|
| A | Conifer boundary hedge, preferably *Thuja lobbii*, which can be clipped more satisfactorily than other conifers | O | Lawn |
| B | Concrete path with adjacent water supply | P | Herbaceous borders with graduated plant height, the shortest being towards the lawn |
| C | Vegetable garden | Q | Small formal pond with waterlilies and marginal aquatics |
| D | Fruit cage | | |
| E | Paved area for manure or leaf-mould stacks | R | Main terrace opposite lounge with French windows |
| F | Oil tank with screen and oil supply pipe to house boiler | S | Seat opposite bay window feature |
| | | T | Path with lawns either side |
| G | Greenhouse with standpipe by door entrance | U | Brick pillars with brick walls to separate main garden from the front garden |
| H | Cold-frames for plant propagation and frost protection | V | Approach path to front door with square plant tubs |
| I | Rose garden | W | Twin access gates and drive to house and double garage |
| J | Double garage with rear workshop | | |
| K | Shrub border with trees backed by beech hedge | X | Three formal beds for spring and summer bedding |
| L | Garden seat | Y | Brick arch with wrought iron gate |
| M | Bird bath on stone plinth | Z | Water supply pipe to garden and garage |
| N | Orchard standard trees with bulbs | | |

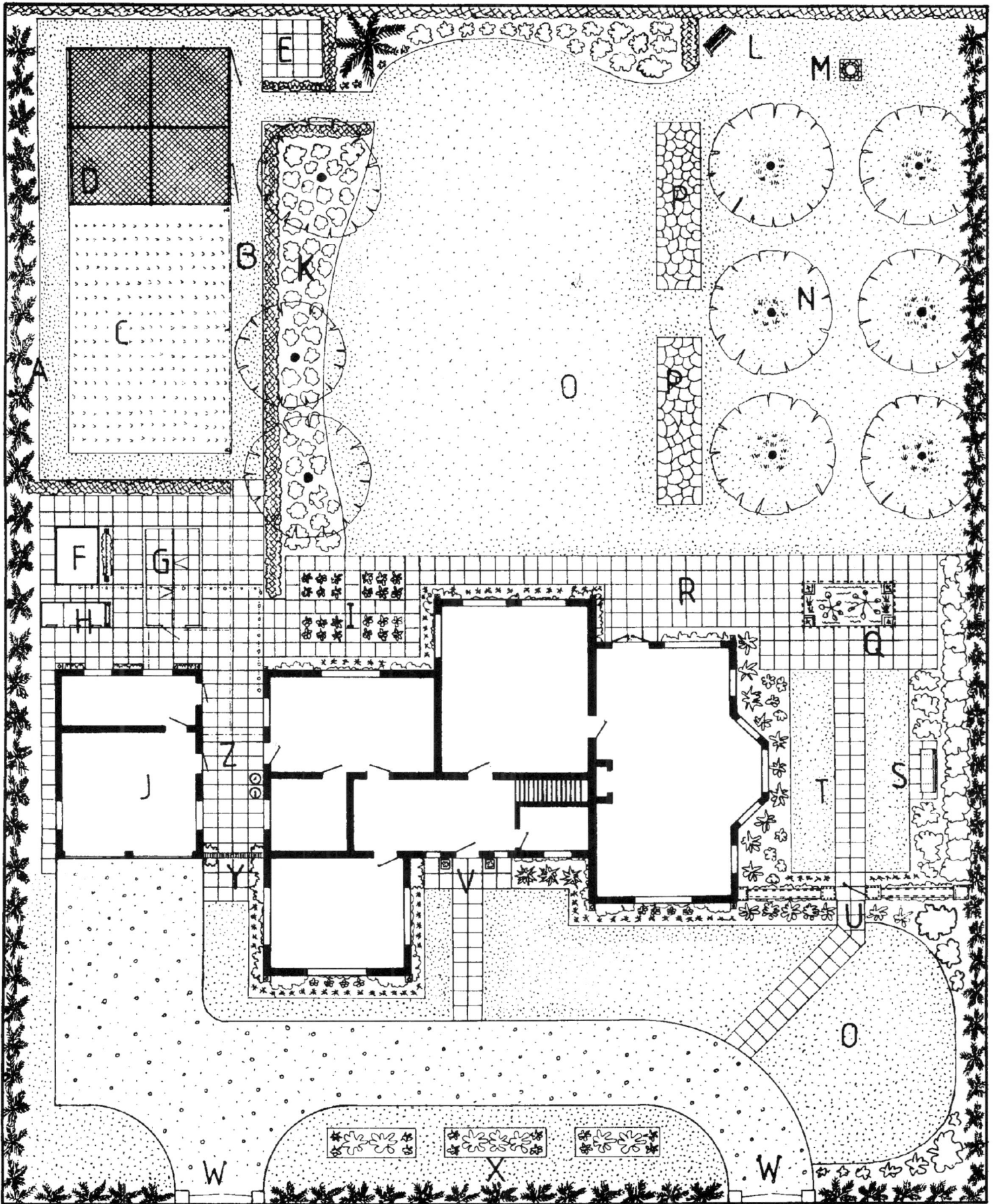

SCALE 1:200

## A design incorporating large existing trees

This large property, with two separate garages (A and B), has been built on what was previously a field and has the benefit of several existing trees (S) along its frontage and two large trees (Y and Z) in the corner of the back garden. There was a need to grade the site level hence grass banking (O) and retaining walls and steps (M and V) up to the trees. There is an imposing drive (L) which has twin entrance gates (N) enabling there to be space for turning and parking. In the front garden stepping stones (T) link the drive to the front terrace (Q) with the connecting pathways (U) adjacent to which is a large mixed shrub border. In the rear garden there is a terrace (X) and a crazy paving sitting area (V) which provides shade. The back lawn (R) has two trees in it and planting borders on its perimeter.

The functional area consists of refuse container area by a side gate and brick screening wall. There is a rotary washing line (J), fuel bunkers (K), screened by trellis, an oil tank (C), also screened, a greenhouse (D) connected to water and electricity supplies, and a garden shed (E), also connected with electricity. At the further end of the paving (G) is a composting zone (F). The kitchen garden (H) has standpipes and is screened by a hedge (I). The whole of the back garden has a boundary fence, thick hedging, and a retaining wall in stone with weepholes. There are many differently shaped planting areas, including those next to the drive (P). There is a path from the garage (B) to the steps (M) and tree.

## Key

| | | | |
|---|---|---|---|
| A | Garage with wash-down tap | N | Entrance gates to drive |
| B | Second garage | O | Banking to adjust levels |
| C | Oil tank screened by trellis and climbing plants | P | Flower beds with stone edging |
| D | Greenhouse | Q | Paving outside front door |
| E | Garden shed | R | Lawn |
| F | Composting area | S | Part of original field with mixed existing trees and naturalising bulbs in grass which is only occasionally cut |
| G | Service path in 600mm × 600mm concrete slabs | | |
| H | Vegetable garden with standpipes | T | Stepping stones in grass from drive to house pathway |
| I | Hedge screen to vegetable garden | | |
| J | Rotary washing line | U | Side path with adjacent mixed shrubs |
| K | Fuel bunkers | V | Crazy paving sitting area and steps up to tree (Z) |
| L | Garage drive with turning and parking area | | |
| | | W | Corner bed with tree and mixed flowers |
| M | Steps with brick wall surround up to large oak tree | X | Terrace by French windows |
| | | Y | Large oak tree |
| | | Z | Large Spanish chestnut tree |

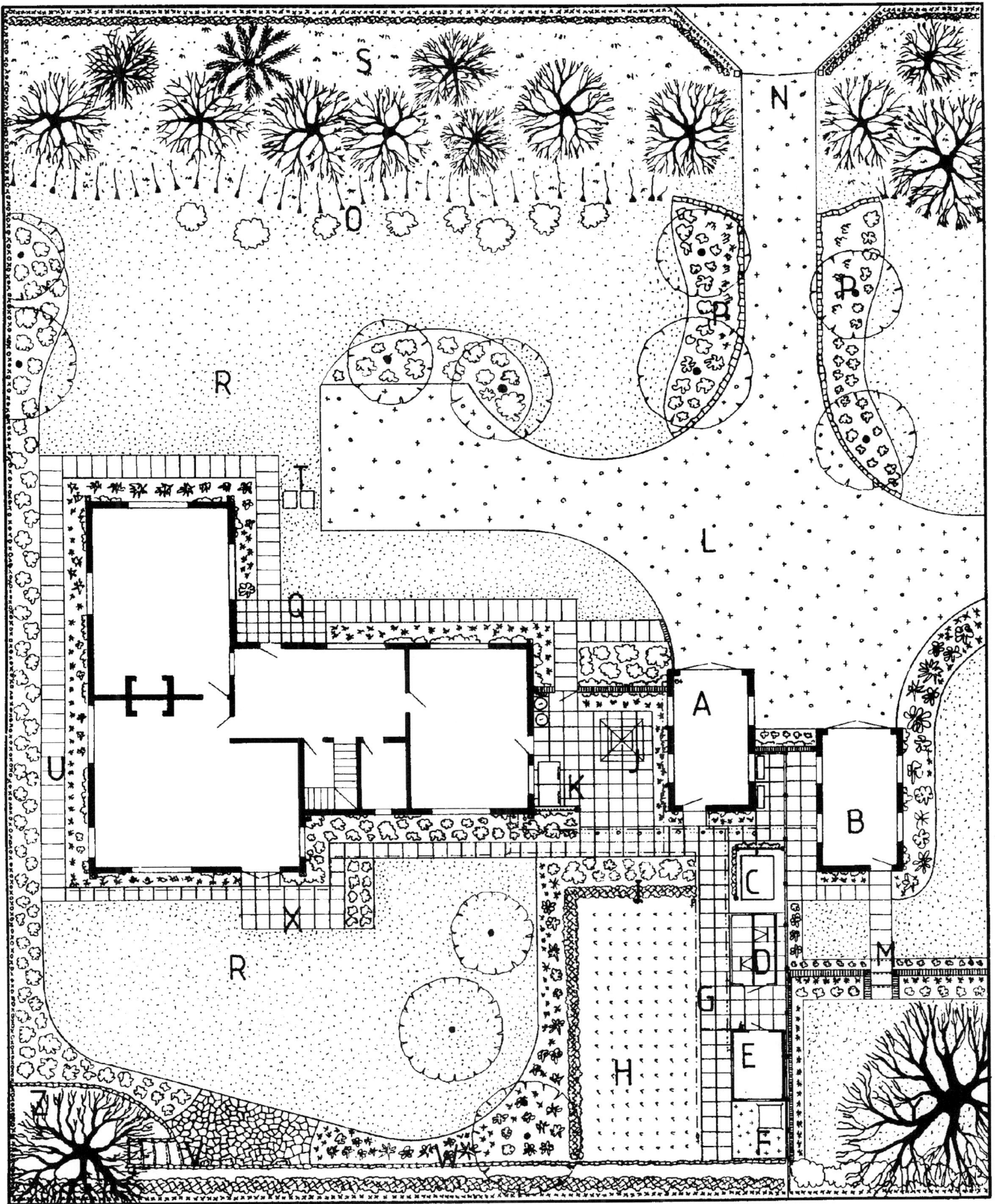

SCALE  1:200

**A modern country house garden**

This modern flat-roofed dwelling with car port is situated in fairly open countryside and is approached by a long drive (B). Halfway up is a mounded area of grass and trees (A). Either side, to fit in with the local topography, are two variably shaped mounded grass areas upon which are planted indigenous trees (C and D). In addition to this, there are two smaller areas of shrubs like double gorse which does not seed itself, wayfarer bushes, and wild briar roses, etc. To complement these three is a belt of larch trees (E).

The dwelling itself has a swimming pool (L) set within the terrace (K) overlooked by wide sliding windows. The terrace is screened by a brick wall (R) which continues to the end of the plant border (M) next to which is the connecting path (S) to the kitchen garden (O). There is a shed (U) and composting zone (V). They are screened by a hedge (Q). Between that and the car port is a grass strip and shrub border (T). There are standpipes nearby (W). There is a terrace (J) by the front door and nearby are low-growing wall shrubs (Y). The whole site is one where the lawns could be maintained by a ride-on mower and the mounded areas trimmed with a strimmer.

---

**Key**

| | | | | |
|---|---|---|---|---|
| A | Mounded central island | | M | Long plant border |
| B | Drive | | N | Oil tank |
| C | Mounded area with naturalising bulbs and trees | | O | Kitchen garden |
| D | Mounded area with naturalising bulbs and trees | | P | Refuse container under car port |
| E | Belt of larch trees | | Q | Hedge |
| F | Entrance gates | | R | Brick wall |
| G | Line of birch trees | | S | Pathway |
| H | Lawns | | T | Shrub border |
| I | Clumps of wild shrubs and roses | | U | Garden shed |
| J | Front terrace | | V | Compost bay |
| K | Main terrace | | W | Standpipes |
| L | Swimming pool with ladder and diving board | | X | Path alongside vegetable garden |
| | | | Y | Low-growing wall shrubs |
| | | | Z | Planting beds |

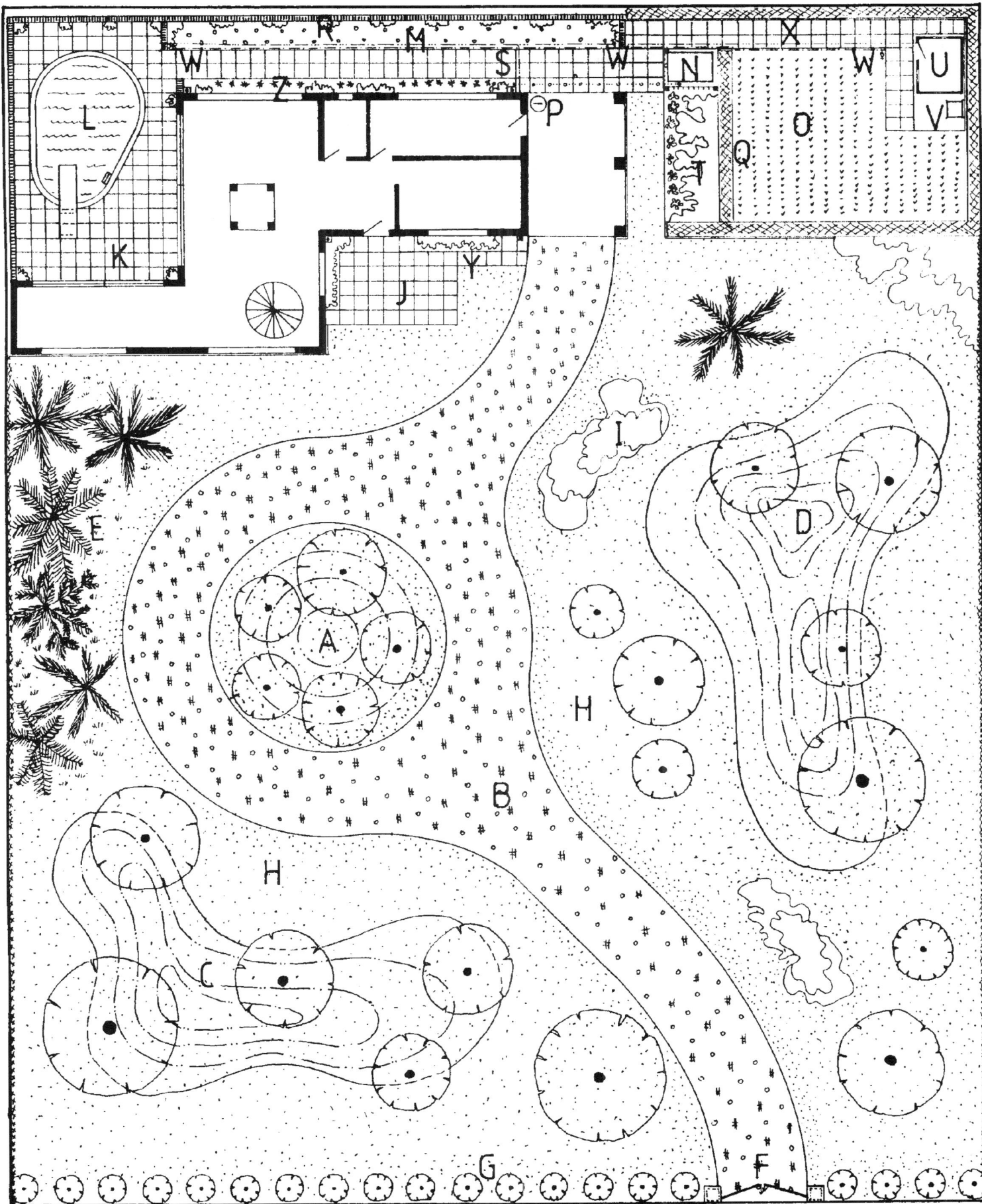

SCALE 1:200

## An irregular-shaped plot with a long drive

This property has been set back from the main road as infill development originating from a very large road-fronted house. This received special planning permission. It is connected to the road by a long drive (S) with wide grass verges either side (W) planted formally with eight specimen standard trees (R). There is a hammerhead turn (N).

The house is surrounded by paving and an irregularly shaped patterned terrace by the French windows. At (Z) paving has had to be cut to join two areas of regular standard-sized slabs. There is a vegetable garden (C) with incinerator (B) composting bay (A) shed (D) close by. Standpipes are located next to the service path (E). There is a screening hedge (X) with a flower border next to it. Electricity is connected to the shed and garage (K). A pair of cold-frames (I) are situated at the far end of the garage. A grass-cuttings dumping area is situated at (F) with a hedge screen (M). The property benefits from large areas of shrubs and trees in the vicinity of the terrace which has a seat nearby.

---

### Key

| | | | |
|---|---|---|---|
| A | Composting bay | P | An irregular line of standard trees in grass area |
| B | Incinerator | | |
| C | Vegetable garden with adjacent standpipes | Q | Boundary hedging |
| | | R | Formal standard specimen trees such as Indian horse chestnut, *Aesculus indica*, set in square earth beds |
| D | Garden shed | | |
| E | Service path | | |
| F | Area for grass cuttings | S | Long drive to house |
| G | Service path with screening hedge | T | Entrance gates and brick capped pillars |
| H | Triangular shrubbery with birch tree | | |
| I | Cold-frames | U | Chain link fence |
| J | Refuse containers | V | Formal specimen bush such as *Magnolia stellata* |
| K | Garage | | |
| L | Oil tank | W | Lawns |
| M | Hedge screen to grass-cuttings dumping zone | X | Screening hedge and flower border |
| | | Y | Bird table |
| N | Hammerhead turn to drive | Z | Paving cut to size as infill to two areas of standard-sized slabs |
| O | Kidney-shaped bed for formal bedding such as dahlias or cannas | | |

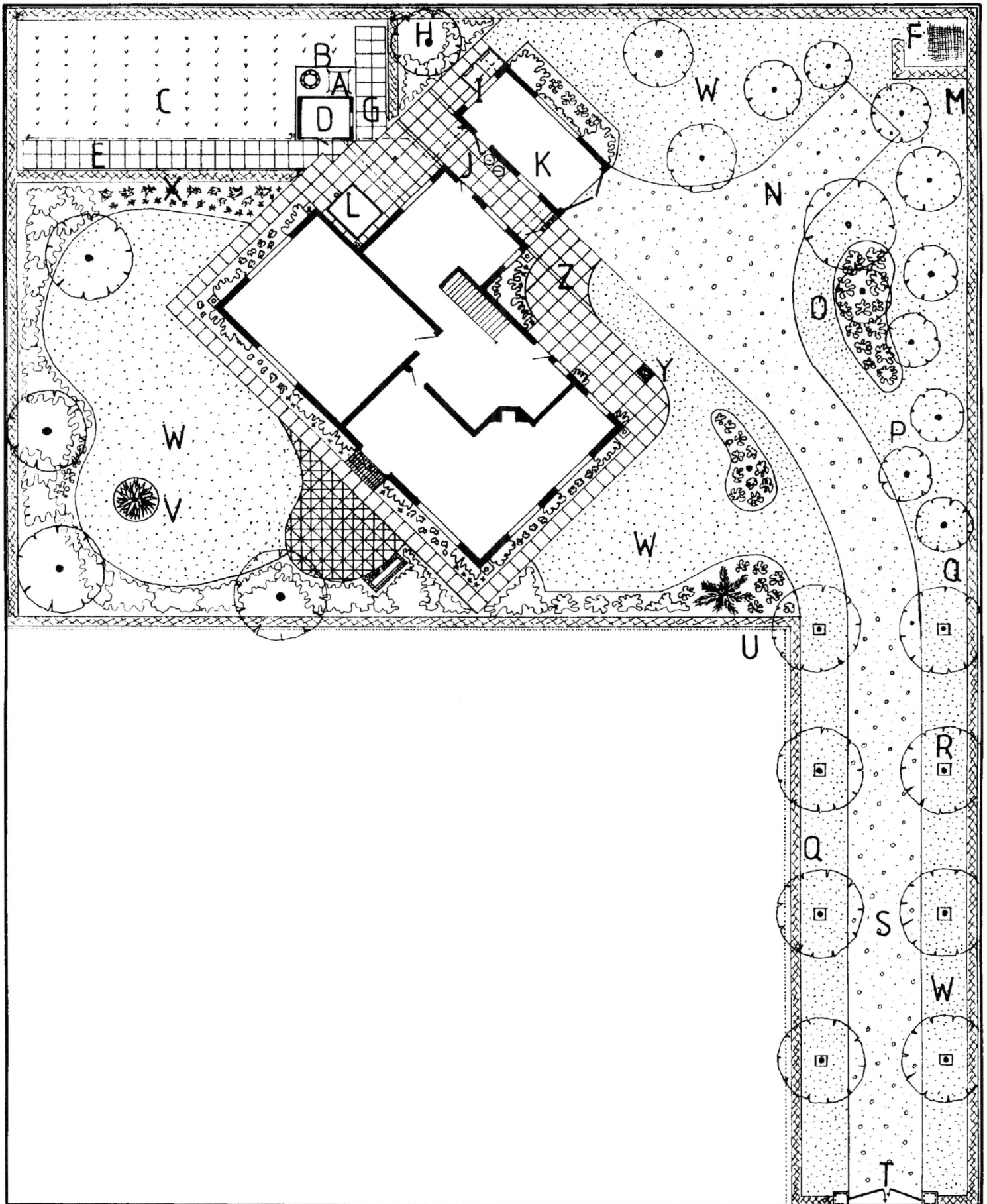

H F M B A C G D E I J K L Z N O Y W V P Q R Q S W U T

SCALE 1:200

## A sunken garden

This dwelling has been centrally sited and has hard surface landscaping on all sides. The drive is wide allowing for extra parking and benefits from a hammerhead turn. There are many borders adjacent to the house for various bedding arrangements plus wall shrubs between windows. Note that the path is sufficiently far away from window swing, when open, thus reducing the possible danger to children running around.

In the front garden there is emphasis on clumps of trees such as naturalising silver birch especially situated on the mounded area (A).

Opposite the lounge there is a feature of a pond (C) with paving surround and, in direct line of viewing, a large garden seat (D). In one corner of the rear garden there is the kitchen garden complex which includes a greenhouse (W), incinerator and compost bay (V), and shed (U), to which electricity is connected. The water supply pipe (K) supplies the garden and kitchen garden.

In the centre of the rear garden is the main feature of a sunken garden with two flights of steps with formal beds and four half standard roses (O). Note the stone retaining wall and adjacent mowing strip.

---

**Key**

A  Contoured mounded area
B  Clumps of silver birch and bulbs in long grass to naturalise
C  Small pond with stone paving surround
D  Garden seat
E  Formal paved approach to front door
F  Service area, coke and coal bunkers, refuse containers and oil tank suitably screened
G  Formal paved terrace area
H  Broad flight of steps with risers
I  Entrance drive with hammerhead turn
J  Electricity supply to garden shed and greenhouse
K  Water supply to greenhouse kitchen garden and garden standpipe
L  Kitchen garden
M  Steps down from lawn area
N  Stone wall and mowing strip

O  Half standard roses in each corner, the rest of the surrounding borders filled with rose bushes
P  Sunken garden requiring timber ramp on steps for mower
Q  Compost area with screens
R  Tree and shrub border
S  Fruit cage
T  Servicing path to vegetable garden and fruit cage with three adjacent standpipes
U  Garden shed
V  Incinerator and compost area screened by low-growing hedge
W  Greenhouse
X  Beech hedge – double row
Y  Lawn
Z  Stone or concrete block backing to shallow rockery and assorted heathers

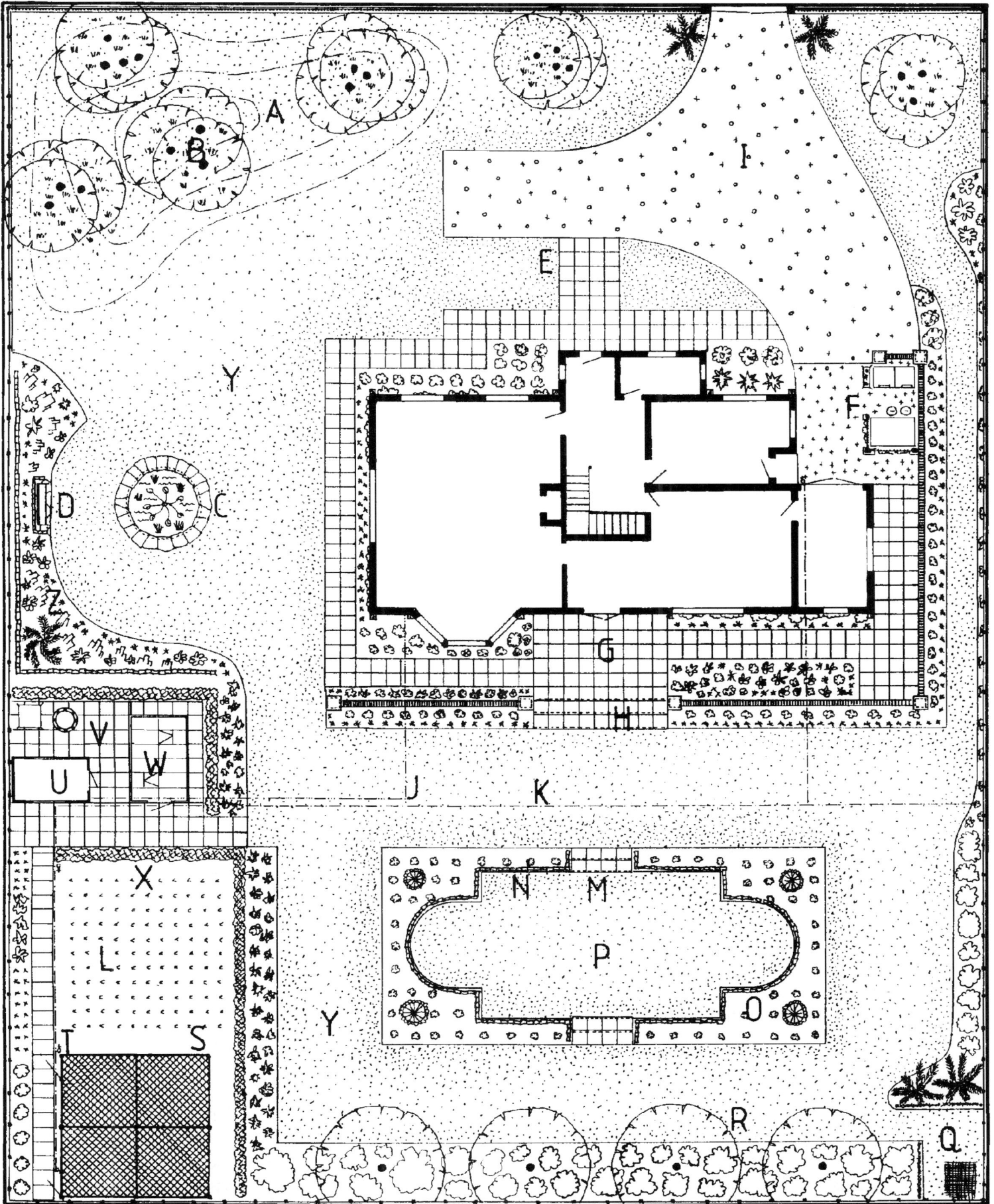

A B I

E

Y

F

D C

Z

G

H

V U W J K

X

L

N M

P

T S Y O

R

Q

SCALE 1:200

## Triangular site

Occasionally there occurs a triangular site which poses problems of design and the separation of the formal garden from the kitchen garden, especially as, in this example, there is gentle rising ground towards the apex. There is likely to be a surface water drainage problem and that is why the terrace (I) has to have an adequate crossfall to its corner by steps (H) necessitating an effective soakaway.

To relieve the severity of the triangular shape it is desirable to form borders with varying curves, quite apart from the interest of what is round the corner. A quantity of edging in stone is shown in random size supplemented by limited pockets of rockery stone (G). It should be emphasised that in this case the dwelling is single-storey and semi-detached. Easy movement without steps for a garden wheelbarrow, roller and lawn mower is essential.

**Key**

| | | | |
|---|---|---|---|
| A | Composting area | P | Refuse container |
| B | Incinerator | Q | Garage |
| C | Concrete path | R | Grid in garage driveway hard-standing |
| D | Area for soft fruit | | |
| E | Vegetable garden | S | Cobble insert bedded in concrete between two strips of strong concrete |
| F | Lawn | | |
| G | Border with occasional rockery stones and stone retaining wall | T | Evergreen hedging as screen such as *Thuja lobbii* |
| H | Circular steps with stone risers | U | One of several specimen flowering trees such as *Prunus hisakura* |
| I | Terrace constructed with random paving with adequate drainage crossfall | | |
| J | Small border within stone surround | V | Small formal borders, e.g., wallflower, salvias, etc. |
| K | Concreted service area | | |
| L | Bunkers for coal and coke | W | Close boarded fence secured to oak posts with pillar caps |
| M | Garden shed | | |
| N | Stone edging to borders | X | Boundary chain link fencing |
| O | Pathway constructed with random paving | Y | Shrubbery |
| | | Z | Beech hedge clipped to suitable height |

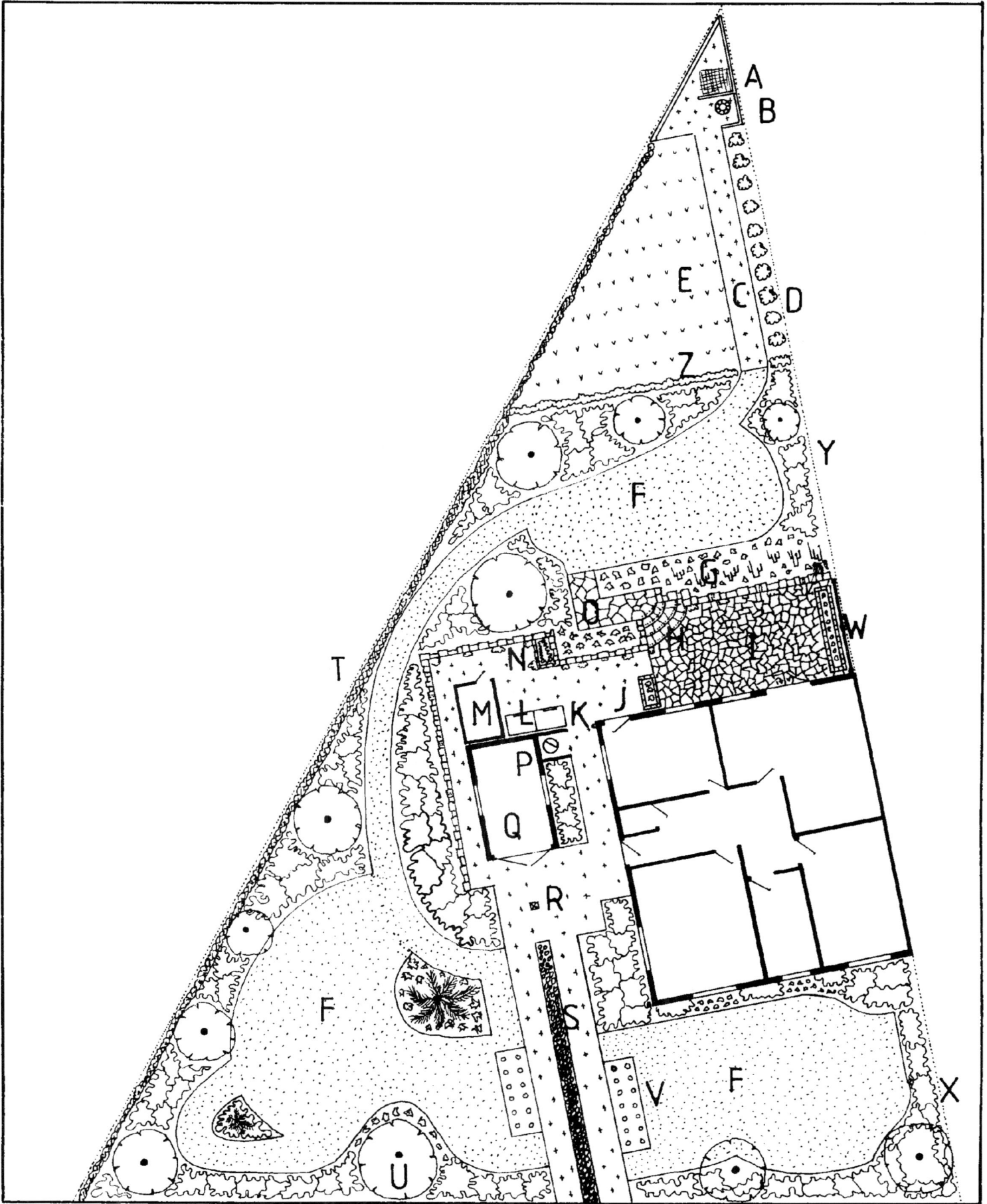

169    SCALE    1: 200

## Formal garden with pond and beech hedges

This garden has a boundary hedge consisting of alternate copper and green beech, both of which will go brown in the autumn, their leaves staying on if the hedge is clipped at the end of July, preventing the abscission layer being formed. There is a high degree of formality in the rear garden, i.e., two equally long herbaceous borders best viewed obliquely. There are also three equal-sized curved beds with ornamental trees behind and eight standard fruit trees. To soften this there is a curved border at (Z) with a low hollow block wall filled with soil for draping alpines.

In the main terrace at the rear of the house there is a large rectangular pond with brick boxes for marginal aquatics and lilies with oxygenating plants in the middle. A garden seat surrounded by evergreen shrubs provides an elongated view.

A good deal of the original topsoil where the house and terrace are situated has been bladed off and used to form interesting raised lawns with gentle slopes either side of the drive. The hammerhead turn has been designed to end opposite the front door. A small vegetable garden with standpipes is near the kitchen door and garden shed (G) and propagating frames (I).

---

**Key**

| | | | |
|---|---|---|---|
| A | Three equal-sized curved beds | M | Mounded area of long grass – naturalising trees with bulbs |
| B | Formal herbaceous borders viewable from all sides | N | Sloped banking either side of drive |
| C | Cedar tree | O | Old hedging and existing trees on top of bank |
| D | Orchard – fruit trees with long grass and bulbs beneath | P | Garden seat providing long view of pond |
| E | Overflow from pond into soakaway in border | Q | Rockery from raised grass area |
| F | Long pond with pockets for aquatics such as iris, plantains, etc. | R | Drive |
| | | S | Paved entrance to house |
| G | Garden shed | T | Garage |
| H | Oil tank screened with access path | U | Low stone edging wall |
| I | Cold-frames for plant propagation | V | Gentle slope to adjust lawn levels |
| J | Coke and coal bunkers | W | Water supply to kitchen garden |
| K | Oil pipe – well protected | X | Neighbour's existing tree |
| L | Gentle grass slope to raised grass area | Y | Screening hedge |
| | | Z | Pocketed walling blocks filled with draping alpines |

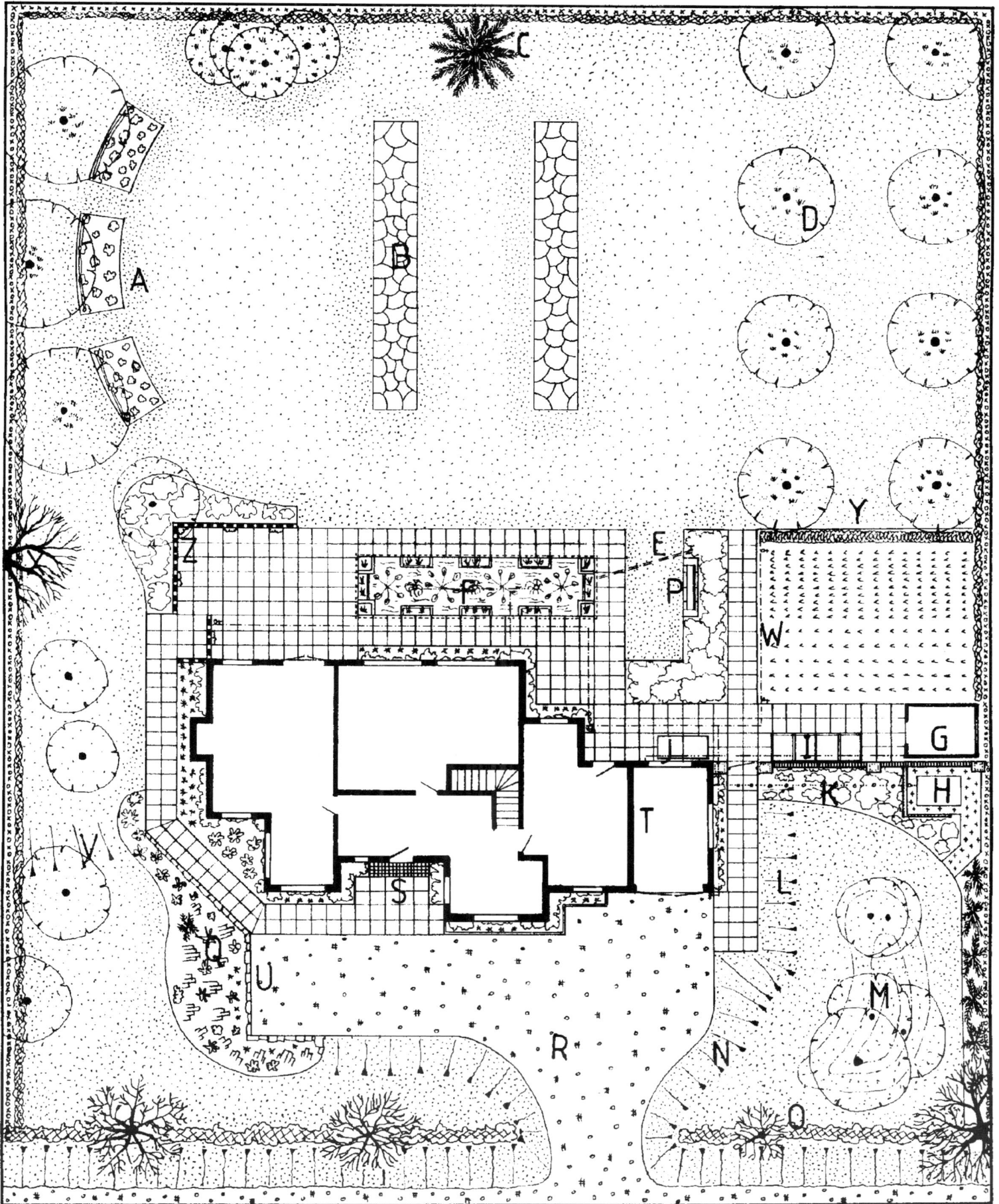

SCALE 1:200

## A ranch-style chalet on clay soil

Far out in the countryside is this ranch-style cedar single-storey chalet. Much care has been taken to landscape the area sympathetically. Being on heavy clay soil there has been a good opportunity to dig out a pond (B) with a fox-proof island (A) in the middle for bird-nesting and preening purposes. There is a bridge (C) which is a feature and stepping stones (G) go from it to the seat (F) nestling into a recess of the bank (D). There are wooden steps (X) to link the bridge with the higher ground. In the main grassed area are two dissimilar-sized raised borders planted with masses of heathers.

Around the edges of the property are many distinctive clusters of indigenous broad-leaved trees (W, Z, V, etc.) while in contrast there are some spruce trees (N). A thatched summerhouse (J) with small paved area (H) gives much scope for wide viewing of the pond and backdrop of trees. There is a paved terrace (S) by the double doors of the chalet accessed by steps down (P). A pathway (O) goes round the dwelling adjacent to which are low-growing and wall shrubs.

### Key

| | | | | |
|---|---|---|---|---|
| A | Fox-proof island for wildfowl nesting | | M | Clumps of rhododendrons and tree heathers, such as *Erica australis* and *lusitanica* |
| B | Pond | | | |
| C | Bridge with handrail over the narrow part of the pond | | N | Group of spruce trees |
| | | | O | Pathway of different sizes of paving around chalet |
| D | Sloped ground – bulbs, wild flowers | | | |
| E | Marginal aquatics – great reedmace, yellow iris, purple loosestrife, etc. | | P | Steps down from French window to the main terrace |
| F | Seat to view the pond and bridge | | Q | Main area of grass probably maintained by 'ride-on' rotascythe |
| G | Stepping stones in grass between seat and bridge | | | |
| | | | R | Long grass kept in control by rotascythe |
| H | Area of irregular crazy paving | | S | Main terrace in different sizes of paving |
| I | Pair of dissimilar mounded beds covered with splashes of assorted heathers | | T | Low-growing and wall shrubs |
| | | | U | Weeping willow |
| | | | V | Clump of silver birch |
| J | Thatched summerhouse | | W | Clump of autumn colour/berried trees |
| K | Mounded grass area with bulbs and birch trees | | X | Steps from bridge to higher ground |
| | | | Y | Long grass cut by rotascythe or strimmer |
| L | Clumps of massed azaleas and rhododendrons | | Z | Beech trees in long grass |

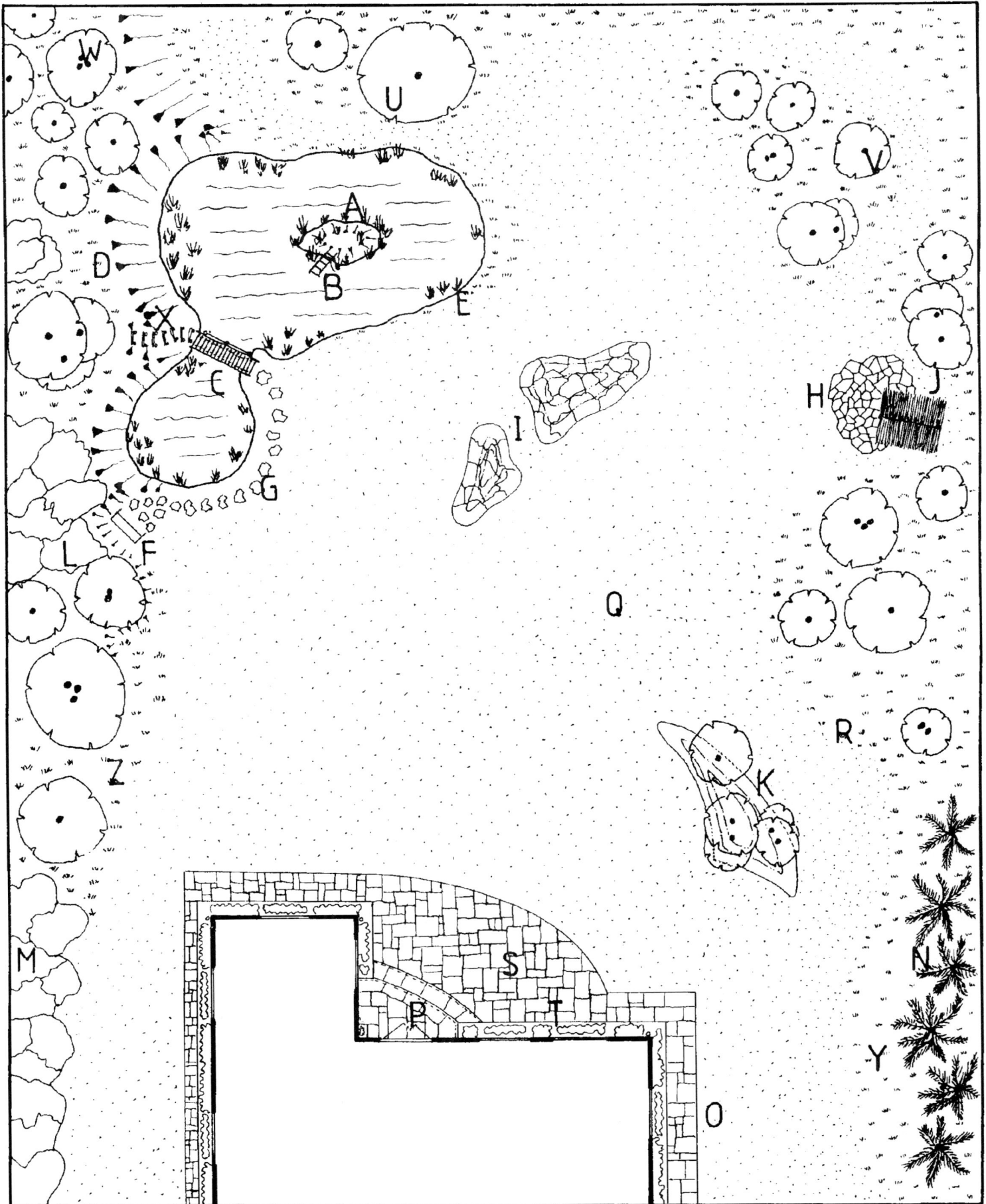

173

SCALE 1:200

## A former farmyard redesigned

This garden has presented many design challenges as the dwelling was a former farmhouse, now renovated with adjacent farm buildings converted into storage and workshops. The old farmyard has been resurfaced and a lean-to constructed against the old walling of blocks or bricks. Part of the kitchen garden is shown with access to the yard.

The terrace (S) is intentionally large since that area was subject to building demolition and there is little or no soil other than imported soil placed in pockets. Attention has had to be given to adequate crossfalls but the paving is open-jointed to allow surface water to percolate down into the rubble base. To break the uniformity there are two dissimilar long beds within the terrace for sympathetic planting, and to reduce intensive maintenance to the garden, shrubbing with associated trees is given high priority.

On the boundary with the road there are existing trees between hedging which may require limbing and balancing. Note that there is a water supply pipe going from house via the kitchen garden to the main lawn areas with occasional standpipes.

## Key

A  Kitchen garden with surrounding path and access to yard
B  Oil tank
C  Lean-to greenhouse with water laid on
D  Former farm buildings, some with stable doors, converted to stores with ornamental flower troughs under the windows – an opportunity for mangers filled with flowers
E  Former oast-house converted into a garage
F  Former farmyard with hard surfacing
G  Entrance drive with hammerhead turn
H  Irregular shaped pond
I  Sloped bed with rockery and stone backing
J  Paved surround to pond with weeping birch tree
K  Path from terrace to old farmyard and flight of steps
L  Sloped bed with rockery and stone backing plus trees
M  Group of firs

N  Area for composting screened by thick evergreen shrubs such as *Viburnum lauristinus*
O  Three groups of mixed floral shrubs and trees
P  Specimen winter flowering cherry – *Prunus autumnalis*
Q  Steps from drive to extensive terrace, stone pillars with coping stones
R  Paved area next to French window
S  Extensive area of crazy paving with many pockets for cushioning alpines such as thyme
T  Semi-circle of walling with mowing strip with double earth-filled walls filled with alpines
U  Steps from terrace to lawn
V  Wide archway of preserved timber allowing movement between two grassed areas
W  Dividing hedge
X  Gateway from drive to old farmyard
Y  Stone wall with pillars encompassing drive area gardens
Z  Main lawn area

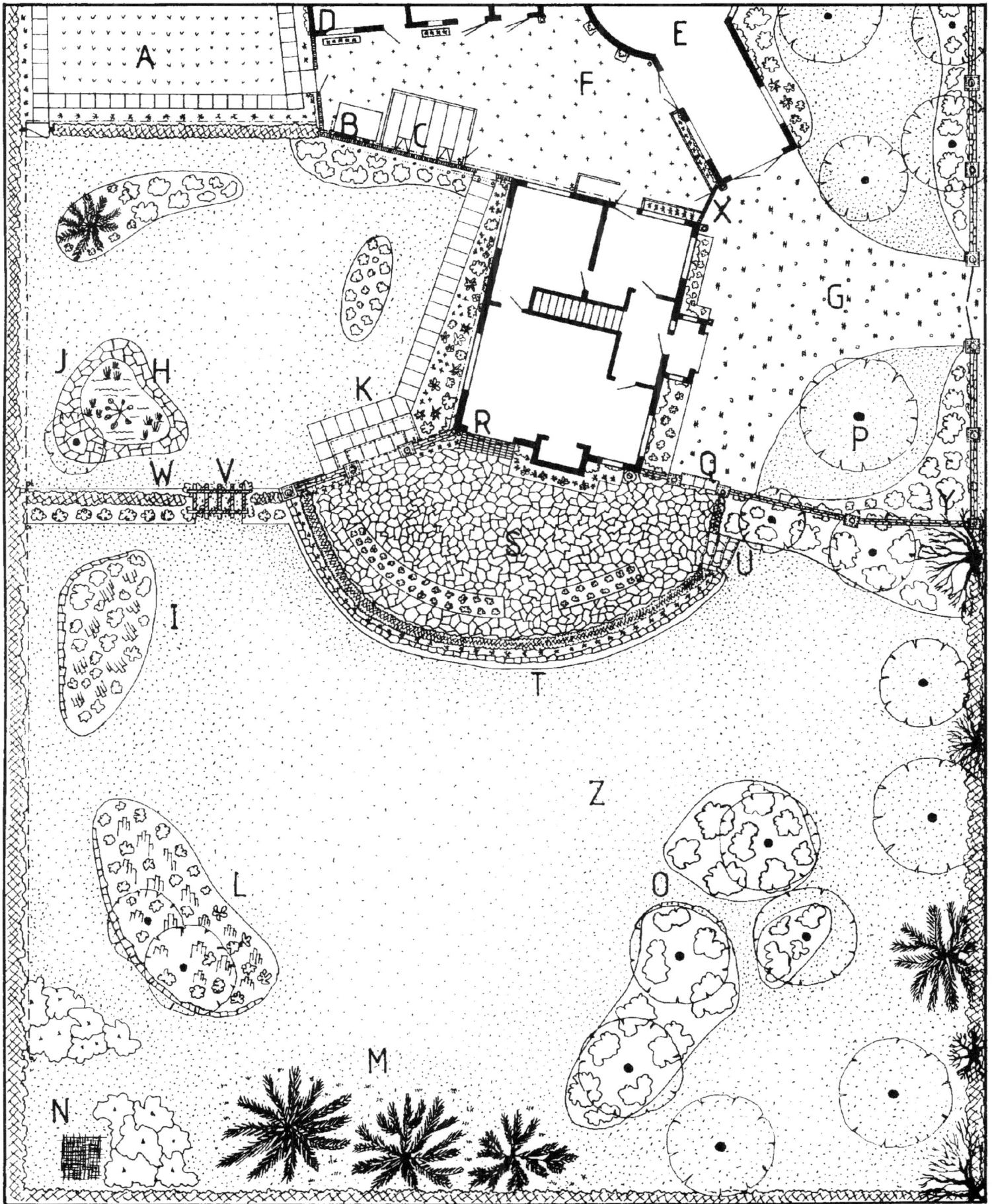

175

SCALE 1:200

## Large-scale formal garden

This large property is set in a big garden. There is so much detail shown that initialling of every feature is impossible. The house is surrounded by a terrace and paving. Oil, water and electricity supplies have been installed. (A) is a summerhouse with thatched roof which looks out on to strategically located formal beds (B), a sundial (C), wrought iron gates (D), large herbaceous border with good height graduation of plants (E) to a seat on paving surrounded by birch trees (F). A specimen Indian cedar (G) is set into the main lawn (Z). The macadam drive (W) is contained within low stone walls on two sides.

The functional area consists of a fuel bunker (N), oil tank (O), shed (M), greenhouse (L), cold-frames (K) leading up to a large vegetable garden (J) screened by hedge (T) and a soft fruit garden (I). At the far end is an asparagus bed (H). There are many standpipes servicing these areas. Lawn mowings can be off-loaded at two locations (V). There is linkage between the main lawn area and the functional zone by a wide grass path (S) with formally planted beds either side. Manure and compost stacks (P) are near to the vegetable garden. On one boundary there is a belt of larch trees either side of a seat.

---

**Key**

| | | | |
|---|---|---|---|
| A | Thatched summerhouse with semi-circular terrace | M | Shed |
| B | Four formal beds for bedding plants | N | Fuel bunker |
| C | Sundial on circular area of crazy paving | O | Oil tank |
| D | Wrought iron gates some 900mm high between brick pillars and clipped yew hedge | P | Area for manure and compost |
| | | Q | Double garage |
| | | R | Terrace |
| E | Formal herbaceous borders | S | Formal beds |
| F | Seat on terrace surrounded by silver birch trees and naturalising bulbs | T | Screening hedge |
| | | U | Standpipes |
| G | Well-shaped Indian cedar | V | Area to dump grass cuttings to rot down |
| H | Long asparagus bed | | |
| I | Soft fruit – black, red and white currants, gooseberries, etc. | W | Macadam drive with turning area, edged with low stone walls and wash-down grid/gully |
| J | Vegetable garden | X | Conservatory with sliding doors |
| K | Cold-frames | Y | Pair of gates secured to brick posts |
| L | Greenhouse serviced by water and electricity | Z | Lawn |

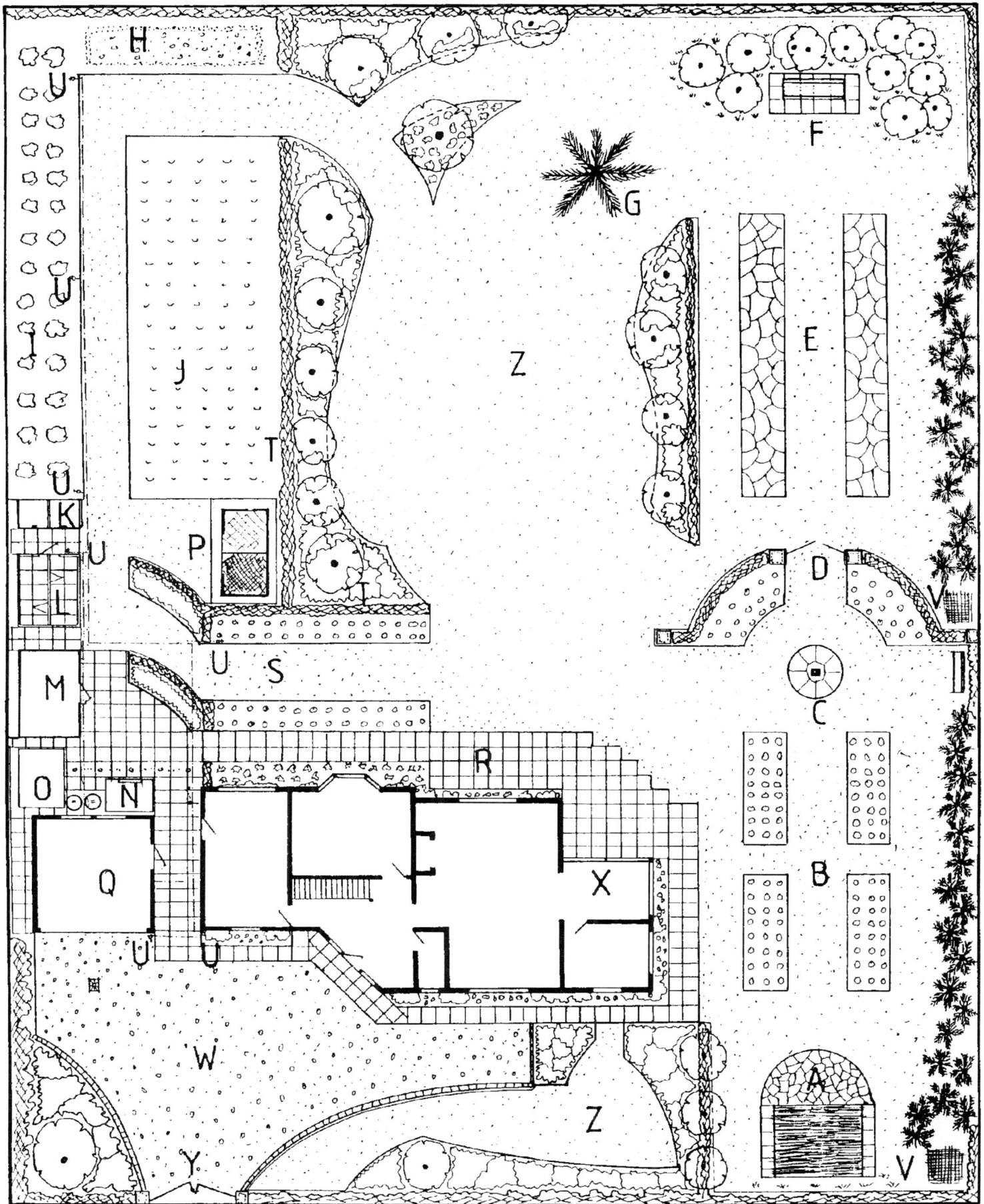

177

SCALE 1:200

## Low-maintenance gardening on a large scale

This large detached house stands in a large area of lawn with minimum maintenance and upkeep. Many of the planted areas contain prostrate plant or ground cover which flow over to the grass up to which the mower reaches. These plants are therefore kept in bounds from exceeding their desired spread. In order to achieve features there is the mounded planted area (O) giving opportunities for naturalising bulbs, daffodils, narcissus, etc.

There is an area set aside for a kitchen garden, the composition of which is as yet undecided, but the framework of servicing pathways is in place. To save a lot of walking there are two designated zones (T) and (P) for the disposal of grass cuttings and swept-up leaves in the autumn. There are several borders adjacent to the house for formal spring and summer bedding. The border opposite the house front door has been thickly planted with assorted deciduous and evergreen shrubs supplemented by trees to give flowers, berries and foliage all the year round.

## Key

A   Service area including incinerator
B   This zone is left undetermined for later usage decisions
C   Greenhouse
D   Garden shed
E   Children's sandpit and play area
F   Water butt with tap
G   Two columnar conifers such as juniper, bays, etc.
H   Formal steps with risers to front door and porch
I   Macadam drive with hammerhead turn
J   Stone edging bedded in concrete with cement joints adjacent to mowing strip
K   Stepping stones suitably spaced, countersunk to grass for easy mowing
L   Rectangular bed for formal bedding – wallflowers, tulips, etc.
M   Paving with brick patterning

N   Garden seat in recess of boomerang-shaped mounded area
O   Evergreen shrubs with trees to provide seclusion
P   Varied shrub border with zone for grass clippings
Q   Irregular shaped shrub border with ground cover type plants overlapping lawn, i.e., no edging
R   Belt of screening conifers, not *leylandii*
S   Heather border using *Erica darleyensis*
T   Zone for grass clippings and rotting leaves in wire surround
U   Area for prostrate shrubs and informal tree planting
V   Formal tree planting
W   Lawn
X   Irregular shaped bed with mass of grouped herbaceous plants
Y   Refuse containers
Z   Pair of elegant gates

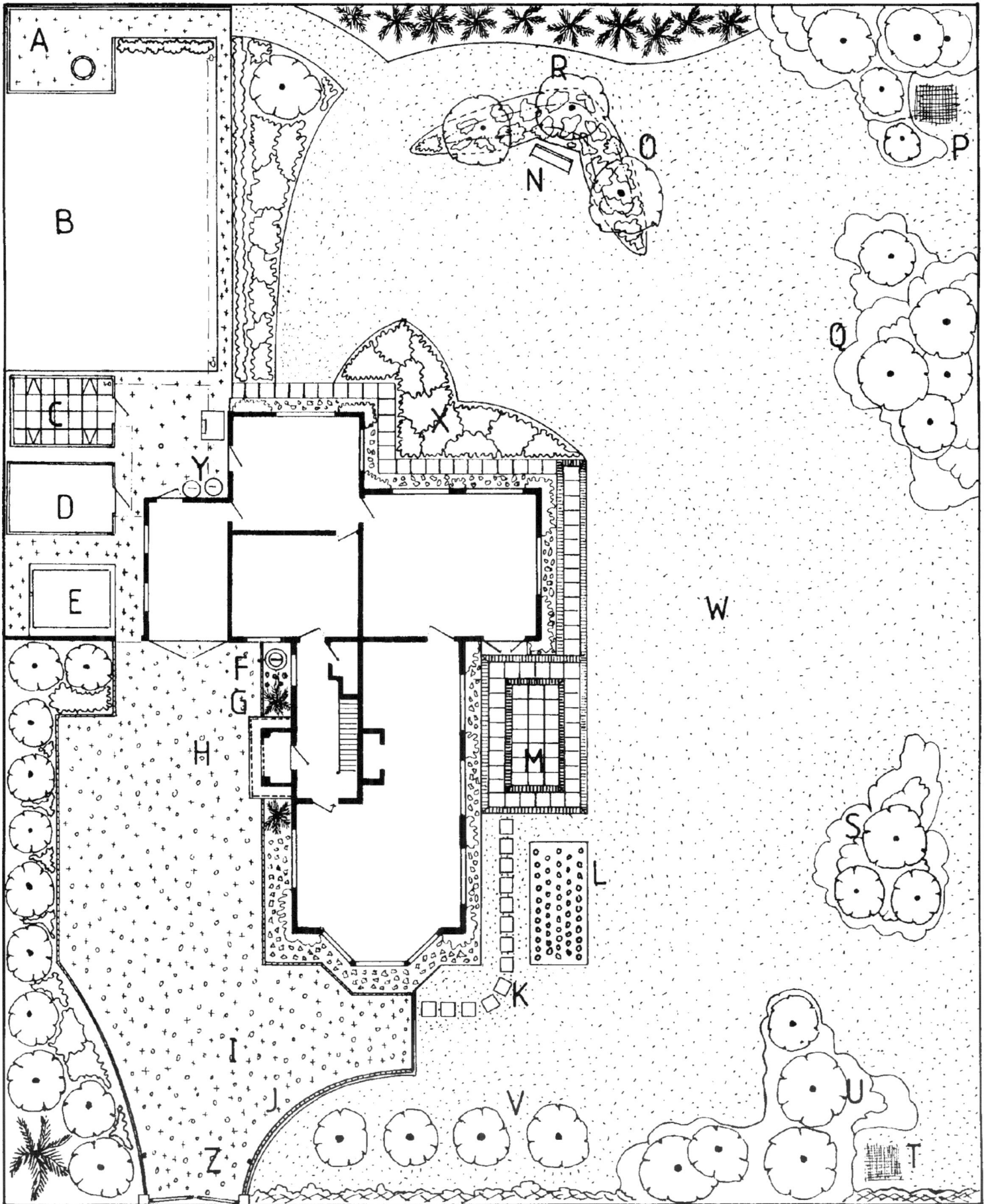

A O

B

C

D

E

F
G

H

I

J

Z

R

N

O

P

Q

X

Y

W

M

L

K

S

V

U

T

SCALE 1: 200

## Creating a large natural pond

This detached house has been built on impermeable clay and therefore there are some problems of surface water disposal. This situation can be used to advantage by establishing a natural pond into which land drainage and roof water is fed with a controlled outfall into an existing area, culverted under the drive.

By calculation of volumes, most of the subsoil needs to be removed off site to suitable finished levels and graded banking, allowing for pondside marginal aquatic planting. A small proportion of the pond area, i.e., low quality topsoil, can be used to provide contoured mounding as shown. The mounded areas and lawn areas will require topsoil after a period of settlement of finished lawn levels and the drain runs. Marginal planting of suitable bushes and trees, which will not clog up the drains, will enhance the natural and beautiful setting, much of the area being planted with naturalising bulbs.

The more formal areas near to the house are laid out extensively with paving and pathways, leaving a small functional area near to the garage. The house and external landscaping have intentionally been located on the higher ground.

---

### Key

| | |
|---|---|
| A | Area for manure or compost screened by evergreen hedge |
| B | Garden seat |
| C | Paving – irregular bonding |
| D | Small border with prostrate shrubs to disguise inspection cover |
| E | Sunken garden |
| F | Tubs planted with standard bay trees or similar |
| G | Water butt to conserve rain-water adjacent to rain-water downpipe |
| H | Bunkers for coal/coke, etc. |
| I | Internal water tap |
| J | Greenhouse |
| K | Garden frames |
| L | Oil tank |
| M | Areas for planting |
| N | Single garage |
| O | Rotary washing line location |
| P | Mounded grassed areas for bulbs and woodland trees, e.g. birch |
| Q | Steps to pond |
| R | Herringbone land drainage system connected to house drainage |
| S | Dammed outlet (adjustable) as overflow to stream |
| T | Gate to drive |
| U | Larch plantation |
| V | Grass pathway between two areas of sloping grass |
| W | Close boarded fence as screen |
| X | Drive in macadam, binding gravel, etc. |
| Y | Concrete pathways |
| Z | Paving – random slabbing with brick infills |

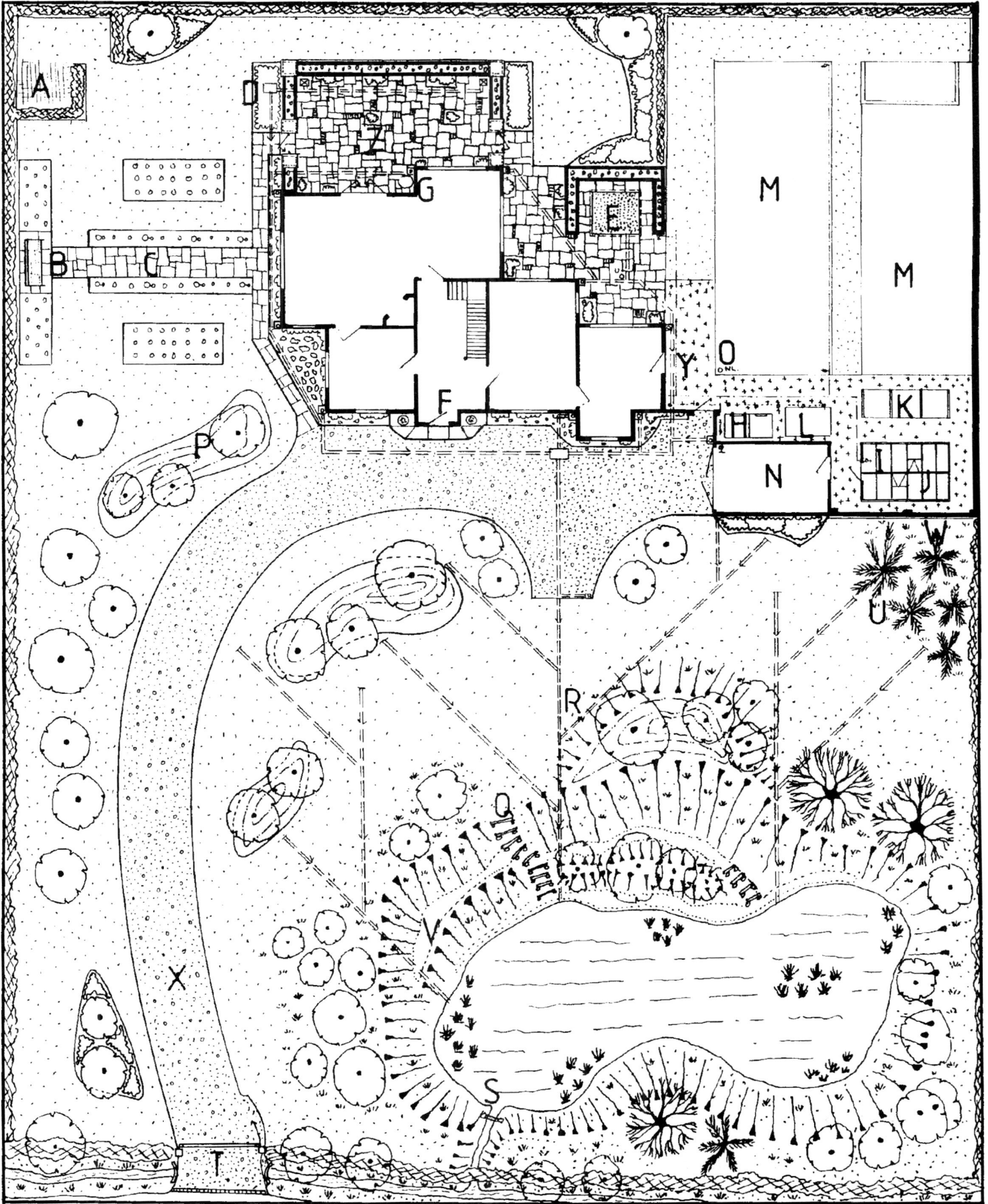

SCALE 1:200

## Large lawns and a panoramic view

This two-storey house has been set well back to allow for an expansive layout of extensive areas of lawn in which several irregular shaped planting borders are situated but with thought given to easy mowing. The main lawn is bisected by a curved path splaying out as it reaches the elliptical steps leading up to the terrace outside the front door. There is a good deal of single course stone edging around the two terraces to allow for alpines or plants such as yellow alyssum, etc. Wall shrubs and edging plants are in abundance, where possible next to the house.

There is a gradual gentle slope from the house to the cleft oak post and rail (T) which adds great panoramic interest especially from the first floor windows. Because of this setting the kitchen garden and neighbouring borders are relatively small.

### Key

| | | | |
|---|---|---|---|
| A | Kitchen garden | N | Pathway from garage to service area |
| B | Fruit cage | O | Terrace with stone edging similar to (J) with elliptical steps to meandering path towards access gate (U) |
| C | Greenhouse | | |
| D | Garden shed as a built-in component of the greenhouse, water and electricity connected | P | Herringbone pattern soil drainage to pond (V) |
| E | Concrete path with water supply pipe to standpipes adjacent | Q | Garage with standpipe and lighting fittings |
| F | Concrete hard-standing with adequate crossfall to drain gully in corner connected to rain-water house drainage network | R | Broken paving path |
| | | S | Incinerator and composting area (one of two) |
| G | Oil tank with oil supply pipe | T | Cleft oak post and rail fence |
| H | Refuse containers | U | Access gate |
| I | Access constructed of pieces of stone set in concrete with cement bonding | V | Pond, irregular shape with naturalising plants such as purple loosestrife, meadowsweet and great reed mace |
| J | Large terrace constructed of random sized York paving with occasional old paving bricks and planting pockets | W | Overflow into perforated pipe outfall for seepage into permeable soils |
| | | X | Curved pathway |
| K | Three formal planting beds | Y | Alternative incinerator and compost bay well screened by hedging and shrubs |
| L | Lawns | | |
| M | Rain-water downpipe to gully drainage network | Z | Avenue of ornamental trees |

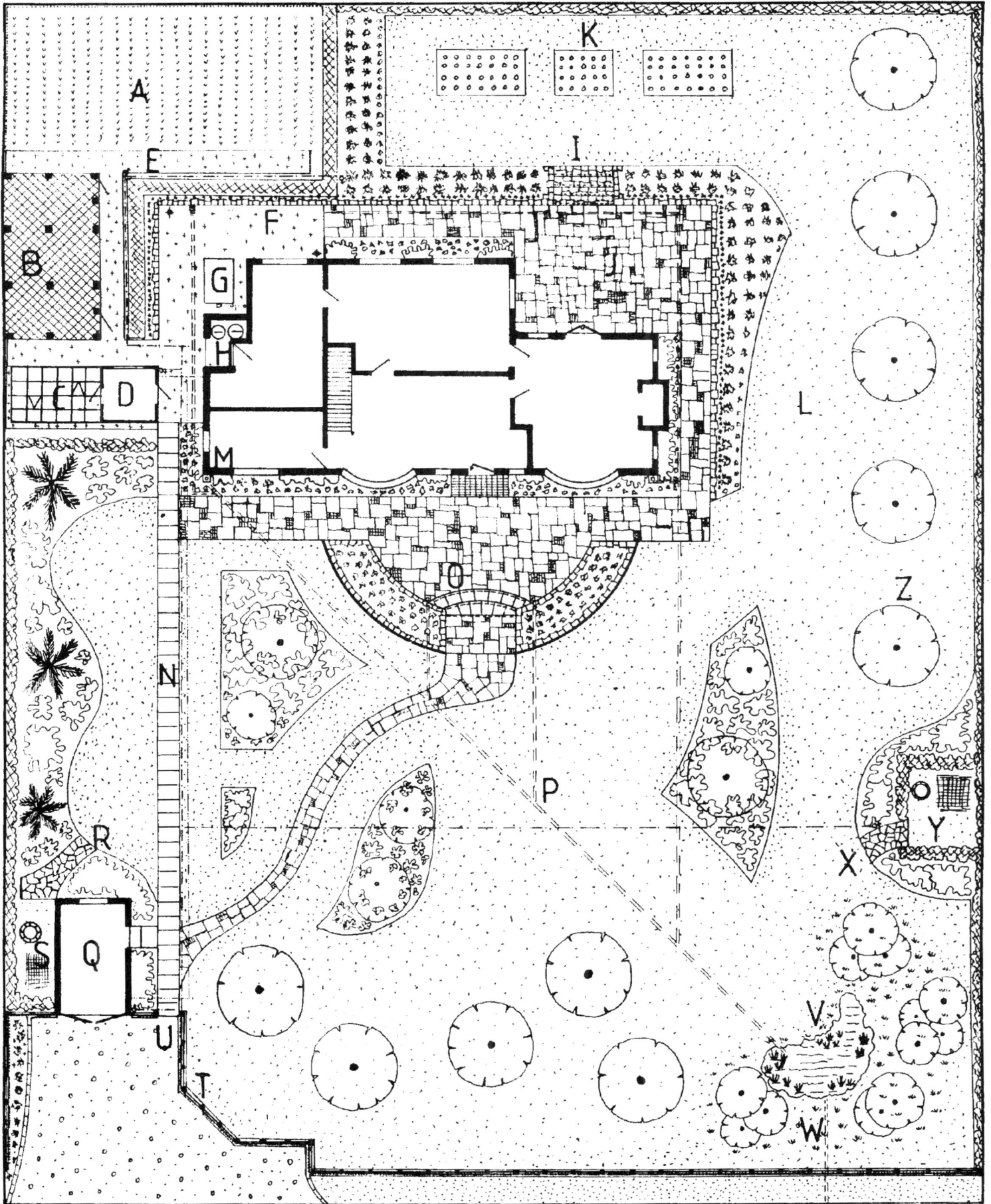

**SCALE 1: 200**

## Heathland planting

This single-storey ranch-type bungalow constructed of timber has been built in an area of outstanding natural beauty. Hillocks with large stone outcrops (S) abound. Frequently trodden grass pathways mingle around the trees, heathers, blueberries, etc., with various sections of wooden steps (B, C, D, E and G). There are rustic seats placed at vantage points (A and H) plus another (J) to achieve panoramic views of the rising ground. There are areas of rhododendrons, azaleas and hydrangeas together with drifts of single and multi-stemmed birch. Carpets of naturalising bulbs abound with interesting patches of snowdrops and primroses. The lawn is not level and in places there are slopes, adding more interest.

The building is enhanced by a large curved terrace in crazy paving with plant pockets. Pathways go round the property up to the front door where there is a terrace. The back door and functional area has not been shown on this plan.

---

**Key**

| | | | |
|---|---|---|---|
| A | Rustic seat | O | Garden swing seat |
| B | Pegged wooden steps | P | Crazy paving pathway |
| C | Pegged wooden steps | Q | Stone edging wall with alpines |
| D | Pegged wooden steps | R | Belt of mixed trees including acers and rowans |
| E | Pegged wooden steps | | |
| F | Clumps of rhododendrons | S | Large outcrops of rock emerging from short wiry grass and earth |
| G | Pegged wooden steps | | |
| H | Rustic seat | T | Margin of mown grass |
| I | Pegged wooden steps next to a larch tree | U | Birch trees |
| J | Rustic seat | V | Mown grass |
| K | Clumps of single and multi-stemmed birch trees | W | Long grass filled with large areas of naturalising narcissus, daffodils and fritillaries |
| L | Long kidney-shaped border full of *Mollis* and *Ghent* azaleas | | |
| | | X | Various contours |
| M | Steps down from terrace | Y | Group of Scots pine trees |
| N | York crazy paving | Z | Painted garden seat |

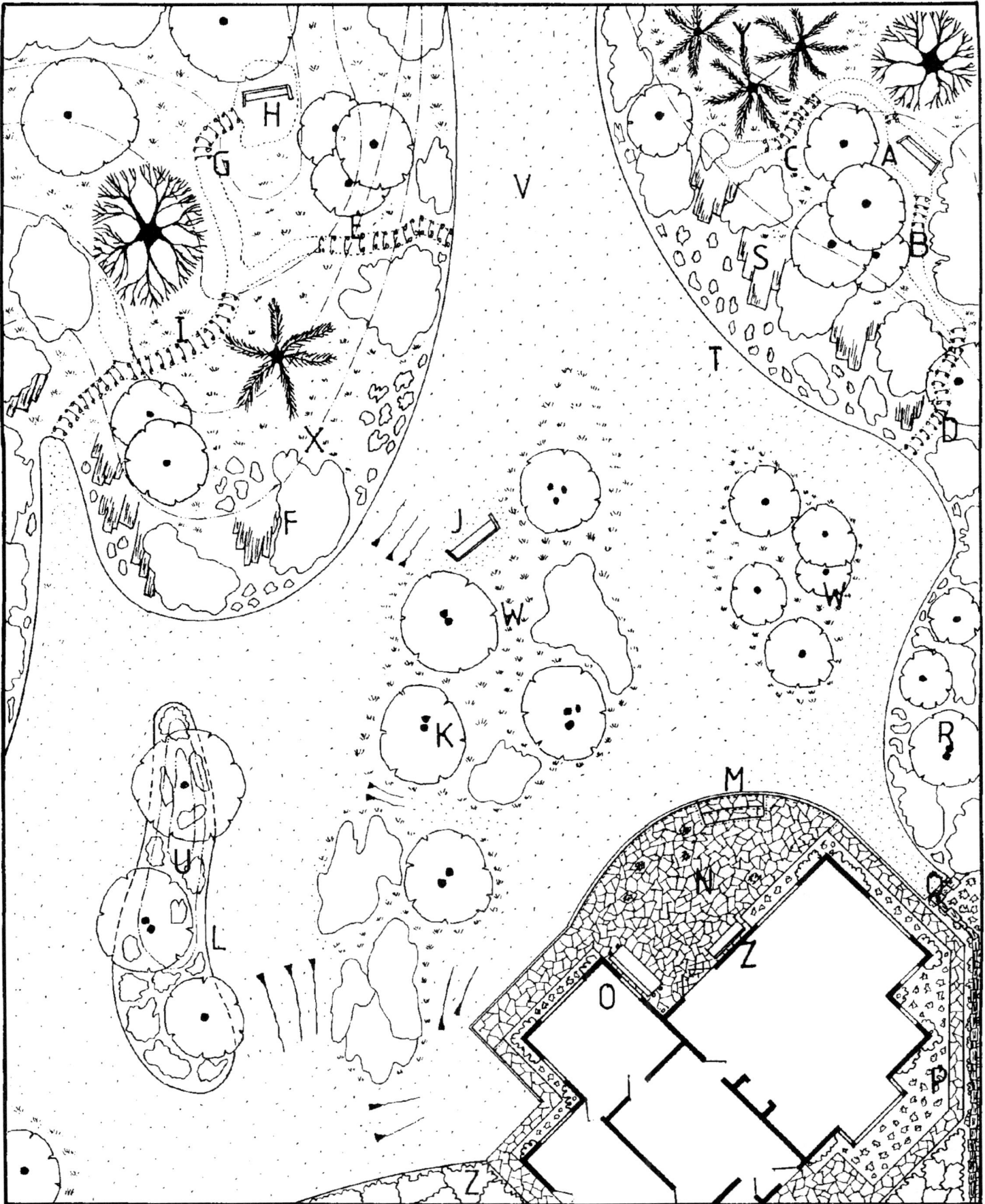

SCALE 1:200

## Two semis sharing a communal garden

This building development is unusual in that two families have chosen to live in adjoining semi-detached bungalows but to have one garden designed in such a way that it can be divided along the centre line (A, B) should the need arise. Each one has its own drive (G and N) with entrance gates. Various borders (W, U, Y and others) are designed to give a curved finish to the lawns (F). Each one has its own vegetable garden (D and P) with access paths (M and Q) and terraces (J and S).

The whole combined site is surrounded by chain link fencing whilst in the front there is a close-boarded fence. Each has its own garage (H and O). Individually there are various flower troughs (L), sheds (I), fuel bunkers (X), refuse containers. In one garden there is a small rectangular pool (K) and sitting area (E). Because the drawing is at 1:200 scale there are many small features which cannot be shown or labelled on the plan.

---

**Key**

| | |
|---|---|
| A ⎫ Location for property division | O Garage |
| B ⎭ demarcation if required | P Kitchen garden |
| C Chain link fencing | Q Access paths and areas of concrete |
| D Kitchen garden | R Shed |
| E Sitting out terrace | S Terrace with planting pockets |
| F Lawns | T Close boarded fence |
| G Drive with entrance gates | U Mixed shrubbery with trees along the |
| H Garage | entire frontage of the gardens |
| I Shed | V Central shrub border with trees |
| J Terrace | W Formal planting beds |
| K Pool with crazy paving surround | X Fuel bunkers and refuse containers |
| L Flower trough | Y Mixed shrubbery with trees |
| M Broken paving access paths | Z Functional area – refuse containers, fuel |
| N Drive with entrance gates | bunkers, etc. |

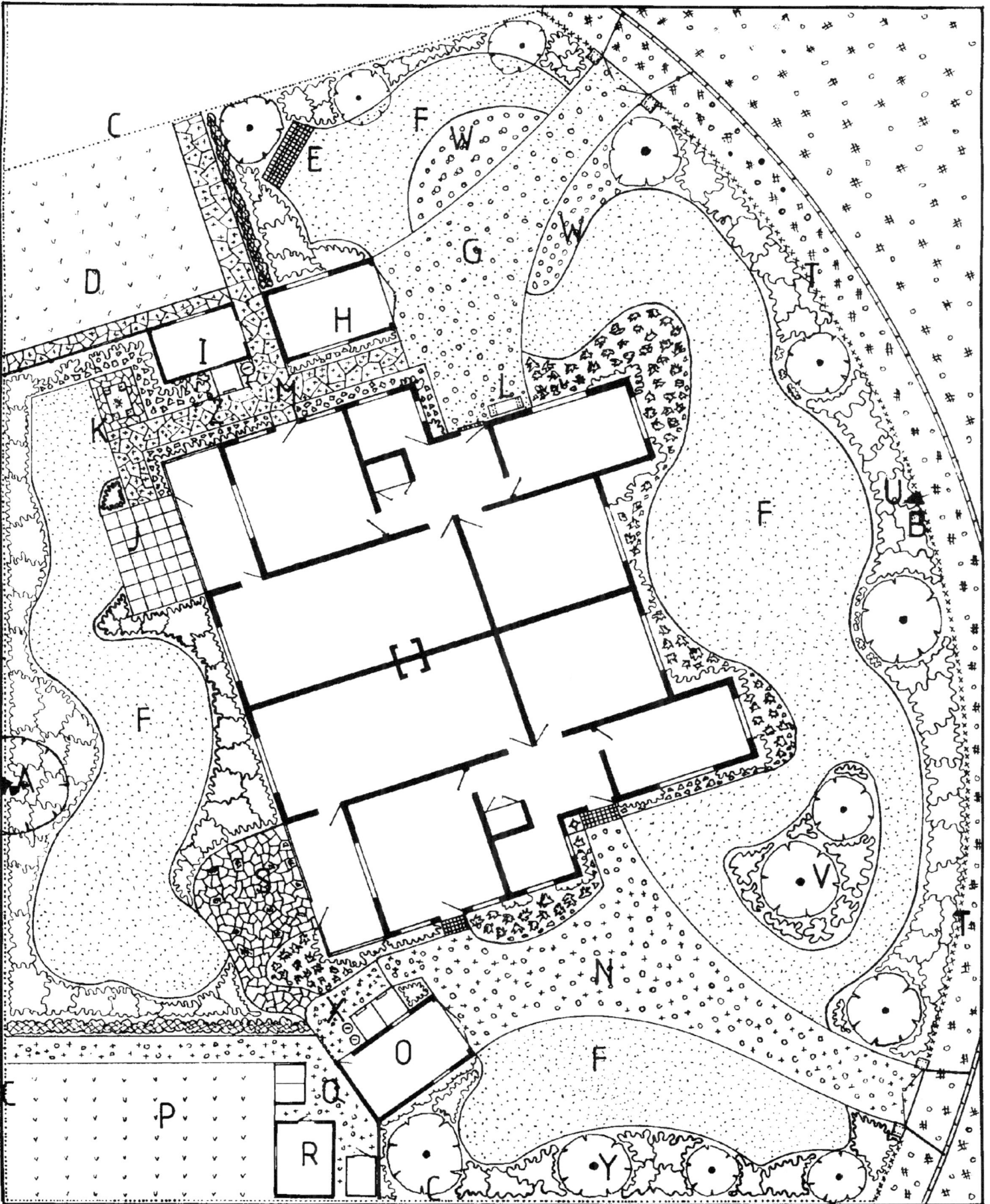

SCALE 1:200

# 5

## *Designing and Constructing a New Garden*

Prior to the new construction, this garden was mainly grassed over as a children's play area and for a dog to exercise in. There were a few shrubs and one or two trees that could be lifted during the dormant season and heeled in prior to planting later in chosen locations. There were patches of bindweed and couch among the rough grass so that the whole area was treated with glyphosate of adequate concentration and left for three months. After that, all the herbage had died down or rotted which made it much easier for constructional work to begin without the problem of tufted grass or the proliferation of invasive weeds. Fortunately there was no marestail or ground elder. Around the perimeter there was a small amount of weed encroachment which required occasional applications of glyphosate in specific locations. As the chemical is translocated through the growing plant tissue, the problem was soon solved.

This garden has been intentionally designed for a partially disabled person, with many raised beds, wall shrubs, slabbed pathways, and shallow wide steps. There was about one metre difference in levels from (A) to (G), and therefore using location (G) as datum point precision levelling and crossfalls had to be set out with level pegs. Luckily the terrace (GH) was already in existence, opposite the French windows, and had an adequate crossfall.

---

**Key**

| | | | |
|---|---|---|---|
| A | Corner of perimeter fence | N | Flight of shallow steps 900mm wide |
| B | Corner of perimeter fence | O | Top of steps at lawn level |
| C | Neighbour's boundary fence | P | End of pathway – beginning of stepping stones to compost bay among birch trees |
| D | Corner of house | | |
| E | Corner of house | Q | Junction of curved interconnecting pathway with main pathway |
| F | Neighbour's fence | | |
| G | Corner of existing paved terrace and datum level point | R | Seat |
| | | S | Compost bay |
| H | Corner of triangular raised bed | T | Corner of pathway |
| I | Corner of triangular raised bed and start of pathway | U | New pathway connected to existing concrete path |
| J | Kitchen window and gully with grating | V | Side border with pergola planted with honeysuckles |
| K | Utility room door | | |
| L | Sliding French windows overlooking terrace with panoramic view of garden | W | Raised border with rockery |
| | | X | Irregular-shaped raised border |
| | | Y | Semi-circular raised border |
| M | Rotary washing line as near as possible to back door | Z | Corner of triangular raised border next to terrace |

# The rear garden of the small house in a modern estate

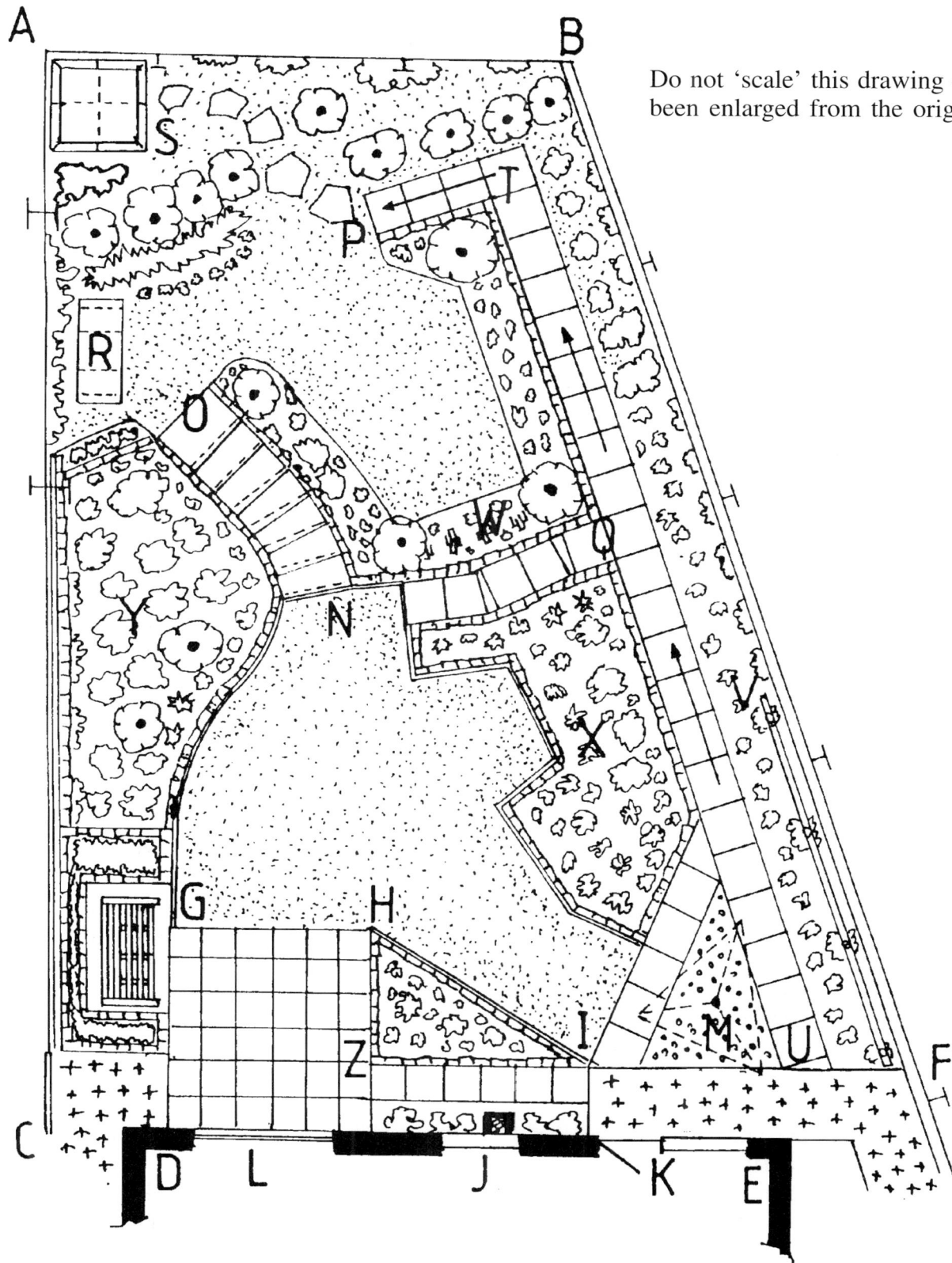

Do not 'scale' this drawing – it has been enlarged from the original.

A B S P T R O U W N Q V G H I Z M U F C D L J K E

N SCALE 1:100

In work sequence, 450mm × 450mm non-slip slabs of similar colour and texture were laid between the existing concrete path (I) to the terrace at (Z). This was followed by laying in stages 600mm × 600mm non-slip slabs similar to those mentioned above, from (I) and (UT) up to (T) and, to cater for a rise in levels, two lengths of four slabs were ramped as shown. At (T) a further three slabs were laid with a slope at right angles to point (P).

The movement of top and subsoil presented many difficulties as quantities were constantly being moved around the site. The next stage was to build the first raised bed (H, I, Z) and then to backfill with suitable soil and thick strata of Irish sphagnum peat.

The lower lawn area (G, H, I, N) was used as a dumping area for surplus soil, while the terrace (G, H) was where walling blocks were stored awaiting selection and use (covered with thick polythene and hessian sacking at night). After this the raised bed (X) of irregular shape was built and back-filled as previously described, followed by a partially curved 600mm wide interconnecting path (QN). The walling (P, T, Q, N) was then constructed to the appropriate levels and a rockery made in area (W) to allow for partial banking.

The interwoven wood panel fence (AC) of joint ownership, was partly covered with soil at ground level so, in order to preserve it, all the existing earth had to be removed to permit the construction of a wall up to ground level using concrete blocks to create an air space where the existing soil levels required it. Most of the soil of the raised border (Y) was dumped on what was to become the lower lawn area during this construction work. At the same time a raised earth border some 1m high was constructed to form a sheltered recessed area of brick paving upon which to place a garden seat.

After estimating the residual soil volumes, the curved wall enclosing the raised bed (Y) was constructed using an inner wall of blocks with reinforced rods for strength and at the same time constructing the curved steps 900mm × 600mm. Upon completion most of the residual soil was put back to form raised border (Y) using copious quantities of sphagnum peat in layers. Soil surplus to requirements was then barrowed to a large skip in the front garden. After all this, the lower lawn area (G, H, I, N) was levelled, gritted and peated prior to turfing, likewise the upper lawn (O, P, Q, N). Much of the area (S, P, B) was graded out to a gentle fall for turfing. The border (B, T, U, F) was then prepared after tanalised shuttering had been installed to allow for an air space to prevent rotting of the timber fence (B, F).

A suitably designed pergola in tanalised poles was constructed (V, F) upon which to train different varieties of honeysuckle as a windbreak and screen from the neighbouring houses. The triangle (M), containing a rotary washing line, was filled with gravel. After a period of settlement borders (H, I, Z) and (X, Y, W) were planted with selected shrubs, of suitable vigour and half-standard flowering trees such as cherry and crab apple.

A compost bay (S), in corner (A), was built with connecting stepping stones (S, P). To screen this and the close-boarded fence (A, B), birch trees approximately 2m high were planted with double staking and cross-bars. Attention was given to their placing, so as not to spoil distant views of the countryside for the neighbours. These, together with double-flowering gorse and Pyracantha to screen the compost bay, formed a good backdrop at the end of the garden.

Plastic covered wiring secured to vine screw eyes was then installed on all perimeter fences (CA), (AB) and (BF), to allow a large number of suitable climbing wall shrubs to be planted to give advantageous embellishment. After the main raised beds were planted with suitable shrubs, providing foliage and blossom colour, leaf and berry, annuals were used in places to give immediate effect while the shrubs grew to a satisfactory size.

Almost the last job after planting was to turf the upper and lower lawns. Note that mowing strips were in place when preparing the concrete foundation for the walling. Many land drains as weepholes were placed during the wall construction to deal with the problem of waterlogged soil behind the walls during the winter. Wiring for wall shrubs was also installed all along the house walls to soften the effect. A waterproofed power point was fixed to the house wall at (E) for mowing purposes. Nearby was an existing, drainable water tap for garden hose watering. Standpipes were not installed as these were unnecessary.

A wooden plank on stone pillars was placed to make a garden seat (R) which gives good views of open countryside. All the trees had rabbit guards fitted to prevent scratching of the bark by cats.

Unfortunately bottle gullies to trap sediment from the roof were not fitted by the builder. Three trays for bird feeding were placed around the garden. The terrace is wide enough for garden furniture (table and chairs) without the need to go on to soft grass.

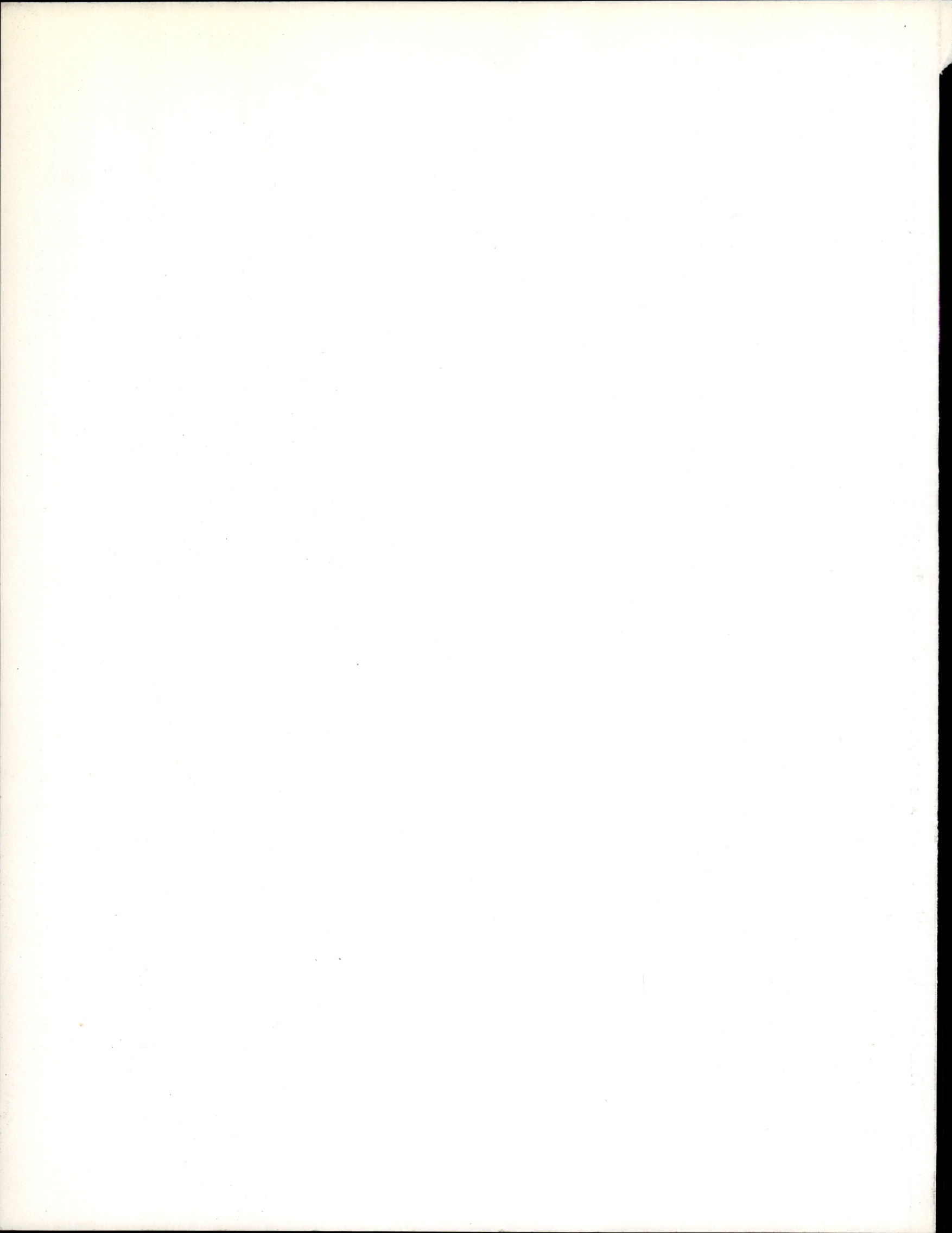